JFK, Conservative

Also by Ira Stoll

SAMUEL ADAMS: A LIFE

JFK,
Conservative

IRA STOLL

Houghton Mifflin Harcourt BOSTON NEW YORK 2013

For information about permission to reproduce selections from this book,
write to Permissions, Houghton Mifflin Harcourt Publishing Company,
215 Park Avenue South, New York, New York 10003.

www.hmhbooks.com

Library of Congress Cataloging-in-Publication Data
Stoll, Ira, date.
JFK, conservative / Ira Stoll.
pages cm
Includes bibliographical references and index.
ISBN 978-0-547-58598-7
1. Kennedy, John F. (John Fitzgerald), 1917–1963 — Political and social views.
2. United States — Politics and government — 1961–1963. 3. Conservatism —
United States — History — 20th century. I. Title.
E842.S825 2013
973.922092 — dc23
2013001595

Printed in the United States of America
DOC 10 9 8 7 6 5 4 3 2 1

For Aliza

Contents

Prelude

"Our Deep Religious Sense"
1946

> Wherever freedom has been in danger, Americans with a deep sense of patriotism have ever been willing to stand at Armageddon and strike a blow for liberty and the Lord.
>
> — JOHN F. KENNEDY, 1946

Boston

JULY 4, 1946, WAS the first peacetime Fourth of July since America had entered World War II four and a half years before, and the city on this morning had an empty, summer feel about it. The holiday fell on a Thursday, so many Bostonians had decided to take Friday off, too, and had left for long weekends in Maine or on Cape Cod. Arthur Fiedler had conducted the big opening-night concert of the Boston Pops on the Esplanade along the Charles River on July 2; some members of the Boston Symphony Orchestra were already in the Berkshires at Tanglewood. The Boston Red Sox were in first place atop the American League, six and a half games ahead of the Yankees, but even the Red Sox were out of town, away from Fenway

Park. Later on July 4, Ted Williams, back with the team after nearly four years as a Marine and Navy aviator, would hit his twenty-first and twenty-second home runs of the season, one in each game of a double-header against the Philadelphia A's.

Among those remaining in the city for the holiday was the mayor, James Michael Curley. At 10 a.m., downtown, in front of City Hall, he hoisted the American flag, and a parade of about five hundred stepped off down School Street. The detachments from the Army, Marines, Navy, Sons of the American Revolution, and Girl Scouts approached the Granary Burying Ground, where Curley's son, Lieutenant George Curley, placed wreaths on the graves of three men who, 170 years earlier, had signed the Declaration of Independence — Robert Treat Paine, John Hancock, and Samuel Adams. Then the parade marched down Tremont Street to the Old State House, where, at 10:45, a student from the Boston Latin School stood on the balcony in colonial dress and read the Declaration aloud to the crowd gathered below. Finally they arrived at Faneuil Hall, the red-brick building where Samuel Adams and the Boston Town Meeting had gathered long ago to protest the taxes on tea. This day's featured speech was to be delivered by a slim, twenty-nine-year-old lieutenant in the Navy Reserve, a veteran of the war in the Pacific named John Fitzgerald Kennedy.

Kennedy began by talking about how religion had shaped Americans and their history, beginning with the original colonists. "Our deep religious sense is the first element of the American character which I would discuss this morning," he said. "The informing spirit of the American character has always been a deep religious sense. Throughout the years, down to the present, a devotion to fundamental religious principles has characterized American thought and action."

He went on to discuss the Declaration of Independence itself: "Our government was founded on the essential religious idea of integrity of the individual. It was this religious sense which inspired the authors of the Declaration of Independence: 'We hold these truths to be self-evident: that all men are created equal; that they are endowed by their Creator with certain inalienable rights.'"

Then he moved to the First Amendment of the Constitution: "Our earliest legislation was inspired by this deep religious sense: 'Congress shall make no law prohibiting the free exercise of religion.'"

He quoted President Washington: "Of all of the dispositions and habits which lead to political prosperity, religion and morality are indispensable supports." He quoted President Lincoln: "that this nation, under God, shall have a new birth of freedom, and that government of the people, by the people and for the people shall not perish from the earth." And he quoted Franklin Delano Roosevelt, who had died the year before: "We shall win this war, and in victory we shall seek not vengeance, but the establishment of an international order in which the spirit of Christ shall rule the hearts of men and nations."

He quoted Alexis de Tocqueville, the French visitor to America more than one hundred years earlier: "You may talk of the people and their majesty, but where there is no respect for God can there be much for man? You may talk of the supremacy of the ballot, respect for order, denounce riot, secession — unless religion is the first link, all is vain."

Kennedy spoke of how the United States had triumphed against assaults on its "essential religious ideas." "The doctrine of slavery which challenged these ideas within our own country was destroyed" in the Civil War, he said. In World War II, "the philosophy of racism, which threatened to overwhelm them by attacks from abroad, was also met and destroyed," he said.

Moving on from religion, Kennedy spoke of America's idealism, and of its individualism:

> The American character has been not only religious, idealistic, and patriotic, but because of these it has been essentially individual.
>
> The right of the individual against the State has ever been one of our most cherished political principles.
>
> The American Constitution has set down for all men to see the essentially Christian and American principle that there are certain rights held by every man which no government and no majority, however powerful, can deny.
>
> Conceived in Grecian thought, strengthened by Christian morality, and stamped indelibly into American political philosophy, the right

of the individual against the State is the keystone of our Constitution. Each man is free.

He is free in thought.

He is free in expression.

He is free in worship.

While the newspapers were describing this day as the first peacetime Fourth of July, Kennedy's speech made clear that America's ideals and freedoms were again under attack. "Today these basic religious ideas are challenged by atheism and materialism: at home in the cynical philosophy of many of our intellectuals, abroad in the doctrine of collectivism, which sets up the twin pillars of atheism and materialism as the official philosophical establishment of the State," he said.

First, Kennedy took aim at the progressive historians at home: "In recent years, the existence of this element in the American character has been challenged by those who seek to give an economic interpretation to American history. They seek to destroy our faith in our past so that they may guide our future. These cynics are wrong, for, while there may be some truth in their interpretation, it does remain a fact, and a most important one, that the motivating force of the American people has been their belief that they have always stood at the barricades by the side of God."

America in 1946 was weary of war. More than 400,000 Americans had died in World War II. Those soldiers and sailors who had survived had recently been reunited with wives, parents, or children from whom they had been separated for months or years. Kennedy himself, like many soldiers, had been injured. His back pain may have been one reason the long bony fingers of his hands were gripping the corners of the wooden podium for support as he leaned toward the newspaper reporters gathered in the front row.

Just as Americans were adjusting to peace, though, Kennedy warned of a new confrontation to come from abroad. He observed that "there are large sections of the world today" where rights that Americans consider universal "are denied as a matter of philosophy and as a matter of government.

"It is now in the postwar world that this idealism — this devotion to principle — this belief in the natural law — this deep religious conviction that this is truly God's country and we are truly God's people — will meet its greatest trial," he said. "Wherever freedom has been in danger, Americans with a deep sense of patriotism have ever been willing to stand at Armageddon and strike a blow for liberty and the Lord."

He concluded:

> We cannot assume that the struggle is ended. It is never-ending.
>
> Eternal vigilance is the price of liberty. It was the price yesterday. It is the price today, and it will ever be the price.
>
> The characteristics of the American people have ever been a deep sense of religion, a deep sense of idealism, a deep sense of patriotism, and a deep sense of individualism.
>
> Let us not blink [from] the fact that the days which lie ahead of us are bitter ones.
>
> May God grant that, at some distant date, on this day, and on this platform, the orator may be able to say that these are still the great qualities of the American character and that they have prevailed.[1]

Introduction

"Not a Liberal"

I'd be very happy to tell them I'm not a liberal at all.
— JOHN F. KENNEDY, 1953

THE PHOTOGRAPHS OF KENNEDY after the July 4, 1946, speech caution of the hazards of drawing too much by way of conclusions from a single talk. His mother, Rose Kennedy, in pearls and a floral print dress, clings to his left arm. His grandmother, Mary Fitzgerald, clings to his right arm. His speech is rolled up in his hand like a baton. His grandfather, John Francis "Honey Fitz" Fitzgerald, a former congressman and mayor of Boston who had been the principal speaker on the same platform exactly fifty years earlier, looks dapper in a bow tie. As for Kennedy himself, the broad white smile is unmistakable, but the skinny young man in a jacket and tie, holding a speech and surrounded by proud and doting elderly relatives, looks less like a fully formed professional politician than like a high school valedictorian on graduation day.

So if, to contemporary ears, the language of "Christian morality" and "the right of the individual against the State" and the attack on the "cynical philosophy of many of our intellectuals" seems off-key for a president who has become an icon of liberalism, there is no shortage of possible explanations.

Perhaps it was the immature speech of a young man who changed his views as he got older.

Perhaps the young politician was being led astray by a speechwriter or staffer with strong views of his own. This, though, is unlikely. Kennedy's White House spokesman, Pierre Salinger, recalled, "Actually, speeches were not written *for* the president but *with* him. He knew what he wanted to say and how he wanted to say it. The role of the speech writer was to organize JFK's thoughts into a rough draft, on which he himself would put the final touches. His revisions would often change it dramatically."[1] Kennedy's secretary in the Senate and in the White House, Evelyn Lincoln, remembered, "He usually dictated a rough draft of his speeches."[2] Though Salinger and Lincoln joined Kennedy's staff some years after 1946, editing marks on drafts of his speeches from this earlier period show a Kennedy who was more than capable of editing either speechwriters' or his own drafts.

Kennedy's secretary from 1947 to 1952, Mary Davis, in an oral history interview that at times is quite negative about Kennedy ("a spoiled young man"), recalls:

> When he wanted to write a speech he did it, most of it. I would say 99% of that was done by JFK himself. I can remember first time he ever called me in — I even forget what the speech was going to be on, but it was going to be a major speech, one of his first major speeches. And I thought, "Oh, oh, this young, green congressman. What's he going to do?" No preparation. He called me in and he says, "I think we'd better get to work on the speech." And I said "Okay, fine." And I thought he was going to stumble around, and he'll *er, ah, um.*
>
> I was never so startled in my life. He sat back in his chair, and it just flowed right out.[3]

Salinger and Lincoln and other Kennedy aides from the presidential years may have had an interest in inflating the late president's reputation so as to enhance, by association, their own, but here their testimony seems to match that of Davis, who quit working for Kennedy in a dispute over her salary.

Perhaps Kennedy's July 4, 1946, speech was a case of political pandering aimed at the electorate. This, though, is also unlikely. Less than a month before, Kennedy had won the Democratic primary for the Eleventh Congressional District in Massachusetts. It was a reliably Democratic district, and if the candidate was trying to appeal to independent or Republican crossover voters, a speech on a holiday weekend, months before the November election, would have been an odd vehicle.[4]

Perhaps Kennedy's words were just rhetoric from a hypocritical politician who, once in office, would, in his public actions and private behavior, disregard his own speech. Maybe the stress on religion was a convenient Cold War shorthand for anticommunism, a way of drawing a contrast between the United States and the atheistic Soviet Union, or a way for an ambitious Catholic to reassure and win the trust of Protestant voters.

Or perhaps, just perhaps — and here is the most dramatic and intriguing possibility of them all — Kennedy actually, deeply, *believed* what he said, and would go on to serve as a congressman and senator and president of the United States according to those principles. He would take a hard line against communism in China, the Soviet Union, Eastern Europe, Cuba, Vietnam, and even in America's own labor unions, weathering protests and criticisms from academia, European intellectuals, and left-wing journalists. He would be supported personally in this struggle by his own strong religious faith, and he would often refer publicly to God and to America's religious history in his most powerful and important speeches. On the home front, he cut taxes. He restrained government spending. His presidency was markedly different from that of Lyndon Johnson's War on Poverty.

Another aide to Kennedy, Arthur Schlesinger Jr., reports that one night Kennedy remarked to him, "Liberalism and conservatism are categories of the thirties, and they don't apply any more."[5] But of course they did, and they still do. The liberalism and conservatism of our two chief political parties have shifted over time, and it is hard for us to remember liberal Republicans or truly conservative Democrats. Yet Kennedy's tax cuts, his domestic spending restraint, his military buildup, his pro-growth economic policy, his emphasis on free trade and a strong dollar, and his foreign policy driven by the idea that America had a God-given mission to defend freedom all make him, by the standards of both his time and our own, a conservative.

This book attempts to recover a basic truth about John Kennedy that in the years since he died has been forgotten — partly because of the work of liberal historians, partly as a result of shifts in American partisanship. Yet John Kennedy's conservatism was hardly a secret during his lifetime. "A Kennedy Runs for Congress: The Boston-bred scion of a former ambassador is a fighting-Irish conservative," *Look* headlined an article in its June 11, 1946, issue. "When young, wealthy and conservative John Fitzgerald Kennedy announced for Congress, many people wondered why," the story began. "Hardly a liberal even by his own standards, Kennedy is mainly concerned by what appears to him as the coming struggle between collectivism and capitalism. In speech after speech he charges his audience 'to battle for the old ideas with the same enthusiasm that people have for new ideas.'"

The *Chicago Tribune* reported Kennedy's election to the U.S. Senate in 1952 by describing him as a "fighting conservative."[6] In a June 1953 *Saturday Evening Post* article, Kennedy said, "I'd be very happy to tell them I'm not a liberal at all," adding, speaking of liberals, "I'm not comfortable with those people."

On December 7, 1958, Eleanor Roosevelt was asked in a television interview what she would do if she had to choose between a "conservative Democrat like Kennedy and a liberal Republican [like] Rockefeller." She said she would do all she possibly could to make sure the Democrats did not nominate a candidate like Kennedy.[7]

On the campaign trail in the 1960 election, Kennedy spoke about economics: "We should seek a balanced budget over the course of the business cycle with surpluses during good times more than offsetting the deficits which may be incurred during slumps. I submit that this is not a radical fiscal policy. It is a conservative policy."[8] Again, this wasn't just campaign rhetoric — Kennedy kept his distance from liberalism right up until his assassination.

"Why are some 'liberals' cool to the Kennedy Administration?" *Newsweek* asked in April 1962. The article went on to explain: "The liberal credentials of young Senator Kennedy never were impeccable

. . . He never was *really* one of the visceral liberals . . . many liberal thinkers never felt close to him."

Even after Kennedy's death, the "conservative" label was used to describe the late president and his policies by some of those who knew him best. One campaign staffer and congressional aide, William Sutton, described Kennedy's political stance in the 1946 campaign as "almost ultraconservative."[9] "He was more conservative than anything else," said a Navy friend of Kennedy's, James Reed, who went on to serve as JFK's assistant Treasury secretary and who had talked for "many hours" with the young Kennedy about fiscal and economic matters.[10] Another of Kennedy's friends, the Washington columnist Joseph Alsop, recalled in a 1964 interview, "The thing that's very important to remember about the president was that he was not, in the most marked way, he was not a member of the modern, Democratic, liberal group. He had real—contempt I'm afraid is the right word—for the members of that group in the Senate, or most of them . . . What he disliked—and here again we've often talked about it—was the sort of posturing, attitude-striking, never getting anything done liberalism . . . This viewpoint was completely foreign to Kennedy, and he regarded it with genuine contempt. Genuine contempt. He really was—contemptuous is the right word for it. He was contemptuous of that attitude in American life." Alsop went on to emphasize "the great success that the Kennedy administration had with an intelligent, active, but (in my opinion) conservative fiscal-economic policy."[11]

In January 1981, in the early days of the Reagan presidency, a group of Kennedy administration veterans gathered at the John F. Kennedy Library in Boston for a private conversation. One of the participants, Ted Sorensen, said, "Kennedy was a fiscal conservative. Most of us and the press and historians have, for one reason or another, treated Kennedy as being much more liberal than he so regarded himself at the time . . . In fiscal matters, he was extremely conservative, very cautious about the size of the budget."[12] Sorensen made a similar point in a November 1983 *Newsweek* article, saying, "He never identified himself as a liberal . . . On fiscal matters he was more conservative than any president we've had since."[13] In a 1993 speech, Kennedy's Treasury secretary, Douglas Dillon, described the president as "financially conservative."[14]

Combine that position with hawkish anticommunism, and it is hard to find much overlap with liberals.

Yet Kennedy's conservatism is by no means a settled point today, nor was it at the time he lived. In January 1962, a columnist in the conservative magazine *National Review* wrote that Kennedy's latest speech had given "further proof of his dedication to doctrinaire liberalism."[15] In 2011, the editorial page editor of the *Boston Globe,* Peter Canellos, wrote of the Kennedy family, "For five decades, they advanced liberal causes."[16] The same year, at a conference marking the fiftieth anniversary of the Kennedy administration, the historian Ellen Fitzpatrick spoke of "the liberalism that he [Kennedy] did stand foursquarely behind."[17] In 2012, the Columbia University history professor Alan Brinkley wrote that John Kennedy "seemed to many people a passionate and idealistic liberal," though he allowed, too, that such a perception was perhaps "surprising."[18] Also in 2012, the biographer of Lyndon Johnson, Robert Caro, could write almost in passing, as if no further explanation were needed, that Johnson's assignment of holding the South for Kennedy in 1960 was a tough one because of "Kennedy's liberalism."[19]

Categorizing Kennedy is made more complicated by the difficulty of defining exactly what was a "conservative" or a "liberal" at the time he lived, and by the shifting definitions of the terms over time, in both foreign and domestic policy. *Political Science Quarterly* once published a twenty-five-page article trying to answer the question "What Was Liberalism in the 1950s?" The author finally punted: "Above all, we must resist the temptation to reduce 1950s liberalism" to "a simple idea."[20] If it is a frustrating point, it is nonetheless a fair one, and so too for the 1960s, when liberalism existed not only in tension with conservatism but also in contrast to radicalism. Yet this book is not primarily about political theory but about the policies, principles, and legacy of a person, John F. Kennedy, whose devotion to the traditional American values he spoke of on July 4, 1946, was sufficiently strong that it was said, "If you talk with a thousand people evenly divided between liberals and conservatives, you find that five hundred conservatives think that Jack is a conservative."[21]

If, after Kennedy's death, there has been confusion about the reality of his politics and principles, it is certainly not the only aspect of his life on which, in spite of all the words written and spoken about it — maybe *because* of all the words written and spoken about it — there are widely divergent views.

Take subjects as seemingly simple and straightforward as how Kennedy dressed, or what he drank. The biographer Robert Dallek describes Kennedy in "khaki pants and a rumpled seersucker jacket with a shirttail dangling below his coat," and quotes a secretary as saying, "He wore the most godawful suits . . . Horrible looking, hanging from his frame."[22] By contrast, the journalist Ben Bradlee remembers his friend Jack Kennedy as "immaculately dressed" in "well-tailored suits" and "custom-made shoes and shirts," and fastidious to the point of castigating Bradlee for the fashion foul of wearing dark brown shoes with a blue suit.[23]

Kennedy "did not drink," the Pulitzer Prize–winning author Garry Wills writes. "During long nights in the Solomon Islands, where there was little to do but drink, Kennedy gave away his liquor coupons."[24] By contrast, Sorensen writes of Kennedy, "When relaxing, he enjoyed a daiquiri, a scotch and water or a vodka and tomato juice before dinner and a brandy stinger afterward."[25] Kennedy "never had brandy in his life," insisted Jacqueline Kennedy.[26]

Some of these differences may be explained by Kennedy's behavior changing over time. But there is a deeper issue, too. Kennedy himself once said that "what makes journalism so fascinating and biography so interesting" is "the struggle to answer that single question: 'What's he like?'"[27] He grappled with this in his own historical writing: the concluding chapter of his book *Profiles in Courage* begins with the observation, "However detailed may have been our study of his life, each man remains something of an enigma . . . shadowed by a veil which cannot be torn away . . . Something always seems to elude us."[28]

The difficulty of coming up with a perfectly clear picture of Kennedy, though, is no reason not to try. It is a matter of more than merely historical curiosity. Kennedy consistently ranks near the top of public polls asking about the greatness of past presidents. His popularity suggests that the American people think of his record as a model worth emulating. Simply to ape Kennedy would be impossible, of course. Some of the issues have changed. The Soviet Union is gone, tax rates now are lower than when Kennedy wanted to cut them, and the state universities of the South have been racially integrated. But if the contours of the foreign policy, tax, and education fights have shifted, Kennedy's course in them may nonetheless inform our choices today, as it has, we shall see, since his death. And other issues of Kennedy's time are still with us, including economic growth, government spending, inflation, and, as he put it, "Christian morality," the "cynical philosophy of many of our intellectuals," and "the right of the individual against the State."

Understanding Kennedy as a political conservative may make liberals uncomfortable, by crowning conservatism with the halo of Camelot. And it could make conservatives uncomfortable, too — many of them have long viscerally despised the entire Kennedy family, especially John F. Kennedy's younger brother Ted.

But the chance of upsetting some preconceived notions is no reason to stop. Instead, it is reason to forge ahead, to try to understand both the twenty-nine-year-old Navy veteran speaking at Faneuil Hall and the president he became. The task is simple: beneath the labels, before the spin, who was John Kennedy at root? As he himself would say, "Let us begin."

CHAPTER 1

PT 109

We, in this country, must be willing to do battle for old ideas that have proved their value with the same enthusiasm that people do for new ideas and creeds.

— JOHN F. KENNEDY, congressional campaign speech, 1946

The Solomon Islands

S WIMMING FOR THREE MILES, a body gets in a rhythm — reach, pull, kick, breathe. When the swim is a matter of life and death, it is both a mental challenge and a supremely physical one.

John F. Kennedy did not leave a record of what he thought about on the afternoon of August 2, 1943, when he swam in the waters of the Blackett Strait in the South Pacific. But he proved he had a great deal of mental and physical capacity.

He had been born with plenty of privilege, of the sort that does not always produce mental and physical toughness. His father, Joseph P. Kennedy, one of the richest men in America, had served President Franklin Roosevelt as the first chairman of the Securities and Exchange Commission and as ambassador to Great Britain. A father like that could help in many ways, and had in the past, but there in the water, John Kennedy was on his own. His mother, Rose, who liked to travel, had done some of the delegating that is inescapable when raising nine children, sending her son John off to boarding school in the fall of 1930, when he was thirteen and a half. First it was a Catholic school, Canterbury, in New Milford, Connecticut, where students attended morning and evening chapel. Then Choate, in Wallingford, Connecticut, where Kennedy left the campus every Sunday to go to Mass, and also was something of a prank-loving rascal, once filling up a neighboring boy's room entirely with pillows.[1] Through it all he had a series of illnesses, so that after his death his widow described him to the journalist Theodore White as "this lonely sick boy . . . this little boy in bed so much of the time."

Illness had also interrupted Kennedy's first semester at Princeton, where he began college. He started again at Harvard, his father's alma mater, where his older brother, Joseph P. Kennedy Jr., was two years ahead of him. There Jack "consistently" attended Sunday Mass and for four years belonged to St. Paul's Catholic Club.[2] He had joked to a friend who had borrowed his hat and had neglected to return it, "You are getting a certain carefree communistic attitude + a share the wealth attitude that is rather worrying to we who are wealthy."[3]

Kennedy's father would have smiled to read that. While he had campaigned with and for Franklin Roosevelt in 1932, he had tried to restrain some of the New Deal's overreaches, opposing the Wealth Tax of 1935, which raised the top income tax rate to above 75 percent, and FDR's effort to eliminate utility holding companies.[4] Joseph Kennedy would soon be giving speeches warning of the loss of independence that could result from what he called "Santa Claus" government: "If the state is to dominate the individual, sustaining him in slavish dependence . . . then the winning of the second World War will have proved a hollow victory."[5]

Rose Kennedy might have smiled, too. When Joseph Jr. had returned from study abroad in England favoring redistribution of wealth, Rose suggested pointedly, as she later recalled, "that in that case he should give up his boat and just fish off the pier or play baseball or do other things that most people do for recreation."[6]

Not that Jack did whatever his parents told him to do. He was already, consciously or unconsciously, doing what all children do, but especially children of powerful parents — figuring out both what to emulate and what to do differently. Joseph Kennedy had spent World War I in the relative safety of a Massachusetts shipyard.[7] On the eve of

World War II, the ambassador had called for "good relations" between democracies and dictatorships, reasoning that "we have to live together in the same world." For this he was widely criticized as an appeaser.[8] But John Kennedy had enlisted and sought a combat assignment.

Now, he had to reach Plum Pudding Island. From the point where Kennedy and his crew abandoned the sinking remnant of PT 109's hull, the island at first was a distant speck on the horizon, growing slowly larger as he approached. There at least he would be safe from sharks, which were so common in the Solomons that back at the Navy base on Rendova, men would go swimming off their patrol torpedo boats only if someone else was standing guard on deck with a rifle.[9]

Kennedy would still have to worry about Japanese bombers. He had already had three close calls. On April 7, 1943, a landing ship he was aboard, approaching Guadalcanal, was attacked. After Americans shot down the Japanese plane, Kennedy noticed its pilot swimming while keeping one hand underwater. As the Americans tried to rescue the airman from the sea, the enemy pilot opened fire on them with a revolver he had been hiding. On July 19, shrapnel from a Japanese bomb drew blood from two of PT 109's crew members, who had to be hospitalized. And on August 1, before Kennedy and PT 109 left for their nighttime patrol, twenty-five Japanese planes attacked the Americans' harbor, blew up one PT boat, sank another, and killed two American sailors.[10]

There was one thing we can be sure Kennedy was thinking about: the badly burned thirty-seven-year-old enlisted man he was pulling behind him — really, on top of him — Patrick "Pappy" McMahon, who had been in the engine room when the steel of the Japanese destroyer sliced through PT 109's eighty-foot plywood hull. McMahon was floating face-up, his back to Kennedy's, as Kennedy swam the breaststroke. Kennedy had a strap of McMahon's life jacket clenched between his teeth, and that was how he towed his crewmate for four or five hours, swallowing salt water along the way.

McMahon was luckier than the two sailors who were missing after the crash. Harold Marney was nineteen, a motor machinist's mate from Springfield, Massachusetts, who had enlisted at age seventeen, a month before Pearl Harbor. Andrew Jackson Kirksey, a torpedoman, was twenty-five and had a wife and a ten-month-old son back home in Georgia.[11]

Kennedy's life experiences, privileged as they were, had provided a kind of mental toughness that separated him from some of his family members. He had spent part of March 1939 with his father in Rome, at the coronation of Pope Pius XII. He wrote to a friend afterward that the pope "gave Dad and I communion with Eunice [JFK's sister] at the same time at a private mass and all in all it was very impressive."[12] In July of 1939, Kennedy traveled with a Rhodes scholar named Byron White to Berlin, Munich, Danzig, Budapest, and Italy.[13] The same year, he visited the Soviet Union, which he found "a crude, backward, hopelessly bureaucratic country."[14]

In the fall, he wrote an unsigned editorial in the *Harvard Crimson*, the student newspaper, urging American leaders to negotiate a peace between Britain and Germany that would disarm Hitler.[15] Once the war in Europe began in earnest, though, he urged American preparedness, seeing Britain's *un*preparedness as having put that country at risk. The president of Harvard, James Bryant Conant, had taken a similar line in a May 29, 1940, nationwide radio speech calling for immediate American aid to the Allies, stating, "I believe the United States should take every action possible to insure the defeat of Hitler," and declaring that the "fear of war is no basis for a national policy."[16] Kennedy made his case in a June 9, 1940, letter to the editor of the *Crimson:*

> In an editorial on Friday, May 31, attacking President Conant's speech you stated that "there is no surer way to war, and a terribly destructive one, than to arm as we are doing." This point of view seems to overlook the very valuable lesson of England's experience during the last decade. In no other country was this idea that armaments are the prime cause of war more firmly held. Lord Grey's statement in 1914 — "the enormous growth of armaments in Europe, the sense of insecurity and fear caused by them, it was these that made war inevitable" — was quoted again and again by the successful opponents of British rearmament. Senator Borah expressed the equivalent American opinion, in voting against the naval appropriations bill of 1928 when he said, "One nation putting out a program, another putting out a program to meet the program, and soon there is war."

If anyone should ask why Britain is so badly prepared for this war or why America's defenses were found to be in such shocking condition in the May investigations, this attitude toward armaments is a substantial answer. The failure to build up her armaments has not saved England from a war, and may cost her one. Are we in America to let that lesson go unlearned?[17]

Kennedy had even turned his Harvard senior thesis on the topic into a book, *Why England Slept,* published in 1940. It was the "poor condition of British armaments" that made the "surrender" at Munich "inevitable," Kennedy wrote. He regretted that welfare advocates and farm interests were stronger than weapons proponents. "There is no lobby for armaments as there is for relief or for agriculture . . . The lobbies of agriculture and relief will oppose it, as it would mean taking money from their cause." And he offered some advice: "We must always keep our armaments equal to our commitments. Munich should teach us that; we must realize that any bluff will be called. We cannot tell anyone to keep out of our hemisphere unless our armaments and the people behind those armaments are prepared to back up the command, even to the ultimate point of going to war. There must be no doubt in anyone's mind, the decision must be automatic: if we debate, if we hesitate, if we question, it will be too late."[18]

Once inducted into the Navy, Kennedy had the chance to explain to new recruits in his own words what he thought the war was about. He did this in a speech delivered on July 4, 1942, in Charleston, South Carolina, titled "For What We Fight." It praised the signers of the Declaration for their "great courage" and "an even greater faith": "Today, 166 years after the signing of the Declaration of Independence, we, in America, are faced with a similar decision. We must decide whether the allegiance which we profess to the principles upon which this government is based is mere lip service, or whether we truly believe in them to the extent that we are ready to die for them."

Kennedy also acknowledged that America may have sometimes fallen short of its principles. "Some may argue that the ideals for which we fight now . . . are likewise impossible to achieve. Indeed, some men argue that Christianity itself has failed. They point to a world aflame with war, and say that the principles that Christ taught are too high, that men will never live their lives according to his precepts," he said. "But that does not mean we should throw these principles aside. They represent ideals and goals worth working for — worth fighting for. A world which casts away all morality and principle — all hopeless idealism, if you will, — is not a world worth living in."

And he reminded the soldiers of "the cause for which our enemies fight": "*We* say that all men are created equal. *They* deny it. *They* believe in the theory of the Master Race, in government by the elite — a government of a chosen few, by a chosen few, for a chosen few. We believe that man has certain inalienable rights. They say that man has no rights — he has duties. Only the state has rights."

The abstractions faded away as the speck of land loomed closer on the horizon. Finally Kennedy stopped swimming and stumbled onto shore. Either from exhaustion or from the seawater he swallowed, he vomited. Then he crawled across the beach to the cover of casuarina trees.

His ordeal had just begun. That night, Kennedy, this time alone, traveled another two or three miles and back, walking along a reef and swimming at times, trying to catch the attention of other PT boats he thought would be patrolling the Ferguson Passage. His idea was to hail one of them to rescue McMahon and the nine other surviving crewmen. But the other PT boats had gone in a different direction.

On the third day, the group swam to a nearby island, Olasana. It had more coconut trees, which were their only source of food. Kennedy again towed McMahon. On the fourth day, Thursday, August 5, Kennedy swam to another island, Naru, where he found a canoe and some fresh water and Japanese candy. The same day, two native scouts working for the British discovered the rest of the American survivors. When Kennedy returned to Olasana, he met the natives. On August 6, Kennedy carved a message into a coconut shell for the scouts to take by canoe to the American base at Rendova, thirty-eight miles away:

COMMANDER NATIVE KNOWS POS'IT
HE CAN PILOT   11 ALIVE   NEED

SMALL BOAT
KENNEDY

On August 7, a group of seven native scouts, sent by an Australian coast watcher who had received Kennedy's message, arrived at Olasana with fish, rice, potatoes, and cigarettes. After midnight on August 8, PT 157 came to rescue the survivors of the August 2 crash.

Was Kennedy lucky to have survived? Or unlucky to have lost his boat and two crewmen? If Kennedy's own thoughts on the matter were mixed, the press portrayed the shipwreck story as nothing short of a miracle. An account of it by John Hersey, whose wife, Frances Ann, was a friend of Kennedy's, ran in the June 17, 1944, *New Yorker* under the headline "Survival";[19] it concluded with the rescued sailors mingling on the deck of PT 157 with the natives, who had been educated by Christian missionaries, and who were singing a hymn they all knew:

> Jesus loves me, this I know,
> For the Bible tells me so;
> Little ones to Him belong,
> They are weak, but He is strong.
> Yes, Jesus loves me; yes, Jesus loves me . . .

A version of the *New Yorker* article, with the same ending, was reprinted in the August 1944 issue of *Reader's Digest,* which at the time had a circulation of 8,750,000.[20] Reprints of the *Reader's Digest* article were mailed to voters in Kennedy's 1946 congressional campaign.

In that campaign, Kennedy spoke to a few veterans' organizations about McMahon's bravery in turning down a medical discharge and remaining in the South Pacific, to work with his painfully burned hands repairing PT boat engines.

Kennedy said in that speech:

The institutions and principles for which we fought will be under a growing fire in the years ahead. We, in this country, must be willing to do battle for old ideas that have proved their value with the same enthusiasm that people do for new ideas and creeds. The tremendous vote in England last year for socialistic collectivism was largely the result of the tremendous enthusiasm that the socialists whipped up with their vigorous propaganda. If you wish to combat a similar move here — because, mark you, you may be sure that there will be such a movement — you must be willing to match your enthusiasm and interest and belief in the old with their interest and enthusiasm and belief in the new and novel.[21]

So the president who coined the phrase "New Frontier" began his career as an advocate of "old ideas." He did not spell out what those old ideas were, but he made it clear enough that they did not include socialism.

If Kennedy's rhetoric changed at times as his political career progressed, PT 109 remained a touchstone. Campaign volunteers distributed gold-colored metal tie clasps in the shape of the lost boat. Some of Kennedy's fellow surviving crew members campaigned with him in 1960, and after the election Kennedy invited them to his inauguration, where part of the inaugural parade was a PT boat painted with the number 109. As president, he read the manuscript of a book on PT 109 written by a newspaper reporter. When the book was made into a Hollywood movie, he screened it at the White House. And on his desk in the Oval Office, President Kennedy kept, preserved in wood and clear plastic, that coconut shell.

It was a symbol of the risks of war, and also of the possibility that, with faith and good fortune, one might survive through perils and hardships and go on to flourish.

CHAPTER 2

Congressman
1946–1952

There can be no compromise with communism or any other "ism" which is contrary to the rights of freedom-loving peoples.

— JOHN F. KENNEDY, broadcast on Polish-American radio, June 16, 1947

Boston

NOT EVERYONE HAD John Kennedy's luck in surviving the war. His older brother, Joe, a naval aviator, was killed on August 12, 1944. A bomber he was piloting, loaded with 21,170 pounds of high explosives, blew up while on a secret mission over Europe. John Kennedy compiled for private publication, in 1945, a volume of reminiscences called *As We Remember Joe.* It began with a beautifully written five-page introductory essay, "My Brother Joe." In it, Kennedy spoke of Joseph P. Kennedy Jr.'s "amazing intensity" and "great physical courage and stamina." The essay concluded: "And through it all, he had a deep and abiding Faith — he was never far from God — and so, I cannot help but feel that on that August day, high in the summer skies, 'death to him was less a setting forth than a returning.'"[1]

To judge by John Kennedy's public statements and actions, his brother Joe's death, far from triggering any crisis of faith, brought a renewed commitment. The congressional candidate's July 4, 1946, speech on the "deep sense of religion" as a characteristic of the American people was followed in August 1946 by Kennedy's presentation of a $650,000 donation to the Boston archdiocese for the founding of the Joseph P. Kennedy Jr. Memorial Hospital in Brighton.[2] The gift was the equivalent of about $7.5 million today. While the donation was a reminder of the candidate's ties to the Catholic Church, it also underscored his reliance on his father's wealth; the gift was far more than anything Kennedy had earned as an author, as a Navy officer, or during a brief stint as a newspaper correspondent.

On October 23, 1946, as the general election campaign drew to a close, Kennedy gave a speech to the Junior League of Boston on the topic "Why I Am a Democrat." It offered something short of impassioned ideological clarity. Rather, the candidate explained, "The easiest and fairest answer to why I am a Democrat is to say, 'Because I was born one'"—in other words, it was an "accident of birth." He sounded almost nostalgic in recalling that "the Democratic Party, as intellectually inaugurated by Thomas Jefferson, stood firmly opposed to a strong centralized government . . . Its philosophy was based on the fundamental belief that the people are capable of self government . . . It championed states' rights, and strict constitutional interpretation." While he contended that "the complexity of economic affairs, the growth of huge enterprises, national in scope, and the complete interdependence of our whole economy made necessary the abandonment of a narrow states' rights, strict constitutional construction viewpoint," he also spoke for free trade, asserting that the "fight for low tariffs . . . was America's great contribution toward breaking the economic nationalism that was strangling world trade."

Although Kennedy's wan remarks can be read as pandering to a Republican-leaning group, the words probably were not far from the truth. Urban Irish Catholics in 1946 America were overwhelmingly Democrats, and so was John Kennedy, the grandson of a former Democratic mayor of Boston and the son of an official in Franklin Roosevelt's administration.[3]

Once elected to Congress, Kennedy worked for federal aid for parochial school students. The archbishop of Boston, Richard Cardinal

Cushing, who said he "spoke frequently" with Kennedy on this subject, later recalled, "He thought that private or church-related schools should be accepted as part of the educational system of the country and, if it was constitutional, these schools should receive some kind of aid that had no relation to religion."[4] The Kennedy biographer Michael O'Brien notes that as a young congressman Kennedy supported federal aid to parochial school students for bus transportation, textbooks, and salaries of school nurses.[5]

If Kennedy was looking out for Boston's Catholics, he was also paying attention to its Jewish community. On June 14, 1947, he gave a speech titled "A Free and Democratic Jewish Commonwealth in Palestine." "Today the United Nations has before it the solution of the Palestine Problem," he said. "It is my conviction that a just solution requires the establishment of a free and democratic Jewish commonwealth in Palestine, the opening of the doors of Palestine to Jewish immigration, and the removal of land restrictions, so that those members of the people of Israel who desire to do so may work out their destiny under their chosen leaders in the land of Israel."

By far the central issue and organizing principle of Kennedy's career in Congress was a hard line against communism, both at home and abroad. As we shall see, and as Kennedy touched on in his July 4, 1946, speech, his anticommunism had religious elements. But it was an animating political and ideological force for Kennedy in its own right. It was also a powerful tide in American politics that would reach a high point — or low point of sorts — in 1950, when Senator Joseph McCarthy publicly denounced what he said were dozens of card-carrying Communists serving in the State Department.[6]

As a freshman congressman, Kennedy, along with another newly elected former Navy officer from California named Richard Nixon, served on the House Committee on Education and Labor. McCarthy was an obscure, newly elected senator. Winston Churchill had given his "Iron Curtain" speech in 1946, but the Cold War between the United States and its World War II ally the Soviet Union had barely begun. On March 12, 1947, President Harry Truman would give a speech setting forth the Truman Doctrine of supporting "free peoples who are resisting attempted subjugation." The National Security Council's Report 68, which set America's strategy of containment of the Soviet Union, would not come until 1950.

As a cold warrior, Kennedy was ahead of the curve. On Saturday morning, March 1, 1947, at a hearing of the Education and Labor Committee, he grilled the president of a United Auto Workers union local in Milwaukee, Robert Buse, about Communist influence in his union, which represented workers at the Allis-Chalmers plant that made turbines for American Navy destroyers, and which had gone on strike between January 22 and April 7, 1941. The issue in 1947 was not so much the effect of the strike on the war effort; the war, after all, had already been won, and the strike was six years past. The issue, rather, was Communist involvement in the American labor movement.

This was very much a live issue. When the CIO — which stood for the Committee for Industrial Organization, later the Congress of Industrial Organizations, and which included the United Auto Workers — had split from the American Federation of Labor in the late 1930s, the new labor umbrella group had initially welcomed Communist involvement.[7] But by 1946 and 1947, the CIO unions were trying to root out the Communists in their midst.[8] To the irritation of the labor unions, Congress was about to try to help the process along by passing the Taft-Hartley Act, which included a provision requiring union leaders to pledge that they were not members of the Communist Party.[9] It was a delicate moment for labor-management relations overall, as management anticipated the end of the wage and price controls and of a union no-strike pledge that had been in effect during the war, while labor faced demobilization, which meant less work at defense plants just as more would-be workers returned home from military service.[10]

Kennedy had served fewer than one hundred days in Congress, but he was already demonstrating a classic political skill, the ability to make a speech in the form of a question at a congressional hearing. "I think I would like to inform you what I believe to be the main difference between socialism in England and socialism in Russia," Kennedy said to the UAW's Robert Buse. "They have a freedom of opposition which they do not have in Russia. Do you not think that is important?"

Buse replied, "I would not know if they have any opposition or not in Russia."

Kennedy shot back: "Well, I do not think you are equipped to tell whether a member of your union is a Communist if you do not know the answers to any of the things that I have asked you . . . I think that your lack of information on communism and on the things that make up the Communist is terrible for the head of a union."

The next witness at the hearing was R. J. Thomas, vice president of the United Automobile, Aircraft, and Agricultural Implement Workers of America. Kennedy asked him, "I think that the problem of communism in trade-unions is an important one, do you not, do you agree with that?" Thomas replied that he thought the matter had been overblown. Kennedy followed up with questions about specific individuals, including one organizer for the heavily Communist United Electrical Workers who was an openly acknowledged member of the Communist Party: "Would you say that Mr. William Sentner is a Communist?"

The final witness at the hearing was a former president of the Allis-Chalmers UAW local in Milwaukee, Harold Christoffel. He had missed the Saturday morning session, explaining to the committee chairman that "my stomach kicked up a little bit." The committee asked Christoffel to stay over until Monday, March 3, when Kennedy pressed him to explain why, in July 1941, after Nazi Germany invaded Russia, Christoffel's union changed from opposing American aid to Great Britain to supporting it. "Do you know what a party liner is, a Communist Party liner?" Kennedy asked.[11] The question seemed less designed to elicit an answer from Christoffel than to establish or burnish Kennedy's reputation as a hawk, fighting communism abroad and at home.

After the Washington hearing, three members of the committee — Charles Kersten, Thomas Owens, and Kennedy — traveled to Milwaukee for a follow-up hearing on "Communistic Influences in Labor," which took place at the federal building on March 17, 18, and 19, 1947. The group's mission, Kersten announced at the opening session, was "to investigate fully whether or not perjury has been committed in hearings in Washington before the full committee with respect to such Communistic activities."

Most of the questioning of witnesses at the Milwaukee hearing was conducted by the committee's counsel, Irving McCann. But on March 19, as the committee heard from Owen Lambert, an Allis-Chalmers employee and union committeeman who had run for the Wisconsin Assembly as a Communist, Kennedy asked some of the questions himself. "Did you ever attend Communist meetings after the time you became a Communist?" Kennedy asked. "You said that you became a Communist because of the working conditions . . . Why didn't you stop working there and start working some place else?" Kennedy went on, "Do you know of the slave labor in Russia? . . . Do you know how many people are in the slave labor camps of Russia?"

Later in the hearing, Kennedy focused on documents indicating the union had changed its position on aid to the Allies after Germany attacked Russia. "It marked a definite conformity with the party line, and that is one of the proofs that Christoffel was a Communist sympathizer," Kennedy said. He summed up the case against Christoffel as follows, putting a sinister interpretation on the evidence the committee had gathered, which was highly suggestive but by no means entirely conclusive: "At the direction of the Communist Party Mr. Christoffel called a strike in the early part of 1941. To get the strike he stuffed or caused to be put in at the time of the election more than 2,000 forged ballots in order to secure the strike, and it slowed our defense program and it slowed up our Navy destroyer program for six months, is that correct?"[12]

The July 11, 1947, issue of the *Dispatcher,* the newspaper of the International Longshore and Warehouse Union, carried an article about the case: "I asked the third member of the subcommittee, the handsome, boyish-looking John Kennedy, son of the former Ambassador to Great Britain, why a perjury charge was being pushed against labor witnesses only while the company wasn't being bothered. Kennedy told me: 'The 1941 Allis-Chalmers strike was a commie strike. It hurt the government. It hurt the union. So we've got to use any technicality we can, just like the government did when it got Al Capone on an income tax evasion.'"[13]

The same article complained that when the subcommittee made its report to the full committee, "not a single one of the five liberal

Democratic members" of the full committee was present. That group of "liberal Democratic members" apparently did not include Kennedy, who was a hard-liner even by the standards of the broad and bipartisan anti-Communist consensus emerging at the time.

On July 23, 1947, a grand jury charged Christoffel with perjury. A Washington, D.C., jury heard evidence during a two-and-a-half-week trial and, on March 3, 1948, found Christoffel guilty of six counts of perjury.[14] Government exhibits filed in the trial showed that under Christoffel's leadership, the Milwaukee County Industrial Union opposed lend-lease aid to the Allies, then reversed course soon after Germany attacked Russia.[15] Christoffel, a thirty-five-year-old journeyman electrician with wire-rimmed glasses, a prominent chin, and a wife and two young children, was sentenced to a term of two to six years in federal prison.[16]

Kennedy and one of his colleagues on the Education and Labor Committee, Richard Nixon, went on to other battles. In April 1947, Nixon and Kennedy appeared at a debate in McKeesport, Pennsylvania. Afterward, as Chris Matthews recounts in his book *Kennedy & Nixon,* the two politicians went to a local diner, where they ate hamburgers before catching a midnight train back to Washington. They drew straws for the lower berth (Nixon won) and sat up much of the way home talking about foreign policy.[17]

The foreign policy issue at hand was the Soviet Union, whose dictator, Joseph Stalin, after a turn as an American ally against Nazi Germany in World War II, was consolidating control over Eastern Europe. Kennedy's questions at the Christoffel hearing and at the follow-up session in Milwaukee indicated he grasped the essential points. Stalin's ban on political opposition, combined with a vast system of slave labor camps, known as the Gulag, that were used to enforce the ban, meant that the Soviet Union was a threat to the Russian people and to any other peoples who might have the misfortune to fall under its domination. Here Kennedy's speeches and legislative actions show he had no illusions about the stakes.

In a June 16, 1947, broadcast on Polish-American radio, Kennedy reached into history, to 1683, when Polish soldiers had defeated the Turkish Muslim invaders at the Battle of Vienna. "History shows that on many occasions, Poland saved the continent of Europe from being over-ridden by aggressors and saved Christianity and civilization. Russia and Germany knew of this and they knew from history of the brave feats of John Sobieski and his brave Polish warriors, who turned back the Turks at the Gates of Vienna," Kennedy said. Russia and Germany knew, he said, that "by breaking Poland, they would snap the strongest link in the chain which surrounded Christianity and Western Civilization in Europe."

Kennedy's broadcast concluded, "Today, the sinister forces of Communism are hard at work. The greatest bulwark against the spread of Communism is the strength of the democracies, in which are enjoyed the fundamental rights of individuality. There can be no compromise with communism or any other 'ism' which is contrary to the rights of freedom-loving peoples. We must support those countries fighting communism."

Kennedy's notations on a typewritten draft of the radio speech show that the congressman edited it to make it more hawkish. That early draft included a nod to multilateralism in the line "We cannot stand alone in this." Kennedy deleted it. Another line in the draft, a conciliatory note apparently directed at the Soviet leadership, asserted, "We as American people are tolerant and understanding and have a great deal of patience." Kennedy deleted that, too. A line in the draft said, "Vigilance is the price of safety." Kennedy deleted the word "safety" and replaced it with "liberty," making clear which one, in his view, was the priority.

On March 7, 1948, Kennedy again took to the radio to address the plight of Poland and its people. He offered a series of policy proposals. "The possibility of invoking the Genocide Treaty against Russia for her actions in Poland and elsewhere must be thoroughly and vigorously pursued," he recommended. He called for revamping the "harsh and discriminatory" laws restricting Polish immigration to America.

He said the conflict between the United States and the USSR must end with the Soviets' defeat. "We realize that the liberty of Poland and the other nations who have fallen victim to Soviet domination depends upon the eventual outcome of the vast world-wide conflict in which we are presently engaged," Kennedy said. "Enslaved nations can be free and independent again, only if the West continues to build its strength, only if the expansion of the Soviet Union is so vigorously controlled and contained that eventually the totalitarian system, which in its denial of God and freedom contradicts the most basic instincts and beliefs of all mankind, is transformed, as eventually it must be."

Kennedy concluded, "We must not forget. We must not give up . . . We will continue to work for that time when all peoples will be free to choose their own government, free from oppression, and free from fear."

Yet again, Kennedy's handwritten edits of the speech show he revised it to make it more hawkish. Where the first draft had said, "Enslaved nations can be free and independent again, only in the atmosphere of a peaceful world, and not in the ruins of another World War for which they would be the battlefield," Kennedy deleted the reference to the peaceful world and the warning against another world war, replacing it, in his own hand, with the reference to Western strength and with the denunciation of totalitarian "denial of God and freedom."

Where the initial draft twice warned that the fate of Poland "is not . . . an issue for political exploitation," Kennedy twice edited that out, suggesting, perhaps, that he felt it was a legitimate issue for American politics.[18] It certainly was an issue at the time for the American political right, as were Communists in labor unions and in China.

Kennedy's anticommunism extended beyond Europe, to Asia, as well. On that front, Kennedy faulted President Truman, his State Department, and their academic advisers for the loss of much of mainland China to the Communists. On January 30, 1949, speaking in Salem, Massachusetts, Kennedy delivered remarks that were later entered into the *Congressional Record*. "In 1948 we appropriated $468,000,000 for China, only a fraction of what we were sending to Europe, and out of this $468,000,000 only $125,000,000 was for military purposes," Kennedy complained. "The end was drawing near; the assistance was too little and too late; and the nationalist government was engaged in a death struggle with the on-rushing Communist armies."

The congressman went on to directly criticize Truman, who was the sitting president from his own Democratic Party. Truman had kept the Chinese leader's wife, Madame Chiang Kai-shek, waiting for nine days before granting her an audience, in which she pleaded with him for additional aid, to no avail.[19] Kennedy said, "The indifference, if not the contempt, with which the State Department and the President treated the wife of the head of the nationalist government, who was then fighting for a free China . . . was the final chapter in this tragic story."

As if that were not brazen enough, the young congressman from Massachusetts, a Harvard graduate, went on to attack a Harvard professor of Chinese history, John King Fairbank, along with a professor at Johns Hopkins, Owen Lattimore, for being too tough on the Chinese nationalists and for giving the advantage to the Communists. Kennedy said, "So concerned were our diplomats and their advisers, the Lattimores and the Fairbanks, with the imperfections of the diplomatic system in China after 20 years of war, and the tales of corruption in high places, that they lost sight of our tremendous stake in a noncommunist China."

To the claim that Chinese communism "was not really communism at all but merely an advanced agrarian movement which did not take directions from Moscow," Kennedy was unequivocally dismissive, quoting a report by a Republican congresswoman from Ohio, Frances Bolton, that concluded: "Its doctrines follow those of Lenin and Stalin. Its leaders are Moscow-trained . . . Its policies and actions, its strategy and tactics are Communist. The Chinese Communists have followed faithfully every zigzag of the Kremlin's line for a generation."

Arthur Schlesinger Jr., a special assistant to President Kennedy who had been a colleague of Fairbank's in the Harvard history department, wrote in 1965 that "as late as 1960" Kennedy "separately expressed both to Theodore H. White and to me his sorrow that he had ever given" the China speech.[20] White, a journalist and author, had been a student of Fairbank's at Harvard. Perhaps Kennedy did regret his attack on the scholars. Yet his public position was clear. In a November 29, 1961, presidential press conference, Kennedy was asked about the 1949 speech. He replied, in essence, that, had he to do it over again, he might not have singled out Fairbank or Lattimore, both of whom were called in 1952 before a Senate committee investigating Communist subversion in America. (As late as 1953, Kennedy told a job applicant to his Senate office that he thought it likely that Lattimore had some

sympathy with the Chinese Communists.[21]) But he stuck by the under-
lying point that America should have done more to keep China from
falling to the Communists, and he made no apologies for it. "I always
have felt that we did not make a determined enough effort in the case
of China. Given the problems we now see, I think a more determined
effort would have been advisable. I would think that in my speech in
'49 I placed more emphasis on personalities than I would today," the
president said. "And I would say that my view today is more in accordance with the facts than my view in '49. But my — I've always felt,
and I think history will record, that the change of China from being
a country friendly to us to a country which is unremittingly hostile
affected very strongly the balance of power in the world. And while
there . . . is still, of course, room for argument as to whether any United
States actions would have changed the course of events there, I think
a greater effort would have been wiser. I said it in '49, so it isn't totally
hindsight."

Kennedy's concerns about Communist advances applied to the
home front as well as to Europe and Asia. In an October 18, 1949,
speech before the Miami Junior Chamber of Commerce, Kennedy repeated some of his earlier language about China. "So concerned were
our diplomats and their advisers with the imperfections of the Democratic system in China after twenty years of war, and the tales of corruption in high places, that they lost sight of our tremendous stake in
a non-communist China. They forgot that the independence of China
and the stability of the national government were the fundamental ob-
jects of our Far Eastern Policy," he said, warning, "The Communist
assault on the rest of Asia has already begun."

Kennedy went on to speak of the risks facing America. "As the responsibilities of government become enlarged, there has been a cor-
responding assumption of authority by the state," he said. "It is obvious
from the history of the past twenty years that whether we like it or
not, whether we be Republicans or Democrats, the government will
continue to play an increasingly large part in our lives. The theme of
today — the scarlet thread that runs throughout all of the thoughts and
actions of people all over the world — is one of resignation of great
problems to the all-absorbing hands of the great Leviathan — the state.

This trend is not divisible. We in the United States suffer from it, if less intensely."

Kennedy repeated a version of the "scarlet thread" and "Leviathan" line a few months later, on January 29, 1950, when he spoke at the commencement exercises of the University of Notre Dame. He added another conclusion: "It is therefore vital that we become concerned with maintaining the authority of the people, of the individual, over the state."

Nearly four years after that July 4, 1946, address in Faneuil Hall, at which Kennedy had spoken of "the right of the individual against the State" as "one of our most cherished political principles," here was Kennedy again voicing concern with the authority "of the individual, over the state." The Kennedy Library has a list of the books the president kept in his apartment at 122 Bowdoin Street in Boston, which was his voting address and where he stayed when he was in town. Among them were at least two books that relate to this theme: *Our Enemy, the State,* by a now obscure libertarian writer named Albert Jay Nock, and *The Man Versus the State,* by Herbert Spencer, an edition of which was brought out in 1940 with an introduction by Nock.

That introduction, with its distinction between the early, and admirable, classical liberals and their more modern namesakes, is a likely source for some of Kennedy's thinking and words. It said:

> Statism postulates the doctrine that the citizen has no rights which the State is bound to respect; the only rights he has are those which the State grants him, and which the State may attenuate or revoke at its own pleasure. This doctrine is fundamental; without its support, all the various nominal modes or forms of Statism which we see at large in Europe and America — such as are called Socialism, Communism, Naziism, Fascism, etc., — would collapse at once. The individualism which was professed by the early Liberals, maintained the contrary; it maintained that the citizen has rights which are inviolable by the State or by any other agency. This was fundamental doctrine; without its support, obviously, every formulation of individualism becomes so much waste paper. Moreover, early Liberalism accepted it as not only fundamental, but also as axiomatic, self-evident. We may remember, for example, that our great charter, the Declaration

of Independence, takes as its foundation the self-evident truth of this doctrine, asserting that man, in virtue of his birth, is endowed with certain rights which are "unalienable"; and asserting further that it is "to secure these rights" that governments are instituted among men. Political literature will nowhere furnish a more explicit disavowal of the Statist philosophy than is to be found in the primary postulate of the Declaration.

The Hebert Spencer essay *The Man Versus the State* makes a similar distinction between the good old classical liberals and the newer, big-government liberals: "It seems needful to remind everybody what Liberalism was in the past, that they may perceive its unlikeness to the so-called Liberalism of the present . . . In past times Liberalism habitually stood for individual freedom *versus* State-coercion."

Nock's *Our Enemy, the State,* published in 1935, distinguished between government — a necessary evil for the goal of freedom and security — and the state, which "is not based on the idea of natural rights, but on the idea that the individual has no rights except those that the State may provisionally grant him."

It would be a mistake to make too much of the presence of *Our Enemy, the State* and *The Man Versus the State* on Kennedy's bookshelf. Many of us have books on our shelves that we have never read, and many of us have other books on our shelves that we have read but with which we do not agree. But given the congruence between Nock's language and Kennedy's, it would be a mistake to make too little of these books, either. There is a distinct possibility that Kennedy read them and was influenced by them, not only in his speeches, but also, at least to some extent, in his actions in office.

At Notre Dame, Kennedy warned specifically of the growing federal government. "The ever expanding power of the federal government, the absorption of many of the functions that states and cities once considered to be the responsibilities of their own, must now be a source of concern to all those who believe as did the Irish Patriot, Henry Grattan: 'Control over local affairs is the essence of liberty.'"

Kennedy at Notre Dame, just as he had at Faneuil Hall, connected this idea of the individual against the state to religious faith. "You have been taught that each individual has an immortal soul, composed of an intellect which can know truth and a will which is free," Kennedy said. "Because of this every Catholic must believe in the essential dignity of the human personality on which any democracy must rest. Believing this, Catholics can never adhere to any political theory which holds that the state is a separate, distinct organization to which allegiance must be paid rather than a representative institution which derives its powers from the consent of the governed."

As a final argument that Catholicism and statism are contradictory, Kennedy added, "A Catholic's dual allegiance to the Kingdom of God on the one hand prohibits unquestioning obedience on the other to the state as an organic unit."

Kennedy seemed comfortable discussing these almost theological issues not only before Catholic audiences such as the one at Notre Dame but also before audiences that were not Catholic, or even Christian. The congressman spoke, on April 30, 1950, to the Hebrew Immigrant Aid Society. Correspondence in advance of the event suggested the society would welcome from the congressman some remarks on refugee resettlement policy, an area in which the Jewish nonprofit agency worked. Instead, the congressman launched into a discourse on faith. "One of the greatest characteristics of the Jewish people is their faith," Kennedy said. "What is this faith . . . what is faith? It is that which gives substance to our hopes, which convinces us of things we cannot see . . . It is faith that lets us understand how the worlds were fashioned by God's word, how it was from things unseen that the things we see took their origin."

It was a speech that, while respectful of Judaism, also offered a revealing view of Kennedy's own Christian beliefs. "Abraham showed faith, when he was put to the test, by offering up Isaac. He was ready to offer up an only son," Kennedy said. "God, he argued, had the power to restore his son even from the dead, and indeed, in a hidden sense, he did so recover him." It was in faith, Kennedy said, that Moses "performed the paschal rite, and the sprinkling of the blood, to leave Israel untouched by the angel that destroyed the first-born, in faith that they crossed the Red Sea as if it had been dry land, whereas the Egyptians, when they ventured into it, were drowned.

"Theirs was the faith which subdued kingdoms, which served the case of right, which made promises come true," Kennedy continued. "They shut the mouths of lions, they quenched raging fire, swords were drawn on them, and they escaped. How strong they became, who till then were weak, what courage they showed in battle, how they routed invading armies! There were women, too, who recovered their dead children, brought back to life. Others, looking forward to a better resurrection still, would not purchase their freedom on the rack . . . May you always cherish that faith!"

Kennedy did not mention communion ("sprinkling of the blood") or the resurrection of Jesus ("restore his son even from the dead") in this speech to a Jewish audience, but the references are hard to miss. At a time when some Jews and Protestants were still suspicious of Catholics or unfamiliar with them, Kennedy's remarks, like some of his other religious references in later speeches, put himself and his own religion into a reassuringly common, more general category, that of faith.

If Kennedy seems to have spent a lot of time as a congressman giving speeches, well, that is what congressmen do. The words of the speeches are worth reviewing at length because of the evidence they offer of what Kennedy actually believed. Certainly, politicians are capable of delivering speeches in favor of positions that they do not believe, and politicians are also capable of expressing views that they later reconsider and abandon. But the speeches were a significant element in shaping how audiences at the time viewed Kennedy.

The young congressman was not just a talker, though. He also used the power he had as a lawmaker to introduce legislation that advanced his hawkish views.

In the summer of 1950, the Cold War turned hot, with tens of thousands of American troops battling to defend South Korea against Chinese- and Soviet-backed North Korean Communists. Kennedy criticized the Truman administration for not doing enough to prepare Americans for a nuclear attack. "The federal government has been inexcusably late in giving proper leadership to the states and cities of the nation in setting up an adequate national civil defense program," Kennedy said. He introduced a resolution authorizing $53,000 in federal spending to print additional copies of a report called "The Effects of Atomic Weapons," whose ten-thousand-copy first printing had sold out by noon on the day of its release. "Here is an opportunity for the Congress to enable local civil defense planners to properly prepare and protect the country's citizens against an atomic attack," Kennedy said in an August 23, 1950, press release.

On May 9, 1951, Kennedy spoke on the floor of the House of Representatives to announce that he had introduced a bill "providing for an embargo on the shipment of all war material, within the limits of national security, from the United States to Communist China or to Hong Kong." To prevent China from simply buying the armaments elsewhere, he included in the legislation a secondary embargo that banned American economic assistance to countries that exported such materials to the Chinese Communists.

On April 9, 1952, Kennedy again took to the floor of the House to criticize the Truman administration and his colleagues on the House Appropriations Committee for failing to spend enough on the Air Force. The Air Force, he explained, had requested $24 billion, which the president's budget bureau had slashed to $22.4 billion, and which the Appropriations Committee had reduced further, to $20.9 billion. Kennedy offered an amendment to spend an additional $1.435 billion, to be devoted entirely to aircraft procurement, describing the committee's cut as taking a "risk with our national security." He explained that "last year the United States built an estimated 4300 airplanes; the Soviet Union at least 12,000, and a large portion of the 12,000 were jet fighters."

On domestic issues, Kennedy's record did not always match his rhetoric when it came to the rights of the individual against the "Leviathan" of the state, which may suggest that at times either the rhetoric or the votes were less expressions of Kennedy's beliefs than attempts to align with the voters. He backed rent control and broader price controls that told individuals what they could charge for property they owned. Kennedy's support for rent control and public housing dated back to his first campaign, when large numbers of returning veterans boosted demand for apartments. He described the issue as one of America supporting its returning soldiers. Though the price controls were statist and counterproductive, they were driven by Kennedy's conservative desire to preserve the value of the dollar and to combat inflation. "Kennedy said the problem that is foremost in the country is the upward swing of the cost of living. This cost rise, he remarked, threatens to destroy all that the people have earned," said a 1952 press release from Kennedy's congressional office. Another press release from the same year quoted the congressman as saying, "The inflation danger, instead of passing, is now more threatening than ever before . . . We must check this spiral before it totally wrecks our economy."

Kennedy took on General Electric over its attempt to win a $25 million federal tax break for a transformer plant in Rome, Georgia. The congressman warned that GE planned to move jobs from Pittsfield, Massachusetts, to the South, "where labor can be hired more cheaply and where companies can escape — at least temporarily — from the principles of trade unionism." Kennedy wrote to the federal official in charge of the tax break, "Of course, nothing can prevent the General Electric Co. from moving out of Pittsfield, if it so desires, but I strongly believe it should not be encouraged to do so by the granting of tax favors from the Federal Government." Kennedy succeeded in briefly stalling the approval of the federal tax breaks, though GE did eventually build the factory in Georgia.

As 1952 approached, the context of Kennedy's policy pronouncements was increasingly his Senate race against the Republican incumbent, Henry Cabot Lodge Jr. Pittsfield, for example, was in western Massachusetts, outside Kennedy's Boston-area congressional district. But the GE employees in Pittsfield would vote in the Senate contest.

As a Democrat, Kennedy was running against the national tide in 1952. The Republican ticket of General Dwight Eisenhower and his running mate, Richard Nixon, was on its way to a landslide victory over the Democratic ticket, Adlai Stevenson and John Sparkman, carrying 39 of the 48 states and winning 55 percent of the popular vote nationwide, 53 percent in Massachusetts. Republicans won a majority in the House of Representatives.

Even putting aside the national trend, Kennedy had a tough race. Lodge's grandfather Henry Cabot Lodge Sr. had defeated Kennedy's grandfather John "Honey Fitz" Fitzgerald in an election for U.S. Senate in 1916. Lodge's family lineage went far beyond that. Henry Cabot

Lodge Jr.'s great-great-great-grandfather, George Cabot, had also served in the Senate. A historian who wrote a book about the 1952 Lodge-Kennedy Senate race, Thomas Whalen, reports that "no fewer than five" of Lodge's family members had served in the Senate.[22] These were the Cabots who inspired the toast given in 1910 at a Holy Cross College alumni dinner:

> And this is good old Boston,
> The home of the bean and the cod.
> Where the Lowells talk only to Cabots,
> And the Cabots talk only to God.

God, however, was not registered to vote in Massachusetts elections. If He were, He would have been outnumbered by the Bay State's growing roll of voters who, like Kennedy, were descended from immigrants who arrived more recently than the Cabot forebears. Polish Americans remembered Kennedy's appearances on their radio programs. A letter from the Albanian American Citizens Committee spoke of Kennedy's "deep hatred for atheistic communism."[23] Ads in Jewish newspapers touted Kennedy's commitment to Israel.[24]

Kennedy made immigration an issue in the campaign, condemning Lodge for being absent from the Senate when only three votes were needed to kill the McCarran-Walter immigration bill. "Representative Kennedy charged the act was un-American and discriminatory and said that the present limit of 154,000 immigrants is but 1-10th of 1 per cent of the nation's present population," the *Boston Post* reported on October 2, 1952. Ralph Dungan, who later worked on Kennedy's Senate staff, recalled that "Kennedy spotted immigration as an important thing, and I suppose it was for Massachusetts politicians for a long while."[25]

Kennedy would eventually write a book, *A Nation of Immigrants,* that outlined his thinking on the subject. Immigrants, he wrote, "helped give America the extraordinary social mobility which is the essence of an open society . . . This has been the foundation of American inventiveness and ingenuity, of the multiplicity of new enterprises, and of the success in achieving the highest standard of living anywhere in the world."

He had seen that social mobility in his own family. His grandfather Patrick Joseph Kennedy was a Boston saloonkeeper and the son of Irish immigrants. Patrick Kennedy's son Joseph became the Senate candidate's father, a stock market player, liquor importer, and movie industry investor who amassed a fortune, becoming the Rolls-Royce–driving former American ambassador to the Court of St. James's.[26] Conservatives today are divided on the subject of immigration, but those voices of the conservative movement that see a restrictive immigration policy as intrusive government interference with the free-market movement of labor often sound as if they are echoing a version of Kennedy's argument that immigration leads to dynamism and economic growth.

In October 1952, Kennedy also used the China issue against Lodge. Whalen reports that Kennedy faulted Lodge for being complacent regarding America's China policy. "I happen to have been among those who in 1949 were critical of our China policy," Kennedy said. "I believed then and have said since that our diplomats were frittering away the victories our young men won for us."[27]

In his campaign against Lodge, Kennedy sought and received the support of conservative Republicans who had backed Robert Taft for the 1952 Republican presidential nomination and who were angry because Lodge had supported Dwight Eisenhower over Taft.[28] Among these conservative Republicans was the chairman of the Massachusetts Taft-for-President Committee, Basil Brewer, who was the publisher of the New Bedford and Cape Cod *Standard-Times.* Those newspapers endorsed Kennedy for the Senate over Lodge, praising JFK for his anti-Communist activism.[29]

Also endorsing Kennedy for Senate was the *Boston Post,* a usually Republican-leaning newspaper that was a supporter of the anti-Communist campaign of Joseph McCarthy, the Republican senator from Wisconsin. Accounts of the *Boston Post* endorsement tend to focus on a loan from Joseph Kennedy to the owner of the newspaper.[30] More interesting, perhaps, is the substance of the October 25, 1952, endorsement editorial itself, which praised John Kennedy for his actions in the Christoffel case and for trying to stop the flow of arms to China. "He fired one of the first shots for the American people against communist infiltration away back in 1947 when he routed-out the leader of a communist-inspired strike at a Wisconsin plant engaged in secret defense work," the editorial said. "While the high-altitude global thinkers were ready to abandon Formosa to the communists and close their eyes to war material shipments to Red China, Mr. Kennedy fought it." The editorial concluded that the young congressman "has his own head on his shoulders, and a keen and very capable brain of his own."

The newspapers looking to endorse a liberal in the 1952 Senate race in Massachusetts backed not Kennedy, but Lodge. The *Berkshire Eagle's* endorsement editorial described Lodge as "an invaluable voice for liberalism," and the *Springfield Union* quoted the *New York Herald Tribune's* judgment of Lodge: "No one represents better than he the liberal forces of the Republican Party."[31]

Kennedy's voting record from the self-described liberal group Americans for Democratic Action shows the degree to which he was willing to stray from the liberal line as a congressman. On a May 19, 1948, vote on the Mundt-Nixon Bill to Combat Un-American and Subversive Activities, the ADA wanted Congress to defeat the measure, which among other things would have required Communists to register with the U.S. attorney general. Kennedy was absent. In June of 1948, he voted to exclude from Social Security certain workers, such as life insurance salesmen and truck drivers, who were paid on commission rather than on salary. The ADA wanted them included in Social Security. On August 29, 1950, Kennedy voted for the Wood Anti-Subversive Bill (offered by Congressman John Wood of Georgia), which the ADA complained "was opposed by all liberal and labor groups as an indiscriminately repressive measure which would threaten the rights of loyal Americans." That vote suggests that Kennedy's earlier absence on the Mundt-Nixon bill, a measure similar to the Wood bill, was not merely due to a scheduling conflict or illness but was driven by the substance. In September 1950, Kennedy voted to override Truman's veto of the bill, which became law as the Internal Security Act.

Biographers have also noted that in Congress, Kennedy departed from the Democratic Party line by voting to cut spending for the Department of Agriculture and of the Interior.[32] As a congressman, Kennedy had also voted to cut funding for the Tennessee Valley Authority, objecting that New Englanders were being taxed to subsidize cheap energy for the South.[33]

When the votes in Massachusetts were finally counted in November 1952, the Republican Eisenhower carried the Bay State in the presidential election, but Kennedy won a narrow victory over Lodge, 1,211,984 votes to 1,141,247.[34] When John F. Kennedy returned to Congress, it would be as Senator Kennedy.

WON BY: 51.5%

CHAPTER 3

Senator Kennedy

1953–1959

> I believe religion itself is at the root of the struggle, not in terms of the physical organizations of Christianity versus those of Atheism, but in terms of Good versus Evil, right versus wrong.
>
> — JOHN F. KENNEDY, commencement address at
> Assumption College, Worcester, Massachusetts, June 3, 1955 — 40 yrs

ANYONE WHO EXPECTED Kennedy to pivot to the left or the center after having won the election was to be disappointed. One historian, Sean Savage, wrote, "Kennedy initially compiled a Senate record as a fiscal conservative who supported Eisenhower's budget cuts, especially for agricultural subsidies and federal water and power programs."[1]

On July 29, 1953, the Senate voted on a proposal by Senator Joseph McCarthy to cut American aid to countries that traded with Communist China. Kennedy voted with McCarthy and Barry Goldwater for the proposal, which the Eisenhower-Nixon administration and Americans for Democratic Action opposed. Senators Prescott Bush of Connecticut, Hubert Humphrey of Minnesota, Albert Gore Sr. of Tennessee, Lyndon Johnson of Texas, and Leverett Saltonstall of Massachusetts all opposed punishing the countries that traded with the Communist Chinese, and the measure was defeated, 34 to 50. It was another example of Kennedy's readiness to side with conservatives on foreign policy issues.

/ 38

On September 12, 1953, Kennedy was married. Officiating was Archbishop Cushing of Boston, a prelate so fiercely anti-Communist he called communism the antichrist, spoke out against "parlor pinks" in the United States, and devoted headlines in the archdiocese newspaper, the *Pilot,* to articles like "Chinese Communists Express Fond Hope of Conquering America."[2] Kennedy's bride, Jacqueline Lee Bouvier, had been "born and reared a Republican."[3] The wedding took place in Newport, Rhode Island, at Hammersmith Farm, the summer home of Jacqueline's mother and stepfather, Mr. and Mrs. Hugh D. Auchincloss. Auchincloss was an heir to the Standard Oil fortune, and the 300-acre estate featured a three-story house with five chimneys, a turret, vast lawns, a wide sandy beach, a private pier, and "a sizable herd of Black Angus Aberdeen cattle."[4] Also sizable was the number of guests at the wedding: more than 1,200.[5] (The bachelor party for Kennedy, held at the Parker House hotel in Boston ten days before the wedding, had attracted 350 guests.[6])

The Kennedys returned from their honeymoon in Mexico in time to attend Senator Joseph McCarthy's wedding to Jean Kerr on September 29, 1953.[7] By mid-1954, McCarthy's national popularity had plunged, he was drinking heavily, and even some anti-Communists had concluded he had become a liability to their cause. The nationally televised Army-McCarthy hearings had featured a lawyer for the Army condemning the Wisconsin senator for what the lawyer called his recklessness and cruelty, and asking him, "Have you no sense of decency, sir?"[8] On December 2, 1954, the Senate voted, 67 to 22, to condemn McCarthy. Kennedy was hospitalized with back-related problems at the time, but he could have announced a position or, as Senate rules allow, "paired" his vote with another absent senator's on the other side of the issue.[9] Instead, he was absent and silent.

On August 2, 1955, Kennedy voted to confirm Harold C. Patterson, an Eisenhower nominee, to the Securities and Exchange Commission. The liberal Americans for Democratic Action protested that Patterson's appointment meant that every commissioner was from the securities industry, and urged "that a public-interested member be appointed in his stead, so that the public might be protected in the current wave of business mergers and proxy fights."

Throughout this period, Kennedy kept breaking with the liberal line, not only in votes but in his speeches as well. Among the most memorable and stunningly eloquent of these was his June 3, 1955, commencement address at Assumption College in Worcester, Massachusetts. It expressed fully and clearly the same ideology he had sketched in both his July 4, 1946, speech at Faneuil Hall and his 1950 address at Notre Dame — what might be called religious anticommunism but what arguably extended beyond anticommunism to religious individualism, or religious skepticism of all state power.

He began by saying that Assumption "stands as a bulwark on the North American continent in the battle for the preservation of Christian civilization." Kennedy also made reference to John Henry Newman (1801–1890), an Anglican priest in Great Britain who converted to Roman Catholicism:

> I say this and not because I believe Christianity is a weapon in the present world struggle, but because I believe religion itself is at the root of the struggle, not in terms of the physical organizations of Christianity versus those of Atheism, but in terms of Good versus Evil, right versus wrong, in terms of "the stern encounter" of which Cardinal Newman so prophetically wrote: "Then will come the stern encounter when two real and living principles, simple, entire, and consistent, one in the church and the other out of it, at length rush upon one another contending not for names and words or half views, but for elementary notions and distinctive moral characteristics."
>
> . . . We tend to forget those ideals and faiths and philosophical needs which drive men far more intensely than military and economic objectives.
>
> This is not to say that we have overlooked religion. Too often we have utilized it as a weapon, broadcast it as propaganda, shouted it as a battle cry. But in "the stern encounter," in the moral struggle, religion is not simply a weapon — it is the essence of the struggle itself. The Communist rulers do not fear the phraseology of religion, or the ceremonies and churches and denomination organizations. On the contrary, they leave no stone unturned in seeking to turn these aspects of religion to their own advantage and to use the trappings of religion in order to cement the obedience of their people. What they fear is the profound consequences of a religion that is lived and not merely

acknowledged. They fear especially man's response to spiritual and ethical stimuli, not merely material. A society which seeks to make the worship of the State the ultimate objective of life cannot permit a higher loyalty, a faith in God, a belief in a religion that elevates the individual, acknowledges his true value and teaches him devotion and responsibility to something beyond the here and the now. The communists fear Christianity more as a way of life than as a weapon. In short, there is room in a totalitarian system for churches — but there is no room for God. The claim of the State must be total, and no other loyalty, and no other philosophy of life can be tolerated.

Is this not simply an indication of the weakness of the communist position? If the ultimate struggle is indeed a moral encounter, then are we not certain of eventual victory?

Kennedy, sounding more like a religious leader than a conventional politician, went on to warn against American secularism, and, as he had in the July 4, 1946, speech, cynicism:

At first glance it might seem inevitable that in a struggle where the issue is the supremacy of the moral order, we must be victorious. That it is not inevitable, is due to the steady attrition in our faith and belief, a disease from which we in the West are suffering heavily. The communists have substituted dialectical materialism for faith in God; we on our part have substituted too often cynicism, indifference and secularism. We have permitted the communists too often to choose the ground for the struggle. We point with pride to the great outpourings of our factories and assume we have therefore proved the superiority of our system. We forget that the essence of the struggle is not material, but spiritual and ethical. We forget that the purpose of life is the future and not the present . . . We cannot separate our lives into compartments, either as individuals or as a nation. We cannot, on the one hand, run with the tide, and on the other, hold fast to Catholic principles.

One might attempt to dismiss Kennedy's Assumption College speech, as well as the Notre Dame speech, using some of the same arguments that could have been raised about the speech he gave in 1946. It might be mere rhetoric, or pandering, trying to please Catholic audiences by telling them what he thought they wanted to hear. It could be just the voice of a young politician who abandoned these views as he got older and as he began speaking to national and international audiences rather than to Catholic college graduates and their families. But it could also be true, or even instead, that Kennedy felt most comfortable expressing his own deeply held beliefs in front of an audience of his fellow Catholics. And it could be true, too, that as Kennedy's career advanced he made similar remarks before non-Catholic audiences. For so he would.

The rest of Kennedy's pre-presidential career was packed with important developments in the senator's political and personal life.

In 1954, Kennedy told friends he voted for Republican incumbent Leverett Saltonstall over Democrat Foster Furcolo for Senate. The decision seems to have been more personal and political than ideological.[10] In 1956, Kennedy took on his state's Democratic establishment again when he launched a hard-fought battle to unseat William H. "Onions" Burke as the chairman of the Massachusetts Democratic State Committee. Burke was an onion farmer from western Massachusetts, and Kennedy's fight against him was a risky, high-stakes one. Jacqueline Kennedy later remembered it as "the worst fight in his life . . . the only time in all of the fights he'd been through in his life when I'd really seen him nervous when he couldn't talk about anything else . . . It really was on his mind all the time."

In a footnote to Jacqueline Kennedy's comments, the historian Michael Beschloss describes Burke as "conservative" and writes that John F. Kennedy "wished to avoid putting an illiberal face on the Massachusetts party."[11] The first of these is technically true, but Beschloss's footnote does not fully capture what triggered Kennedy's anger against Burke. For that we have to go to a book about Kennedy written by two of his close political aides at the time, Kenneth O'Donnell and David Powers. They recall that the Soviet spy Alger Hiss, a State Department official who had become president of the Carnegie Endowment for International Peace before being tried for perjury in connection with espionage accusations, "was in the newspapers that week, making a speaking appearance at Princeton University after his release from prison."

"Anybody who's for Stevenson," Burke said, making it plain that he was referring to Kennedy, "ought to be down at Princeton listening to Alger Hiss."

Then we saw a side of Jack Kennedy that none of us had seen before. The gloves came off.

What really irked Kennedy, in other words, was not that Onions Burke was conservative or illiberal, but that Burke had accused him of being an acolyte of Alger Hiss, with all the attendant implications that he was some kind of Ivy League, State Department, left-wing, soft-on-communism pantywaist. What really got under Kennedy's skin was not that Onions Burke was a conservative; it was that he dared to suggest, falsely, that Kennedy was not one.

The control of the Massachusetts party that Kennedy gained by unseating Burke positioned him for a run at the vice-presidential nomination at the 1956 Democratic National Convention. In the second round of balloting, Kennedy had the lead until Albert Gore Sr. of Tennessee announced his state's support of Estes Kefauver.[12] The near-victory was nonetheless a useful marker for Kennedy's future ambitions.

In Kennedy's 1958 race for reelection to the Senate, he faced only token opposition from Republican Vincent Celeste. Kennedy won by a 73 to 27 percent margin.[13] By now the senator had solidified his inner circle, a handful of aides who would remain alongside Kennedy during the presidential campaign and presidency that followed. Ted Sorensen, who at this time was on Kennedy's Senate staff, was among the most ambitious, eloquent, and hardworking. He explained the lopsided victory: "Republicans were frequently reminded of his cooperation with Senator Saltonstall, his support of Eisenhower foreign policy measures and his independent voting record . . . Budget-cutting advocates were told of his Senate leadership on behalf of the Second Hoover Commission Report, and given the reprints of a warm letter of appreciation from another old friend of his father's, Herbert Hoover."[14]

Sorensen, a self-described "Danish Russian Jewish Unitarian," was the son of two Nebraskan peace activists who had opposed American entry into World War I. His father, C. A. Sorensen, served two

two-year terms as a Republican attorney general of Nebraska, favoring Prohibition, opposing the death penalty, and backing publicly owned rural electric power. As a young man, Sorensen followed his parents' aversion to war, filing with the draft board in 1946, at age eighteen, as a conscientious objector seeking noncombatant service. He did share Kennedy's anticommunism, advising the founders of one civil liberties group that one "cannot work with Communists to achieve civil liberties . . . I am convinced that such cooperation inevitably destroys the very objective sought, as well as the usefulness of the organization." Within the context of the Kennedy team, Sorensen was a liberal — so much so that he was concerned before taking a job on the senator's staff that Kennedy's views were too conservative relative to his own.[15]

Kenneth O'Donnell, a key aide whose responsibilities included handling Kennedy's schedule, was, like the senator, an Irish Catholic and a Harvard graduate from Massachusetts. He had grown up in Worcester, the son of the football coach at Holy Cross. At Harvard, he was Robert F. Kennedy's roommate. During World War II, he flew more than thirty missions over Germany and, Chris Matthews recounts, "once had to climb down and kick loose a bomb stuck in the doors."[16] O'Donnell, by Sorensen's account, "fiercely opposed" the creation of the Peace Corps as a "kooky, liberal idea."[17]

David Powers had been helping Kennedy since the 1946 congressional campaign, when he accompanied the candidate knocking on doors of three-deckers in Boston's Charlestown neighborhood. Powers's father, an immigrant from Ireland, had died when Powers was two. In World War II, Powers spent three years in the Pacific, in the Army Air Force.[18]

The closest aide of all was Kennedy's brother Robert. He was eight years younger but in some ways seemed ahead of John. Robert F. Kennedy had a law degree from the University of Virginia. He had married three years before JFK had, and he and Ethel had five children before JFK and Jacqueline had one. Robert Kennedy was just as anti-Communist as his brother John; in 1954, he wrote a letter to the *New York Times* critical of Franklin Roosevelt's deal with Stalin at Yalta, asserting that the agreement "caused some of the heartbreak and problems of postwar Europe" and had been made by FDR "without adequate knowledge and without consulting any of the personages, military or political, who ordinarily would have had the most complete knowledge of the problems involved." At the time, it drew a scathing response from Arthur Schlesinger Jr., who criticized Robert Kennedy's "astonishing mixture of distortion and error."[19]

What Sorensen, O'Donnell, Powers, and Robert Kennedy shared most of all was a fierce and primary loyalty to John Kennedy, and a readiness to subordinate any policy preferences of their own to his final judgment. Nevertheless, with the exception of Sorensen, Kennedy chose to surround himself with hawkish, centrist Democrats who fought against their own party establishment as often as they worked within it.

On foreign policy and national security, Senator Kennedy's speeches and votes were consistent with those of the young congressman who faulted the Truman administration for losing China to the Communists and who in 1952 wanted to spend more on jet fighters. In 1954 and 1958, Kennedy worked for increased defense spending on conventional weapons, criticizing President Eisenhower for wanting to cut the size of the Army.[20] In two speeches about Vietnam, Kennedy took a hard line on an issue that would eventually challenge him as president. In an April 6, 1954, Senate speech, Kennedy warned against "the menace of Vietminh communism disguised as nationalism."[21] And in a June 1, 1956, speech to American Friends of Vietnam, Kennedy called South Vietnam "the keystone to the arch, the finger in the dike." He went on, "This is our offspring — we cannot abandon it, we cannot ignore its needs. And if it falls victim to any of the perils that threaten its existence — Communism, political anarchy, poverty and the rest — then the United States, with some justification, will be held responsible; and our prestige in Asia will sink to a new low." Kennedy had visited Vietnam in October 1951 when it was still under French control; he had also met an exiled anti-French, anti-Communist Vietnamese politician, Ngo Dinh Diem, while Diem was living for three years at a Catholic seminary in New Jersey in the early 1950s.[22]

In a July 2, 1957, speech, Kennedy irked the former colonial power in Vietnam, France, by expressing support for another soon-to-be-former French colony, Algeria. The most powerful force in the world,

Kennedy said in his Algeria speech, is "man's eternal desire to be free and independent."[23] In 1959, Kennedy supported American economic aid to another former colony, India, seeing that country even then as a counterweight to Chinese Communist power. "We want India to win that race with China," he said. "If China succeeds and India fails, the economic-development balance of power will shift against us."[24]

When it came to domestic policy, Kennedy's aversion to nondefense government spending put him at odds with various interest groups and, at times, his colleagues. Arthur Schlesinger reports that Senator Kennedy "for a while, opposed farm price supports."[25] In 1955, a major conflict arose between Senate Democrats and the Eisenhower administration over how to finance the interstate highway system. Eisenhower wanted state and local governments to pay more than 70 percent of the cost, while the Democrats, led by Senator Gore, wanted the federal government to pay for nearly 70 percent of the highway program by tripling the federal gasoline tax. The Eisenhower proposal was defeated in the Senate by a vote of 60 to 31; of the 31 senators who favored it, there were 30 Republicans and a lone Democrat, John F. Kennedy.[26]

Sorensen explained Kennedy's overall approach: "He found that economy in government was a principle in the Senate but not always a practice. In the House Kennedy had taken pride in being one of a handful of Democrats who had upheld President Truman's vetoes of unjustified veterans' pensions . . . When a New England business group which had badgered him mercilessly about reducing federal spending insisted that he vote more funds for airport construction, he voted against the increase partly for that reason. But when, after careful study, he openly attacked 'pork barrel' river and reclamation projects, their sponsors resented his role and overrode his protests."[27]

Spending was not the only domestic policy area where Kennedy showed conservative tendencies. He opposed a constitutional amendment to lower the voting age to eighteen. In 1956, Kennedy voted against a bill, backed by Americans for Democratic Action, to replace the Electoral College with direct popular election of the president and vice president. Opposing another constitutional amendment, he cited a "classic definition of conservatism": "When it is not necessary to

change, it is necessary not to change."[28] In 1957, Kennedy voted with
southern Democrats (and against northern liberal Republicans) on a
couple of civil rights measures, including one that added a jury trial
provision to a civil rights bill. Civil rights groups feared the provision
would empower white southern juries and make the entire law unen-
forceable. On June 25, 1959, the Senate voted to reduce the oil deple-
tion allowance tax break. Kennedy was absent.

Kennedy's signature domestic issue was labor reform, rewriting the
law to make it more difficult for unions to fall under the sway of organized crime or corrupt labor leaders. "It was one of the toughest kinds
of issues for a prospective Democratic candidate," his Senate staffer
Ralph Dungan explained — there was a risk of alienating the politically powerful labor unions. "At the same time he himself was convinced, and the public, a substantial part of the right and center right
elements in the body politic were urging labor reform."[29]

Kennedy himself laid out the issues in an April 4, 1957, speech to
the Lynchburg, Virginia, Chamber of Commerce. It was no accident
that he was speaking to a business group in a southern right-to-work
state. While he took pains to distinguish at the outset between "a few
dishonest, disreputable men" and "the legitimate activities of the great
mass of union leaders and members," the bulk of the speech was devoted to detailing instances of union corruption and violence — what
Kennedy called "the cancer of labor racketeering."

"Labor racketeers are getting labor organizations, founded originally to protect the worker's welfare, into the fields of vice, gambling,
prostitution, and other rackets; using union funds to finance and extend these illegal or questionable activities, and to influence or corrupt
public officials into permitting them," Kennedy said. "Labor racketeers
are using their positions with a union to practice extortion, shake-
downs and bribery; threatening strikes, labor trouble, physical violence or property damage to employers who fail to give them under-
the-table payments, personal gifts, or other contributions which the
union members never see."

Kennedy's speech went on to accuse "labor racketeers" of "abusing
and manipulating for personal gain union pension, welfare and health
funds" as well as "converting union treasuries for their own personal

use and profit; financing their investments, hobbies, private affairs and even their homes with dues contributed by members to strengthen their union; and obtaining this money through questionable loans, so-called gifts, or outright larceny." He singled out the president of the Teamsters Union, Dave Beck, who had invoked his Fifth Amendment right against self-incrimination 117 times before the Senate's special committee on labor racketeering. (Beck's 1993 *New York Times* obituary reported that he "was convicted in 1959 of Federal income-tax evasion and state embezzlement charges for stealing $1,900 from the sale of a union-owned Cadillac," and that he "served 30 months in prison before being paroled in 1964" and was pardoned in 1975 by President Ford.[30]) Robert Kennedy, as counsel to the Senate select committee investigating the unions, also pushed this issue, writing a book about the corrupt Teamsters, *The Enemy Within,* that was published in 1960. Its epigraph was a quote from Thomas Jefferson: "I have sworn upon the altar of God, eternal hostility against every form of tyranny over the mind of man."

John Kennedy took the lead in drafting legislation to require detailed financial disclosure at the federal level for labor unions and their leaders. The 1958 Kennedy-Ives labor reform bill passed the Senate, 88 to 1, but was buried in the House. The 1959 Kennedy-Ervin labor bill passed, 90 to 1.[31] (The one dissenter was Barry Goldwater, who, in his book *Conscience of a Conservative,* called the vote "the most important of my Senate career."[32] Goldwater complained that the bill, "in terms of its effect on the evil conditions it professes to cure, is like a flea bite to a bull elephant."[33]) The AFL-CIO, the large American labor federation, initially backed Kennedy-Ervin, but eventually came out in opposition. The law that finally passed, the Labor Management Reporting and Disclosure Act of 1959, carried many of the Kennedy-Ervin provisions but is known as the Landrum-Griffin Act after two sponsors on the House side.

Even when it came to federal action, however, Kennedy maintained a highly conservative awareness of its limits. He told the Lynchburg Chamber of Commerce that while labor racketeering had been "the chief domestic issue before the Congress," the problem "is not one for the Federal Government alone, or even primarily — the responsibility for cleaning up this foul situation is divided also among union members, employers, local government, and the general public." Seven years after his Notre Dame speech about how "control over local affairs is the essence of liberty," Kennedy was still reminding audiences that not every problem needed a solution from Washington.

Not that Kennedy saw no role at all for the federal government, particularly in providing a safety net for poor or vulnerable Americans. He cast a series of votes in favor of spending on public housing. He voted for expanding federal disability benefits as part of Social Security, for funding the construction of public schools, and for extending unemployment benefits. Particularly as 1960 approached and Kennedy sensed the political need to court the Democratic Party's liberal wing, his voting record became more similar to that of potential rivals such as Hubert Humphrey.[34]

Kennedy engaged in politics not only as a voting senator but also as an author. In 1956, sixteen years after the publication of *Why England Slept,* a second book by John F. Kennedy arrived in bookstores. *Profiles in Courage* tells the stories of eight senators who exhibited political courage while in office. The first was one of Kennedy's predecessors as a senator from Massachusetts, a fellow Harvard graduate, John Quincy Adams. Like John F. Kennedy, John Quincy Adams had a famous and powerful father who had served as American ambassador to Great Britain. Kennedy wrote approvingly of John Quincy Adams: "His guiding star was the principle of Puritan statesmanship his father had laid down many years before: 'The magistrate is the servant not of his own desires, not even of the people, but of his God.'" Another politician whose courage was singled out for praise in a chapter of Kennedy's book was Robert Taft — "Mr. Republican," as *Profiles in Courage* described him. Perhaps Kennedy had not forgotten how the Taft supporters helped him defeat Henry Cabot Lodge Jr. in the 1952 Senate race. *Profiles in Courage* ended on a reflective note: "The stories of past courage," Kennedy wrote, "can provide inspiration. But they cannot supply courage itself. For this each man must look into his own soul."

Here was a topic Kennedy knew all too well. He wrote *Profiles in Courage* while he was staying in Palm Beach. His parents' six-bedroom oceanfront estate, at 1095 North Ocean Boulevard, featured a swimming pool and tennis court as well as a private beach. While writing the book, Kennedy was undergoing a painful recovery from a surgery intended to repair his back, which had been a source of recurring pain since he had injured it getting tackled at Harvard and then again when PT 109 was hit. In a way, the physical agony in the luxury of Palm Beach encapsulated Kennedy's personal life, the paradox of his privileged existence. He managed to be both cursed and blessed at the same time.

Having a choice of salubrious retreats was definitely one of the blessings. If Kennedy wanted to relax and gaze out at the sea, he had the option not only of the Palm Beach house and the Hammersmith Farm estate at Newport, where he was married, but also of the six-acre Kennedy compound at Hyannis Port on Cape Cod. The main house there had fourteen bedrooms, nine baths, a basement theater, a sauna, and an outdoor tennis court, the Kennedy biographer Robert Dallek reports, though in fairness some of the bedrooms were servants' quarters, and other sources count only eleven bedrooms.[35] John and Robert Kennedy each had his own cottage on the property in addition to the main house. For visits to New York City, the senator kept a two-bedroom penthouse apartment on the thirty-fourth floor of the Carlyle Hotel, on Manhattan's Upper East Side. It had a view of Central Park.[36] And he also maintained, over time, a series of townhouses in Washington's Georgetown neighborhood.

The expense of these residences could at times drive the senator to frustration. "What's the point of spending all this money? I mean a chair is a chair and it's perfectly good the chair I'm sitting in. What's the point of all this fancy stuff?" he once complained to a friend.[37]

Not that money was a problem. Sorensen said John F. Kennedy "was worth an estimated ten million dollars, owing primarily to the vast trust funds his father had established many years earlier."[38] That would be about $80 million today.[39] Fortune estimated Joseph Kennedy's net worth in 1957 at between $200 million and $400 million, making him the ninth-richest man in America.[40] That amounts to between $1.6 billion and $3.2 billion today and is a lot of money even if one accepts the criticism that the Fortune estimate was somewhat inflated.[41]

Nor did John Kennedy always differentiate sharply between the family business and his own. Pacing his Senate office one evening, he declared, "You know what I need in this office? I need a couch." He ordered his secretary, "Get the Mart on the phone." The senator proceeded to have a couch delivered to the Capitol from the Chicago Merchandise Mart, a wholesale warehouse and showroom owned by his father, who had installed, on pedestals outside the main entrance, eight bronze, four-times-life-size busts of such merchants as Marshall Field, Edward Filene, Frank Woolworth, and Julius Rosenwald of Sears, Roebuck.[42]

Joseph Kennedy's fortune, immense as it was, was never quite sufficient to gain him admittance to places where Irish Catholics or the newly monied were unwelcome. His application to the Cohasset Country Club, south of Boston, was not accepted. Neither was his application to the Everglades Club in Palm Beach.[43] Joseph Kennedy moved his family to New York, partly in hopes of finding a more open elite than Boston's. In Palm Beach, he stayed at and joined the mostly Jewish Palm Beach Country Club.

It all left John Kennedy with an anti-elitist streak. Ben Bradlee, the former *Washington Post* editor from a Boston Brahmin family, tells the story of how Kennedy, a few weeks after moving into the White House, came over for dinner with Bradlee's father: "Kennedy made us tell the story of how we had been unable for two years to get our daughter, Nancy, accepted into some posh dancing class, despite references that had included Mrs. Borden Harriman, Mrs. Gifford Pinchot, and a host of other acceptables. Kennedy loved that story, because in Boston, he said, people like the Bradlees had kept people like the Kennedys out of many more significant institutions than dancing classes. At the end of the story, he turned to my father and said, 'If that had happened to Dad, he would have moved the whole family out of Boston.'"[44]

If vast wealth could not buy social acceptance, neither could it purchase health or happiness. Joseph Kennedy Jr.'s death still affected John Kennedy. At Sunday Mass, he once asked a friend to wait a minute: "I want to go up and light a candle for Joe."[45] The other two Kennedy siblings who were closest in age to JFK also met unfortunate fates.

Rosemary, the third-born child after Joe and JFK, was from birth what we would now call developmentally disabled. The young Kennedys were good about including her. "They took her everywhere," recalled Robert Morgenthau, who spent two summers in Hyannis when he was sixteen and seventeen and JFK was two years older.[46] In 1941, though, a brain surgery performed in the hope of improving Rosemary's condition wound up worsening it, and she was institutionalized at St. Coletta, a Catholic group home in Jefferson, Wisconsin.[47] (Today, lobotomy procedures are widely rejected, but at the time they were not uncommon.)

The fourth Kennedy sibling, Kathleen, had moved to England and married William Cavendish, a British nobleman — his parents were the Duke and Duchess of Devonshire — who himself died in the war. In May 1948, Kathleen, too, perished in an airplane crash in France.

Meanwhile, as JFK's younger brother Bobby and his wife were reproducing prolifically, John and Jacqueline were having a difficult time. First came a miscarriage, then, on August 23, 1956, a stillborn daughter. In November 1957, Jacqueline gave birth to a baby girl, Caroline. At the age of forty, John F. Kennedy finally became a parent.

It would not be long before the new father became the president. But first, he would have to win an election.

CHAPTER 4

Presidential Campaign
1960

This is not a struggle for supremacy of arms alone — it is also a struggle for supremacy between two conflicting ideologies; freedom under God versus ruthless, Godless tyranny.

— JOHN F. KENNEDY, campaign speech at the Mormon Tabernacle in Salt Lake City, September 23, 1960

Chicago

WHAT EVERYONE REMEMBERS is the sweat. Watching on television, a voter begins by glancing at Richard Nixon's receding hairline, then notices the shadows under the eyes, the slack jaw, the suit with its ill-fitting collar and lumpy shoulders. Before long, though, the viewer cannot avoid focusing on the moisture pooling under Nixon's lip, shining there, demanding attention as if it were a third candidate in the debate.

"No picture in American politics tells a better story," Theodore White wrote in his classic account *The Making of the President 1960.*

Nixon's opponent in the September 26, 1960, presidential debate, John F. Kennedy, by contrast, "looked like a young Adonis," recalled the CBS producer who directed the face-off, Don Hewitt.[1] When the debate was over, even Nixon's mother called to ask the candidate if anything was wrong, because he did not look well.[2]

But memories, like looks, can be deceiving. Debates are not beauty contests. Americans, whether they saw that first Kennedy-Nixon debate as it happened or read about it in a book or watched it on You-Tube years later, have remembered how Nixon and Kennedy appeared but may have forgotten what the candidates actually said.

So here is a reminder.

One candidate in the debate railed against criminal control of America's largest labor union, raised the specter of the "dangerous" Chinese Communists, and warned of the "serious" threat of Communist subversion in America. "I don't believe in big government," this candidate said.

The other candidate boasted of his record of "programs" for "housing," "health," "medical care," "schools," and "the development of electric power."

"I favor higher salaries for teachers," this candidate said, also backing federal aid for school construction. "I know what it means to be poor," this candidate said.

The anti-Communist, anti–big government candidate was John F. Kennedy. The one touting government programs and higher salaries for public employees was Richard Nixon.

Nor was that debate an outlier. The next time the two candidates met in a televised debate, on October 7, one of them called for "a revitalization of our military strength." This candidate criticized the administration for losing ground in the international effort to prevent "the admission of Red China into the United Nations." That was Kennedy, the senator from Massachusetts, the Democrat.

The other candidate said, "I think it may be necessary that we have more taxes," and called for more funding, staffing, and power for a government committee to make sure that government contractors did not discriminate on the basis of race. That was Nixon, the Republican from California who was serving as vice president under Eisenhower, and who, this time around, had learned from his experience and agreed to use makeup to fight his perspiration problem.

And so it went for the next two debates in the series of four. Kennedy laced into Nixon for having "never really protested the Communists seizing Cuba, ninety miles off the coast of the United States."

Nixon warned that Kennedy's proposal to support the opponents of Fidel Castro's Communist dictatorship was "dangerously irresponsible," and that it risked violating the United Nations charter, which, in "its Preamble, Article I, and Article II," provides "that there shall be no intervention by one nation in the internal affairs of another."

Nixon credited his party, the Republicans, for having kept America out of war, in contrast to "three Democratic presidents who led us into war."

Kennedy faulted the Eisenhower-Nixon administration for spending excessively on farm subsidies: "We've spent more money on agriculture in the last eight years than the hundred years of the Agricultural Department before that."

The pattern, in other words, in all four debates was that Nixon sounded like a tax-and-spend peacenik, and Kennedy sounded like a hard-liner against both federal spending and communism. As Nixon put it in his memoirs, "Kennedy conveyed the image — to 60 million people — that he was tougher on Castro and communism than I was."[3]

The conventional account of the 1960 campaign, enshrined by Theodore White in *The Making of the President,* is that, as White wrote, "rarely in American history has there been a political campaign that discussed issues less or clarified them less."[4] White had a front-row seat, so it is hard to argue with him. White himself, though, conceded in the author's note at the start of his book that "later historians would tell the story of the quest for power in 1960 in more precise terms with greater wealth of established fact."

From the perspective of this later historian, the 1960 campaign seems to have been full of issues — so much so that it is possible to re-tell the story of the entire campaign, not according to the conventional chronological narrative of the Wisconsin and West Virginia Democratic primaries, then the political conventions, then the debates, and then Election Day itself, but rather by focusing on three big issues: religion, national security, and economic growth.

Today it seems hard to believe that religion was an issue at all. But it was, and a significant one. It was not simply that until Kennedy, the United States had never had a Catholic president. The issue reached well beyond that, down to the deep roots of anti-Catholic feeling in American history. That history, often overlooked, is worth a brief review here, to help explain exactly what Kennedy was up against.

The first and arguably most important wave of European settlers in North America, the Puritans, had left England in protest of Catholicizing tendencies in the Church of England after King Charles I (r. 1625–1649) married a French Catholic. The first minister at the first church in Boston, John Cotton, spoke of the Roman Catholic Church as "the mother of Harlots and Abominations of the earth." In 1689, Bostonians rebelled against their British-appointed governor, complaining that he was contaminating their pure Protestant society with "the great Scarlet Whore" of Catholicism. The "Rights of the Colonists" statement approved by the Boston Town Meeting in 1772 recommended mutual toleration for adherents of different religions, with the exception of Catholics, whose allegiance to the pope rather than to local government was said to lead "directly to the worst anarchy and confusion, civil discord, and blood shed." Thomas Paine's influential 1776 pamphlet, *Common Sense*, rejected monarchy as "the Popery of government."[5] John Adams wrote that "Liberty and Popery cannot live together."[6]

The picture for Catholics was not entirely hostile. A Catholic, Charles Carroll of Carrollton, Maryland, was among the signers of the Declaration of Independence. The Constitution included not only a First Amendment guaranteeing the free exercise of religion, but also, in Article VI, an emphatic ("no . . . ever . . . any") prohibition on religious tests for office. Neither provision, though, was sufficient to put anti-Catholicism to a final rest. In August 1834, a crowd of Protestants in Charlestown burned a convent to the ground. In the 1850s, an anti-Catholic political movement, the American Party, or Know-Nothing Party ("I know nothing," its members were supposed to respond to inquiries), elected governors in six states, including Massachusetts.[7] In 1855, following a dispute over a block of marble that Pope Pius IX had donated, the Know-Nothing Party took control of the committee in charge of building the Washington Monument; partly as a result, construction ground to a halt.[8] The Ku Klux Klan is today remembered primarily for its antiblack bigotry and violence, but the historian Kenneth Jackson writes in his book about the Klan that at the time of the group's resurgence in the 1920s, anti-Catholicism was the dominant motive: "Among Klansmen in almost every state and section, the most basic and pervasive concern was the Pope. Catholics were regarded not simply as communicants of an idolatrous church, but as citizens who placed their love and devotion to the Vatican above their allegiance to the United States."[9]

The anti-Catholic bias spread to other minority groups. Paul Samuelson, a Jewish MIT professor with a Ph.D. from Harvard who later won a Nobel Prize in economics, confessed that before supporting Kennedy, he had to resolve in his own mind what he characterized as "a problem that he was a Catholic." The attitude was typical of liberal academics at the time. James Tobin, an economics professor at Yale who was also to win a Nobel, recalled, "I can remember I think in May of '60 a dinner party with quite a group of liberal intellectuals in New Haven — law school people mainly — at which my wife and I were the only ones who were for Kennedy at all, even in the sense of being willing to vote for him in the election, should he be nominated . . . They were so much concerned about the Catholic issue."[10]

The bias also infected the African-American community. At one point in the campaign, Senator Kennedy called Coretta Scott King to express concern about her husband, the civil rights leader Martin Luther King Jr., who was languishing in a Georgia jail. In response, the pastor of the Ebenezer Baptist Church in Atlanta, Martin Luther King Sr., announced, "I had expected to vote against Senator Kennedy because of his religion. But now he can be my president, Catholic or whatever he is." Kennedy was as stunned by the comment as he was glad of the endorsement, telling an aide: "That was a hell of a bigoted statement, wasn't it? Imagine Martin Luther King having a bigot for a father."[11]

As for Kennedy's own father, Sorensen reports that Ambassador Kennedy, "asked how many states his son would have carried had he been an Episcopalian, snapped without hesitation, 'Fifty!'"[12]

As with many hatreds in history, it is hard to know whether to focus on the power of the hatred or on the power of the hated group or individual to overcome the prejudice. Before Kennedy, the Catholic who had come closest to the presidency was a governor of New York, Al Smith. Denied the Democratic Party's presidential nomination in 1924, he received it in 1928, only to lose the general election to Herbert Hoover. Was Smith's nomination proof of progress for Catholics? Or was Smith's loss a sign of enduring voter bias? The answer is probably a bit of both. During the 1928 campaign, virulently anti-Catholic litera-ture targeting Smith included photographs of the recently completed Holland Tunnel between New York and New Jersey, describing it as the route the pope would take to America from Rome.[13] In any event, by the time Kennedy arrived in 1960 to put the nation's tolerance to the test, the Irish were, anti-Catholic bias notwithstanding, well on their way to achieving their status, as described by the sociologist Andrew M. Greeley, as "the most successful educational, occupational, and economic gentile ethnic group in America."[14]

The first place where the Kennedy presidential campaign was to meet this challenge was Wisconsin, where JFK faced a primary contest against Hubert Humphrey, the senator from neighboring Minnesota. Humphrey was forty-eight years old to Kennedy's forty-two. The Min-nesotan had served four more years in the Senate than had the man from Massachusetts, but Kennedy had the advantage in wartime ser-vice; Humphrey had failed a draft-related physical exam on account of what a doctor described as a "right scrotal hernia."[15]

When it came to anticommunism, the candidates were evenly matched. While Humphrey was mayor of Minneapolis, his own Democratic Farmer-Labor Party was dominated by Communists who shouted him down at a party convention with cries of "Fascist! War-monger! Capitalist pig!"[16] Humphrey purged them. He went on, as a senator, to sponsor the Communist Control Act of 1954, an outright ban on the Communist Party in America. "The Communist party isn't really a political party, it's an international conspiracy," Humphrey said, describing the Communists as "rats."[17] Theodore White's *The Making of the President 1960* includes an account of Humphrey's speech at the Jewish Community Center of Milwaukee during the Wisconsin pri-mary campaign. America's struggle against communism, Humphrey said there, "is a struggle between good and evil, between tolerance and intolerance, over the very nature of man."[18]

When the Wisconsin primary results were tallied on the night of April 5, 1960, they showed that while Kennedy had won the popular vote statewide, he had lost all four of the predominantly Protestant congressional districts, and won in four more-Catholic congressional districts. The religious "issue" was unresolved, and Kennedy and Humphrey headed south, to more heavily Protestant West Virginia, for another contest.[19]

There the religious issue was even more overt, and, at times, ugly. Andrew J. Houvouras, a Catholic businessman and Navy veteran[20] who was one of three Kennedy cochairmen in Cabell County, West Virginia, recalled, "There was literature that said that if a Catholic was president that they would split open the bellies of Protestant pregnant women and dash their babies' heads upon the stones! Now, this wasn't just hearsay. This literature was passed around." Some Protestant churches played anti-Catholic recordings after services. Driving with Kennedy into the city of Huntington after meeting him at the airport, Houvouras reported to the candidate that one local minister had said "he was worried of the fact that you would popularize the Catholic faith as Eisenhower had popularized golf."

Houvouras remembered, four years after the primary:

On the religious issue — it is hard to look back and actually believe what happened. People whom I had associated with for many, many years — I had been in their homes and they had been in my home — voiced derogatory remarks; would not let their children play with my children because I was active in behalf of Senator Kennedy. As a matter of fact, one of our very best neighbors told my little girl that Catholics should vote for Catholics and Protestants should vote for Protestants. People who I am associated with indirectly in business, in other corporations, said that you must remember that he is a Catholic candidate, not the Democratic candidate.[21]

Kennedy eventually addressed the issue head-on. First, on April 21 he gave a speech in Washington to the American Society of Newspaper Editors. There he backed away from his efforts as a congressman to promote government aid to parochial schools: "Federal assistance to parochial schools, for example, is a very legitimate issue actually

before the Congress. I am opposed to it. I believe it is clearly unconstitutional. I voted against it on the Senate floor this year." He concluded by associating himself with the Founding Fathers: "I believe the
American people are more concerned with a man's views and abilities
than with the church to which he belongs. I believe that the founding
fathers meant it when they provided in Article VI of the Constitution
that there should be no religious test for public office — a provision
that brought not one dissenting vote, only the comment of Roger Sher-
man that it was surely unnecessary — 'The prevailing legality being a
sufficient security against such tests.' And I believe that the American
people mean to adhere to those principles today."

Then — almost as if to hedge against the possibility that Americans,
or at least West Virginians, were *not* going to adhere to those principles — Kennedy took to television on Sunday night, May 8, a pivotal
moment before the Tuesday, May 10, West Virginia primary. Kennedy,
according to White, took about ten minutes of a half-hour paid appearance to answer a planted question on religion. As White recounts
it, Kennedy looked into the camera and said: "When any man stands
on the steps of the Capitol and takes the oath of office of President,
he is swearing to support the separation of church and state; he puts
one hand on the Bible and raises the other hand to God as he takes
the oath. And if he breaks his oath, he is not only committing a crime
against the Constitution, for which the Congress can impeach him —
and should impeach him — but he is committing a sin against God."

White wrote: "Here Kennedy raised his hand from an imaginary
Bible, as if lifting it to God, and, repeating softly, said, 'A sin against
God, for he has sworn on the Bible.'"

This, then, was Kennedy's most effective answer on the religious
issue — not to reject altogether the importance of religion, but rather
to remind voters, subtly or not so subtly, that he, too, was a devout
believer in God. He made clear that "separation of church and state,"
by his definition, did not preclude either swearing an oath of office on
a Bible or invoking God during a presidential campaign. He continued
to do this after his victory in West Virginia, where he had effectively
vanquished Humphrey, and as his focus shifted from winning his party's nomination to winning the general election against Nixon.

Here is Kennedy in his speech at the Democratic National Convention in Los Angeles on July 15, 1960, accepting his party's presidential nomination: "My call is to the young in heart, regardless of age — to all who respond to the Scriptural call: 'Be strong and of a good courage; be not afraid, neither be thou dismayed.'... Recall with me the words of Isaiah: 'They that wait upon the Lord shall renew their strength; they shall mount up with wings as eagles; they shall run and not be weary.'"

Kennedy's September 12, 1960, speech to a special meeting of the Greater Houston Ministerial Association, televised throughout Texas, perhaps left itself open to misinterpretation when it declared, "I believe in an America where the separation of church and state is absolute." The reference was to the First Amendment ban on Congress's establishing an official state religion. But the most important part of the speech was its conclusion, which made clear Kennedy's understanding that the separation of church and state was not as absolute as some might wish to believe. The candidate ended by offering a variation on the formulation that had been so effective the Sunday night before the West Virginia primary. If Kennedy won the election, he promised, "I shall devote every effort of mind and spirit to fulfilling the oath of the Presidency — practically identical, I might add, to the oath I have taken for 14 years in the Congress. For, without reservation, I can 'solemnly swear that I will faithfully execute the office of President of the United States, and will to the best of my ability preserve, protect, and defend the Constitution — so help me God.'"

In the closing days of the campaign, before large audiences, Kennedy at least three times likened his campaign to a divinely inspired mission. On October 26, at a rally in Hamtramck, Michigan, the candidate said, "One hundred years ago in the campaign of 1860, Abraham Lincoln wrote to a friend: 'I know there is a God, and I know He hates injustice. I see the storm coming, and I know His hand is in it. But if He has a place and a part for me, I believe that I am ready.' Now, 100 years later, we know there is a God, and we know He hates injustice. We see the storm coming, and we know His hand is in it. But if He has a place and a part for us, I believe that we are ready."

He used almost identical language in an October 27 speech to a campaign rally in New York organized by the International Ladies' Garment Workers' Union, and again at 3 a.m. on Sunday, November 6, speaking from a hotel balcony to a crowd of thirty thousand gathered outdoors in Waterbury, Connecticut.[22]

At 11 p.m. on election eve, November 7, the Kennedy campaign aired a paid national television broadcast from Boston's Faneuil Hall, where fourteen years earlier the young congressional candidate just back from World War II had given his July 4 oration. Part of the broadcast was a clip from the candidate's appearance before the Houston ministers, including the conclusion about Kennedy's readiness to "preserve, protect, and defend the Constitution — so help me God." Another part featured Kennedy before a live audience at Faneuil Hall, associating himself with both the Founding Fathers — "We are meeting in the old hall which was the scene of Otis' speeches and Samuel Adams's which led up to the American Revolution" — and their Puritan forebears: "This painting behind me is of the first Thanksgiving, December 13, way back. It was painted in 1821, and of course it was of the first Thanksgiving in the Plymouth Colony. They had had a long, hard experience. Many had died. And yet the first harvest came in, they gave thanks to the Lord for His generosity to them. It reminds us of our great history, of what our people have been willing to do in order to build our society."

While Kennedy's Catholicism probably helped him with some Catholic voters, it cost him votes among non-Catholics, and the non-Catholics outnumbered the Catholics.[23] Some might wonder why he did not simply become a Protestant. Other politicians at the time did. The governor of New Jersey, Robert Meyner, a Democrat who himself was considered a possible contender for president in 1960, was "born and brought up a Catholic" but was married in a Congregational church and thus blurred his affiliation with Roman Catholicism. Malcolm S. Forbes, the magazine publisher who was the Republican candidate against Meyner in 1957, was a Catholic in college before becoming an Episcopalian.[24] And JFK's sister Kathleen had married into the Church of England, though she stopped short of becoming a member herself. Perhaps if Kennedy had left Catholicism, he would have alienated Catholic voters in his home state of Massachusetts and elsewhere, and his own devout mother, without fully dispelling doubts in the minds of Protestant voters. Or perhaps he did not view it in terms of such strictly political calculus; perhaps he felt comfortable in his own faith and its rituals as a significant part of his life and identity, embracing its standards even as he sometimes fell short of them in his personal behavior.

In any case, that was the view expressed by the candidate himself. He had agreed to cooperate with a campaign biography by a professor at Williams College, James MacGregor Burns. When a draft came in to the senator's office, Kennedy demanded changes. In an October 27, 1959, letter to Burns, Sorensen wrote: "The charge should not be made in two places that he is not deeply religious — that is not true, in my opinion or his — and it is certainly unverifiable.

"IF THESE CHANGES ARE NOT BEING MADE, PLEASE LET ME KNOW IMMEDIATELY BECAUSE THE SENATOR WANTS TO CALL YOU IN PERSON ON THEM."

Burns backed down in a November 1, 1959, "Dear Jack" reply: "On the references to the depth of your religiousness, I agree that no one but yourself can answer that question and I have taken these out."[25]

The fact that Kennedy considered himself deeply religious does not necessarily mean that he was a conservative. Father Daniel Berrigan, for example, was a Catholic priest who became an antiwar activist. It is true that nowadays, religious intensity is a strong predictor of voting behavior. An analysis of 2008 exit-poll data by the Pew Forum on Religion and Public Life, for example, found that frequency of worship attendance was a more powerful indicator of voting behavior than age, gender, education, income, urban/rural status, region, or union membership: "In 2008, for instance, the predicted probability of voting Democratic among voters who never go to church or other worship services was 41 points higher than among those who said they attend worship services more than once a week (even after controlling for other demographic variables). In 2004, this difference was 38 points, and in 2000 it was 39 points."[26] Another analysis, by Gallup in 2009, found "Republicans outnumber Democrats by 12 percentage points among Americans who are classified as highly religious, while Democrats outnumber Republicans by 30 points among those who are not religious."[27] In 1960 such distinctions mattered less, as the numbers of Americans with no religion was still quite small.[28]

Understanding the influence of Kennedy's religion on his politics, though, does not require exit polling, statistical regression analysis, or speculation about his motives. It just requires listening to what Kennedy himself said, over and over again, connecting religious freedom and the right of the individual against the state to the idea that all people are created by God with certain rights, and connecting all of that to the Cold War between the United States and the Soviet Union, the worldwide struggle between "freedom or slavery," as Kennedy put it in those campaign-closing remarks citing Lincoln. He explained all this in his July 4, 1946, speech at Faneuil Hall when he spoke of how, "strengthened by Christian morality," "the right of the individual against the State" was under challenge abroad by "the doctrine of collectivism." He reprised it yet again in his January 29, 1950, speech at Notre Dame, where he explained that "Catholics can never adhere to any political theory which holds that the state is a separate, distinct organization to which allegiance must be paid rather than a representative institution which derives its powers from the consent of the governed." He had explained it most fully and recently in his June 3, 1955, speech at Assumption College, in which he spoke of the Cold War as "the battle for the preservation of Christian civilization," and elaborated: "I say this and not because I believe Christianity is a weapon in the present world struggle, but because I believe religion itself is at the root of the struggle, not in terms of the physical organizations of Christianity versus those of Atheism, but in terms of Good versus Evil, right versus wrong."

Now, in the heat of the presidential campaign, Kennedy, rather than abandoning this theme, returned to it again, explicitly putting religious liberty at the heart of the Cold War struggle between the United States and the Soviet Union. In doing so, he was connecting the first big issue of the campaign, his own Catholic faith, with the second one, national security. The remarks came, as some of the previous ones did, before a religious audience, although not to a Catholic one. He was speaking, rather, at the Mormon Tabernacle in Salt Lake City, on September 23, 1960. He began with language that made clear he had no illusions about the nature of the adversary: "the enemy is the communist system itself — implacable, insatiable, unceasing in its drive for world domination."

He recalled visiting the Soviet Union in 1939, when it was "barely emerging into the 20th century, isolated in its Godless tyranny, devoid of allies and influence." Then he drew a contrast, implicitly faulting the Eisenhower-Nixon administration, and perhaps Roosevelt and Truman before them, for failing to contain or isolate this enemy:

> Today, 21 years later, the Kremlin rules a ruthless empire stretching in a great half-circle from East Berlin to Vietminh — with outposts springing up in the Middle East, Africa, Asia, and now, only 90 miles from our shores, in the fretful island of Cuba.
>
> The products of their once-backward educational system have surpassed our vaunted science and engineering in launching rockets to the moon and outer space. The growth of their once-backward economy now progresses at a rate nearly 3 times as fast as our own. And the prestige of this once-feared and hated nation now leaves a glittering web entrapping neutralists and nationalists in all corners of the globe.
>
> In almost every area of competition — military, diplomatic, economic, scientific and educational — the communists are now capable of competing with the United States on nearly equal terms.

Yet there was one important competition with the Communists in which Kennedy knew America had clear superiority — religion. He went on:

> But in one area the communists can never overcome us — unless we fall back to their level — and that is the area of spiritual values — moral strength — the strength of our will and our purpose — the qualities and traditions that make this nation a shining example to all who yearn to be free.
>
> This is our single greatest advantage. For this is not a struggle for supremacy of arms alone — it is also a struggle for supremacy between two conflicting ideologies; freedom under God versus ruthless, Godless tyranny. The contest, moreover, is not merely to gain the material wealth of other nations — it is a contest for their hearts and minds. And the challenge to all Americans now is not merely the

extent of our material contributions as tax-payers — but the extent to which we can find greater strength for the long pull in our traditions of religious liberty than the masters of the Kremlin can ever exact from disciplines of servitude.

Here in our land church and state are separate and free — in their lands neither is free, and the church lives in constant fear of the state. In our land the diversity of equality brings strength to our spiritual ties — in their lands the terror of tyranny drives hope and will from the hearts of men.

The communist camp divides over the best pathway to follow to world conquest. In this nation our two parties divide over the best pathway to world peace.

I have advocated the pathway of strength — a stronger America, the strongest sentinel at the gate of freedom — a nation prepared to put force behind law so that we will not be destroyed by the law of force. But I mean spiritually and morally stronger as well . . . We boast to foreign visitors of our great dams and cities and wealth — But not our free religious heritage. We have become missionaries abroad of a wide range of doctrines — free enterprise, anti-Communism and pro-Americanism — But rarely the doctrine of religious liberty.

When Kennedy said, "In this nation our two parties divide over the best pathway to world peace. I have advocated the pathway of strength," he was recalling the peace-through-strength argument he had advanced in his 1940 letter to the editor of the *Harvard Crimson*, and in his senior-thesis-turned-book, *Why England Slept*.

The claim that the Communists had advanced during the terms of President Eisenhower and Vice President Nixon was a staple of Kennedy's campaign. In the senator's acceptance speech to the Democratic National Convention, he said, "Communist influence has penetrated further into Asia, stood astride the Middle East and now festers some ninety miles off the coast of Florida. Friends have slipped into neutrality — and neutrals into hostility."[29]

In an August 24, 1960, speech to a Democratic rally at George Washington High School stadium in Alexandria, Virginia, Kennedy said, "Never before has this country experienced such arrogant treatment at the hands of its enemy. Never before have we experienced a more critical decline in our prestige . . . Never before has the grip of communism sunk so deeply into previously friendly countries. Mr. Nixon is experienced in policies of weakness, retreat, and defeat." He faulted Vice President Nixon for a decline, over the past eight years, in American "defensive strength and retaliatory capacity."

Kennedy said, "We have within 90 miles . . . Castro, who attacks us daily. In the Congo, the most intimate adviser to the new Prime Minister is the Soviet Ambassador."[30]

A Kennedy campaign statement promised to help defeat the Communists in Cuba: "We must attempt to strengthen the non-Batista democratic anti-Castro forces in exile, and in Cuba itself, who offer eventual hope of overthrowing Castro. Thus far these fighters for freedom have had virtually no support from our government." Schlesinger claims Kennedy had not seen this statement before it was issued, and says it had been drafted by campaign speechwriter Richard Goodwin, an account Goodwin confirms in his own memoir.[31]

But there can be no separating Kennedy from his own words, on October 6, 1960, at a Democratic Party dinner in Cincinnati:

> I want to talk with you tonight about the most glaring failure of American foreign policy today — about a disaster that threatens the security of the whole Western Hemisphere — about a Communist menace that has been permitted to arise under our very noses, only 90 miles from our shores . . . In the 2 years since that revolution swept Fidel Castro into power . . . there have been no free elections — and there will be none as long as Castro rules. All political parties — with the exception of the Communist Party — have been destroyed. All political dissenters have been executed, imprisoned, or exiled. All academic freedom has been eliminated. All major newspapers and radio stations have been seized. And all of Cuba is in the iron grip of a Communist-oriented police state . . . He has transformed the island of Cuba into a hostile and militant Communist satellite — a base from which to carry Communist infiltration and subversion throughout the Americas.

As a remedy, Kennedy proposed "encouraging those liberty-loving Cubans who are leading the resistance to Castro" and also "constantly" expressing "our determination" that Cuba "will again be free."[32]

When the Eisenhower administration announced it would confine Khrushchev and Castro to Manhattan during their visit to the United Nations in September 1960, Kennedy shot back, "But they have not confined them . . . in Latin America or around the world."[33]

The Castro line was enough to distress some of the Cambridge academics who had come over to Kennedy from years of backing Adlai Stevenson. The MIT economist Paul Samuelson recalled, "What I winced about, I remember, weren't economic things. It was when he was chastising Nixon for being soft on Castro, which he got a very successful response from and continued it and so forth. That was the sort of reproach about which friends would say, 'Now what about this?'"[34]

Schlesinger recalled that Kennedy stressed Soviet gains in Africa as well as in Latin America: "During the 1960 campaign he repeatedly criticized the Eisenhower administration for its delay of eight months in sending an ambassador to Guinea, pointing out that the Russian Ambassador was there on Independence Day with offers of trade and aid — 'and today Guinea has moved toward the communist bloc because of our neglect.'"[35]

Kennedy's campaign did more than simply fault the Eisenhower-Nixon White House for its failures, however; it laid out an alternative approach, what Kennedy, in a June 14, 1960, Senate foreign policy speech, called a "national strategy backed by strength," to counter "the determined Soviet program for world domination."

To detail that strategy, Kennedy the presidential candidate again drew on Kennedy the author, issuing a book of collected speeches under the title *The Strategy of Peace*. For a book with "peace" on the cover, it was strong stuff. "We need to develop small tactical nuclear weapons," it said. It faulted Eisenhower for having "tailored our strategy and military requirements to fit our budget — instead of fitting our budget to our military requirements and strategy." Kennedy insisted, "We must refuse to accept a cheap, second-best defense." *The Strategy of Peace* made a remarkably prescient call for developing and deploying a missile defense of the continental United States: "Our continental defense system, as already mentioned, must be redesigned for the detection and interception of missile attacks as well as planes." Kennedy called for "more and better missiles" — to close the "missile gap" with the Soviets — and also for increased conventional forces, reminding readers that in 1954 he had offered, unsuccessfully, a legislative measure that would have prevented Eisenhower from reducing the Army to seventeen divisions from nineteen. He wrote, "No problem is of greater importance to every American than our national security and defense. And no aspect of our defense capabilities under this Administration should be cause for greater concern than our lag in conventional weapons and ground forces." When Kennedy dealt with arms control or a nuclear test ban in the book, he stressed that "generally speaking, we are ahead of the Russians in the development of atomic warheads," and warned that resuming nuclear testing might therefore help the Soviets more than America.[36]

Sorensen did his part to try to get some of these same points inserted in the campaign biography of Kennedy by James MacGregor Burns. The Kennedy aide wrote to Burns to complain about a draft in which "nothing is said about . . . the missile gap . . . or his fight to stop the 'new look' reductions in the Armed Forces."[37]

Nixon was on weak ground when it came to countering Kennedy's attacks on Eisenhower's supposed parsimony when it came to defense spending, because his own rivals within the Republican Party were making the same points. So had other Democrats, including Senator Stuart Symington of Missouri, since the mid-1950s. The governor of New York, Nelson Rockefeller, a Republican, called for an additional $3 billion a year in defense spending above the baseline of about $48 billion. Though Nixon deleted that specific proposal, the Republican nominee did end up signing on to a July 23, 1960, Rockefeller statement acknowledging that "speeded production of missiles" was required by the "imperatives of national security," and that "the United States can afford and must provide the increased expenditures . . . There must be no price ceiling on America's security."[38]

The Strategy of Peace also offered Kennedy's views on a variety of conflicts around the world. "Let us be clear that we will never turn our back on our steadfast friends in Israel, whose adherence to the democratic way must be admired by all friends of freedom," Kennedy wrote. Israel "shares with the West a tradition of civil liberties, of cultural freedom, of parliamentary democracy, of social mobility," he wrote, approvingly quoting a description of British mandatory Palestine before the creation of Israel: "The land without a people waited for the people without a land." The Palestinian Arabs had yet to become a celebrated cause among the Democratic primary electorate.

When it came to dealing with the "captive nations" of Eastern and Central Europe, Kennedy said he looked forward "to a free Berlin, in a united Germany." He expressed special interest in Poland, as he had in those Polish radio broadcasts in 1947 and 1948, saying in the book (and in a 1957 Senate speech) that "the people of Poland—because of their religious convictions and strong patriotic spirit, because of their historical hatred of the Russians—are perhaps better equipped than any people on earth to withstand the present period of persecution, just as their forefathers withstood successive invasions and partitions from the Germans and Austrians and the Russians for centuries before them, and just as theirs was the only country occupied by Hitler that did not produce a quisling." He noted that he had cosponsored an amendment that would authorize the president to deliver American aid to countries, like Poland, where there were stirrings of freedom. And he faulted Eisenhower for allowing Soviet tanks to roll into Budapest and crush the Hungarian uprising of 1956, derisively quoting Eisenhower's words at the time: "The United States doesn't now, and never has, advocated open rebellion by an undefended populace against force over which they could not possibly prevail."[39]

A brief section of The Strategy of Peace dealt with communism on the home front in America, and here it seemed that Kennedy was trying to win over some of the liberals who thought he was too close to McCarthy. Included were Kennedy's January 30 and June 29, 1959, Senate speeches seeking to eliminate the loyalty oath provision from the National Defense Education Act of 1958, which required scholars applying for government grants or loans to sign an affidavit "declaring that they do not believe in, belong to, or support any subversive organization." Kennedy called the oath requirement "repugnant," but, perhaps more tellingly, he also argued that it would be ineffective: "Card-carrying members of the Communist party, of course, have no hesitancy about perjuring themselves in such an affidavit."[40] Even in the midst of his attempt to reach out to the intellectual left that already viewed him with suspicion, Kennedy could not help but confess his belief that "of course" any card-carrying Communist would lie without hesitation.

The third major issue of the 1960 campaign was economic growth. Just as the religious issue had been connected to the national security issue through the linkage of the "Godless tyranny" of the Soviet Union, so, too, the question of economic growth was seen not only as a matter of keeping Americans employed and prosperous, but also in the context of the competition with Moscow. Kennedy's approach to the growth issue was similar to his line of attack on the missile gap — to fault the Eisenhower-Nixon administration for its failures while promising that he would do better as president. Walter Heller, an economist at the University of Minnesota who became an adviser to Kennedy, recalls meeting the senator in a hotel suite. Kennedy was running an hour late, and a crowd of fifteen thousand was waiting for him outside. Kennedy was in the middle of changing his shirt, and while scratching his chest, he mused about a $5 billion tax cut and asked the professor, "Tell me, do you really think we can make this 5 percent growth rate we talk about into a platform?"[41]

Kennedy hammered away at the issue. Here he is in a speech at Bethany College in West Virginia, April 19, 1960: "We have declined to a growth rate which is only half the record increases of the Roosevelt-Truman era. And in some states growth has completely stopped."[42]

Then again, speaking at a Democratic rally in Alexandria, Virginia, on August 24: "Last year we had the lowest rate of economic growth of any major industrialized society in the world."[43]

On September 6, Kennedy took a question about the growth issue from an audience member in Seattle, during a statewide television appearance. In his answer, he elaborated on his target of 5 percent annual real growth in gross domestic product, a goal that had been included in the Democratic Party platform and that Kennedy embraced. He also called economic growth and a tax increase "contradictory":

QUESTION. My name is J. T. Hong. Senator Kennedy, I would like to ask you, how do you plan to obtain 5 percent economic growth without raising taxes?

Senator KENNEDY. Let me say that I don't believe that there is an intimate relationship between raising taxes and economic growth. In fact, under the present conditions, I can imagine nothing more deflationary than to increase taxes. I don't say that it is possible immediately to provide 5 percent economic growth. The Democratic platform called for it and the Rockefeller brothers 2 years ago said it was possible. I do think, however, that we can secure a better economic growth than we have today, and we can aim for the goal of 5 percent. It is a fact that Germany, France, and England all had a growth of 5 percent or over last year. We had the lowest rate of economic growth of any major industrialized society in the world . . . I don't think that anyone has suggested that we should increase taxes at the present time in order to stimulate growth. The only time I heard taxes discussed, and I discussed them, would be if we had a serious national emergency requiring a large appropriation for national defense at a time when our economy was booming and we suffered a serious danger of inflation. That would be, in my opinion, the time that you might have to face up to the problem of taxes. But if you are talking about economic growth, there is not an intimate relationship at the present time between a tax increase and economic growth. In fact, in my opinion, they would be contradictory.[44]

With the 5 percent growth goal, as with the need for increased military spending, Nixon had been boxed in by Governor Rockefeller. The same July 23, 1960, Rockefeller statement that Nixon had approved, calling for stepped-up missile production, also said that "the rate of our economic growth must, as promptly as possible, be accelerated . . . As the Vice President pointed out in a speech in 1958, the achievement of a five per cent rate of growth would produce an additional $10 billion of tax revenue in 1962."[45] Nixon, in other words, could neither assail Kennedy's 5 percent goal as unattainable nor disagree with Kennedy's call for improvement over the growth record of the past eight years under Eisenhower and Nixon.

The Republican candidate and his allies were left to fulminating, reactive bluster. In December of 1959, the White House budget director, Maurice Stans, decried "the cult of growth."[46] Henry Hazlitt, a columnist for *Newsweek* who favored Nixon over Kennedy, derided "rate-of-growth fetishists."[47] The October 17, 1960, issue of *Life* magazine carried a side-by-side comparison of the two candidates on the subject. Under the heading "What Nixon has to say about economy," the first sentence was this: "They [our critics] invite us to join them in . . . the most fashionable political parlor game of our time . . . growthmanship."[48] Such dismissive comments were unpersuasive. "Mr. Nixon doesn't understand the problem," countered an editorial in the July 1, 1960, *Tonawanda* (New York) *News,* headlined, "'Growthmanship' Not So Silly, Mr. Nixon." "With a rapidly expanding population, we need the higher growth rate to meet defense and public needs without reducing our standard of living. So 'growthmanship' is not a silly parlor game. It is a vital concern to everyone."

Kennedy did not go into great detail about how exactly he would achieve his target of 5 percent growth, but he offered some broad outlines.

One area was taxes. As he said in answer to J. T. Hong's question in Seattle, he would try to avoid tax increases. He elaborated on the tax question in a December 9, 1959, interview with the editor of *Harper's Magazine,* John Fischer, which was included in *The Strategy of Peace.* "Do we have to pay higher taxes?" Fischer asked. Kennedy did not flatly rule it out, but his answer expressed his preference: "If we had a sufficiently stimulated rate of growth, we would get additional tax revenues — normally, without any increase in taxes . . . If unemployment is high . . . then quite obviously it would be the greatest mistake to try to increase taxes, because such a policy might have a deflationary [that is, contracting] effect." Tax increases, Kennedy was saying, kill jobs; economic growth swells tax revenues without requiring increases in tax rates.

During the campaign, Kennedy also addressed the question of local property taxes. He would not set those rates as president, but his attitude toward them was indicative of his overall perspective on tax issues. In an October 29, 1960, speech at the Valley Forge Country Club in Pennsylvania, Kennedy spoke of "the new frontier of suburbia." He told the group: "The property tax in most urban communities has reached the point of diminishing returns. It has reached in some communities the point of a capital levy, and we cannot expect that the property tax will furnish, in the 1960's, the same income for the sustenance of the public sector that it has sustained in the 1940's and the 1950's. I come from a city where the property tax is about $103 or $104 per thousand dollars, and the assessments reasonably high, and at that point I say it becomes confiscatory." Here was Kennedy, in the closing weeks of the campaign, speaking at a country club to denounce "confiscatory" taxation.

As for the tax break to encourage domestic energy exploration, Kennedy made his position known in an October 13 public letter to the director of the Kennedy-Johnson Texas Democratic Campaign: "I have consistently, throughout this campaign, made clear my recognition of the value and importance of the oil-depletion allowance . . . A healthy domestic oil industry is essential to national security."

Another path to growth was in a balanced budget and federal spending restraint. Kennedy said, in an October 12 speech on economic policy, that he would "seek a balanced budget over the course of the business cycle with surpluses during good times more than offsetting the deficits which may be incurred during slumps." He described this as "a conservative policy." In the same speech, he elaborated further on his approach to government spending, pronouncing himself "opposed to excessive, unjustified or unnecessary government intervention in the economy — to needlessly unbalanced budgets and centralized government." He said, "I do not believe that Washington should do for the people what they can do for themselves through local and private effort. There is no magic attached to tax dollars that have been to Washington and back." And, countering a last-ditch Nixon effort to portray Kennedy as a big spender, Kennedy faulted the Eisenhower-Nixon administration for *its* free-spending ways, for having "expanded the Federal payroll to an all-time high, operated at an $18 billion deficit, increased the debt limit five times, caused the highest peacetime deficit in the history of the United States, and spent two-thirds as much money as all of the previous administrations put together."[49]

The third prong of Kennedy's economic growth platform, after tax and spending restraint, was a monetary policy to fight inflation. In an

October 17 speech at the Biltmore Hotel in Dayton, Ohio, Kennedy said, "I think we can do better . . . in the matter of monetary policy . . . First, account must be taken of the national interest in economic growth. For economic growth is the spring from which there flow high living standards and all public services, including defense. And an interest rate which slows down economic growth ill serves the cause of America and of freedom. Second, account must be taken of the national interest in a sound dollar. Inflation robs every man, but especially the pensioner and the civil servant on fixed incomes of the fruits of hard work. An interest rate that precipitates inflation is no friend of America and the cause of freedom either."

This, then, was how Kennedy won the 1960 election — by standing by his faith and declaring "we know there is a God"; by calling for a bigger military and for more American missiles and for overthrowing Fidel Castro; by defending a sound dollar and denouncing confiscatory taxation; by explaining that tax increases hurt economic growth and criticizing excessive federal spending. As Hazlitt saw it, looking back in a post-election, November 28, 1960, *Newsweek* column: "It was Kennedy who set the 'issues' — economic growth, military strength, American 'prestige.' He succeeded in keeping Nixon on the defensive."

A few additional points on the campaign and election are worth mentioning here. The first is that liberal suspicion of Kennedy and unease with him immediately before and during the campaign was widely recognized and commented upon. Arthur Schlesinger Jr. recalled that JFK "was having his problems with the liberal intellectuals . . . Many liberal Democrats regarded him with suspicion."[50] Kennedy, Schlesinger wrote, was "bored by the conditioned reflexes of stereotyped liberalism, . . . wore no liberal heart on his sleeve,"[51] and had "a detachment from the pieties of American liberalism."[52] In all these aspects, he differed from Adlai Stevenson, who, despite his previous losses, or maybe in some way because of them, was the candidate many liberals would have preferred.

Chester Bowles, a congressman from Connecticut who served in the Kennedy State Department, remembered: "The liberals, somewhat skeptical of Kennedy because they were not sure of his views, were also withholding commitment. I, being the first one to support him, drew a good deal of private fire from some of my liberal friends — they thought I had made a mistake."[53]

This skepticism and suspicion among the liberals was only accentuated by Kennedy's decision to choose a southerner, Lyndon Johnson of Texas, as his running mate. The liberals would have preferred a northerner with better credentials on labor issues and civil rights. Sorensen recalled, "His selection of Johnson had angered the already suspicious liberals."[54] Two other Kennedy aides, Kenneth O'Donnell and David Powers, remember the president of the United Auto Workers, Walter Reuther, and the president of the American Federation of Labor–Congress of Industrial Organizations, George Meany, as being "infuriated" and "violently angry."[55]

"It was a struggle" to get the liberal Americans for Democratic Action to endorse Kennedy in 1960, Schlesinger reported, writing to JFK that he had been unprepared for the "depth of hostility" among grassroots liberals.[56] Hyman Bookbinder, the legislative representative of the AFL-CIO who later joined the Kennedy administration's Commerce Department, recalled, "In the primary period of 1960 and in the election period, I could probably name on my fingers of one hand the number of associates I had who were for Kennedy in a positive way." Bookbinder said, "Until the day of his death, Jack Kennedy was not really loved, at least consciously and knowingly loved, by the great bulk of what we have come to know as the labor and civil rights movement as well as the liberal and ADA movements."[57]

In at least one campaign speech, Kennedy addressed the "liberal" question head-on. On September 14, 1960, he accepted the presidential nomination of the Liberal Party of New York. The party had been founded by the president of the International Ladies' Garment Workers' Union, David Dubinsky, in 1944 after the American Labor Party, which Dubinsky had founded in 1936, fell under Communist sway. A biographer of Dubinsky reports that when Dubinsky quit the American Labor Party to start the Liberal Party, he took a swipe at the president of the rival Amalgamated Clothing Workers of America, Sidney Hillman: "Mr. Hillman can act as a front for the Communists; I never did and never will."[58]

So it was to an avowedly anti-Communist liberal group that Kennedy went in 1960 to deliver a carefully conditioned acceptance of the liberal label.

What do our opponents mean when they apply to us the label, "Liberal"? If by "Liberal" they mean, as they want people to believe, someone who is soft in his policies abroad, who is against local government, and who is unconcerned with the taxpayer's dollar, then the record of this party and its members demonstrates that we are not that kind of "Liberal." But, if by a "Liberal," they mean someone who looks ahead and not behind, someone who welcomes new ideas without rigid reactions, someone who cares about the welfare of the people — their health, their housing, their schools, their jobs, their civil rights, and their civil liberties — someone who believes that we can break through the stalemate and suspicions that grip us in our policies abroad, if that is what they mean by a "Liberal," then I'm proud to say that I'm a "Liberal."

Kennedy went on to make clear that whatever kind of "liberal," he was, he was not a big-spending, big-government one: "I do not believe in a super state. I see no magic to tax dollars which are sent to Washington and then returned. I abhor the waste and incompetence of large-scale Federal bureaucracies in this administration, as well as in others. I do not favor state compulsion when voluntary individual effort can do the job and do it well."[59]

Though Dubinsky was strongly with Kennedy, other labor unions kept their distance. The Teamsters and the longshoremen's unions opposed him.[60] Sorensen reports that during the campaign Kennedy was resistant to some labor policy initiatives. After the president of the United Steelworkers proposed a thirty-two-hour workweek, Kennedy spoke to the union's convention and "said the Communist challenge required this nation to meet its employment problems by creating abundance rather than rationing scarcity."[61]

Abortion in 1960 was not the hot political issue it would later become, but population control was a topic of discussion. In Kennedy's interview with *Harper's* editor John Fischer, the senator was asked, "Do you see any hope at all of slowing up the rate of population increase?"

Kennedy's reply was somewhat dismissive. "Now, on the question of limiting population: as you know the Japanese have been doing it very vigorously, through abortion, which I think would be repugnant to all Americans." Kennedy went on, "Most people consider their families to be their families, and that it is other people's families that provide the population explosion."[62]

For all the talk of the importance of the issues and of television — both of which *were* important — the campaign remained not only abstract or electronic but also relentlessly, gruelingly physical, with long days and extensive travel in all kinds of weather. The crowds along the candidate's travel routes and at his rallies were filled with what the press called "jumpers" — women who leaped into the air to get a better view of Kennedy. The basic physical act of campaigning, the handshake, was repeated so often that it left the candidate's flesh scratched, swollen, calloused, bloody.[63]

For Kennedy and his supporters, it was worth the sacrifices. Voter turnout on Election Day was high. American University's Center for the Study of the American Electorate estimates that 64.8 percent of eligible citizens voted for president in 1960, the highest percentage, in its assessment, of any presidential election between 1920 and 2008.[64] Thirty-four million people voted for John F. Kennedy; another thirty-four million voted for Richard Nixon. If there were such a thing as a tie in American elections, this would have been one.

Kennedy's popular-vote margin was eventually recorded by the National Archives as 118,574 votes, or less than two out of every thousand votes cast for the two major-party candidates. Theodore White's book recorded the result as Kennedy 49.7 percent, Nixon 49.6 percent. As for the electoral vote, Kennedy took 303 to Nixon's 219. Sorensen later observed that Nixon could have won an electoral vote majority with a swing of a total of just 12,000 votes in Illinois, Nevada, New Mexico, Hawaii, and Missouri.[65] A swing of just 28,500 total votes in Illinois and Texas would have had the same effect. But the deployment of the Secret Service around Kennedy's house in Hyannis Port at seven o'clock the morning after the election, while the senator was still asleep, was an official sign that the election result, while close, was clear.[66]

The campaign and election were finally over, but Kennedy's presidency had yet to begin. Would Kennedy govern as he had campaigned and served as congressman and senator? Or would he "grow in office," softening or abandoning his positions now that he had the responsibility of translating them into action rather than simply delivering critical speeches? The president-elect had barely recovered from the fatigue of the campaign before he started to make decisions.

CHAPTER 5

Transition and Inauguration
November 1960–January 20, 1961

> The same revolutionary beliefs for which our forebears fought are still at issue around the globe — the belief that the rights of man come not from the generosity of the state but from the hand of God.
>
> — JOHN F. KENNEDY, inaugural address, January 20, 1961

Washington

ONLY A FEW LIVING AMERICANS know firsthand what it feels like during the less than three months between being elected president of the United States and being inaugurated. The rest of us can only speculate and compare it to other, more familiar liminal states, like being pregnant, being engaged to be married, or working to launch a new business. A person can do his or her best to plan and prepare, but until the baby is born, the wedding day arrives, or the doors of the business open to customers, the sense of anticipation outweighs the actual responsibility.

It was a similarity that John F. Kennedy was in a unique position to appreciate, as he indicated in his comments on November 9 to reporters gathered at the Hyannis Armory. He concluded by saying, "Now my wife and I prepare for a new administration and for a new baby. Thank you."

The new baby, John F. Kennedy Jr., arrived on November 25, earlier than anticipated. The father got the news by radio in the cockpit of a plane in which he was returning to Washington from Palm Beach. He spent the next two weeks visiting his son and his wife at Georgetown University Hospital, while also helping to take care of Caroline, who celebrated her third birthday two days after her younger brother was born.[1]

As for the new administration, the most important work of the transition involved staffing. Some of the choices were obvious. Kennedy's close and longtime aides from the Senate and his campaigns — his secretary Evelyn Lincoln, Kenneth O'Donnell, David Powers, Ted Sorensen — would follow him into the White House.

Other choices were perhaps more surprising, especially given how critical Kennedy had been of the Eisenhower-Nixon record during the campaign. Kennedy chose as his Treasury secretary C. Douglas Dillon, a Wall Street banker (the investment bank of Dillon, Read was eventually acquired and later merged into what is now UBS), Republican, and Eisenhower administration State Department official who, with his wife, had given more than $26,000 to Nixon and the Republicans in the 1960 campaign.[2]

Kennedy had first met Dillon in 1956 at Harvard; Dillon was there for his twenty-fifth reunion, and Kennedy was receiving an honorary degree. After the formal ceremonies they mingled at the Spee Club, of which they had both been members. Following the 1960 election, Kennedy visited Dillon at his home in Washington. Kennedy told Dillon he had noticed his speeches in favor of a faster growth rate in the economy, and he mentioned Dillon's belief in a sound dollar, which, as Dillon later put it, "he very much believed in himself." In the conversation, which lasted an hour, Dillon mentioned his own "deep interest in tax reform . . . far reaching reform which would result in substantially lower tax rates across the board." He recalled, "At that time the President-elect agreed with me that this would have high priority in his administration."[3]

Dillon's appointment was made over the objection of Senator Albert Gore Sr., who complained the appointment was "a signal" that Kennedy "had given up the goals of a truly Democratic administration."[4] Gore pleaded his case against Dillon in person at Kennedy's

Georgetown home, which was serving as transition headquarters: "Why should Dillon, a rich, Wall Street Republican, who contributed $30,000 to Nixon, be in your cabinet?" When Kennedy dismissed the objection and stuck with Dillon, Gore called it a "shocking shame."[5]

Kennedy's defense secretary was Robert McNamara, an Eagle Scout and former Harvard Business School professor who was president of Ford Motor Company. The president's national security adviser, McGeorge Bundy, was a Republican[6] who had worked for Thomas Dewey's presidential campaign in 1948.[7] Kennedy retained Eisenhower's FBI director, J. Edgar Hoover, and his CIA director, Allen Dulles. He also kept Eisenhower's chairman of the Federal Reserve, William McChesney Martin Jr.

Arthur Schlesinger Jr. wrote: "There was spreading unhappiness among the liberals over the failure of any of their particular favorites, except Arthur Goldberg [secretary of labor], to make the cabinet."[8]

Conservatives were more pleased. The editor of the Wall Street Journal, Vermont Royster, who like Kennedy had been a Navy officer who saw combat in the Pacific, wrote to his publisher, Barney Kilgore, on January 5, 1961, about a private meeting over lunch that he, Royster, had had that day with Kennedy at the Carlyle in New York. "Specifically, he insisted that he does not plan to go in for bigger spending," Royster wrote. "This is a very smart young man. He is, for instance, smart enough to recognize that he has got to get rid of the label he acquired in the campaign of the reckless spender with a slap-dash attitude about fiscal affairs. I don't know whether he understands the real fiscal problems here; he does understand the political problems that come with the tag. This shows up not only in the adroitness of his Treasury appointments but (if we can be a bit immodest) by the very fact that he would use a luncheon period on a very busy day to try to sell himself to the WSJ."[9]

More Republicans would join the administration later on. William C. Foster, who had been an executive of Olin Mathiesen, an arms and ammunition manufacturer, was named director of the Arms Control and Disarmament Agency.[10] In September 1961, Kennedy chose as his CIA director John McCone, a Republican from California, who, according to Schlesinger, "had the reputation of a rigid cold-warrior who viewed the world in moralistic stereotypes."[11] The special disarmament adviser was another Republican, New York lawyer John J. McCloy, a former chairman of Chase Manhattan Bank. A special mission to Ghana to clinch American support for the Volta Dam project (opposed by Senator Gore) was led by Clarence Randall, "a steel magnate of profound and well-publicized conservatism."[12] Kennedy's envoy to West Berlin was a retired general, Lucius Clay, another "conservative Republican."[13] Henry Cabot Lodge Jr., Nixon's 1960 running mate and Kennedy's old rival in the 1952 Senate race in Massachusetts, was named in 1963 by Kennedy to the key position of ambassador to South Vietnam.

The newspaper columnist Walter Lippmann explained the Republican appointments by writing of Kennedy, "By temperament and instinct and association, he has never been a partisan Democrat of the Roosevelt or Truman persuasion."[14] The closeness of the election outcome is another possible explanation. The Republican candidate had, after all, received about half the votes, and Kennedy might have felt it appropriate to recognize that in staffing his administration — in the same way that Kennedy reached out to Nixon by visiting him in a poolside cabana at a post-election "Sunshine Summit" in Key Biscayne, Florida. Others have suggested that Kennedy might have liked the idea of having a Republican in some of the more delicate or difficult posts as someone to blame if things went wrong. As a final possible explanation, Arthur Schlesinger Jr. has written of Kennedy's "customary practice of seeking a conservative to execute a liberal policy." Kennedy's friend Ben Bradlee recalls Kennedy remarking, "Boy, when those liberals start mixing into policy, it's murder."[15] Schlesinger is correct that Kennedy had a custom of appointing conservatives, but less so about whether the policies they executed were liberal ones.[16]

Not all of Kennedy's appointments were Republicans or right-wingers. George McGovern, an Air Force veteran who had represented South Dakota in the House of Representatives and ran unsuccessfully in 1960 for a U.S. Senate seat, was head of the Food for Peace program. Bill Moyers, who had worked for Lyndon Johnson in the 1960 campaign, was the number two official at the Peace Corps. But the most prominent liberals were relegated to second-tier jobs, a fact that they surely recognized. Adlai Stevenson, who wanted to be secretary of state, had to settle for permanent representative to the United Nations. Chester Bowles, chosen as undersecretary of state, was eventually ousted by Kennedy from even that post. Bowles later reflected, "Why didn't Kennedy have liberal people around?" He answered his own question as follows: "When the Kennedy people got to Washington, they were all full of belligerence and 'We're not going to let the Russians push us around, we're just as tough as anybody.' And I think Kennedy had a lot of it — this attitude."[17]

Some administration appointees now identified as liberals had their rightward leanings. The Robert Kennedy named by his brother as attorney general was not yet the anti–Vietnam War candidate of 1968. Rather, he was known as the former staff member of Senator Joseph McCarthy, the Robert Kennedy described by Schlesinger in 1965 as "the demon of the liberal imagination," who "regarded (and continued to regard) professional liberals with suspicion."[18]

Even the liberal Schlesinger himself, after all, had served in the Office of Strategic Services as "editor of the weekly intelligence bulletin," in which he observed, and rejected, the "communist slant" in the reports of the Latin American affairs section chief, who in fact turned out to be a Communist Party member, Maurice Halperin.[19] Schlesinger had also contributed, in 1947, to a *Partisan Review* symposium: "The Future of Socialism." "The socialist state is," he wrote, "worse than the capitalist state because it is more inclusive in its coverage and more unlimited in its power."[20] Nevertheless, with Schlesinger Kennedy kept his distance. Evelyn Lincoln writes that the president's "relationship with Schlesinger was never that close . . . The President understood that he [Schlesinger] supported him only because he felt that, as President, Kennedy was in the best position to further his [Schlesinger's] own liberal ideas. He knew that Schlesinger would have preferred to be working for 'President' Adlai Stevenson."[21]

Regardless of their politics, many of the members of the new administration shared with the president-elect the experience of serving their country during World War II. Schlesinger wrote:

Lieutenant Orville Freeman [secretary of agriculture] had had half his jaw shot off by the Japanese in the swamps of Bougainville in 1943. Lieutenant Kenneth O'Donnell had flown thirty missions over Germany as a bombardier for the 8th Air Force; his plane had been shot up, and twice he had made emergency landings. Lieutenants Mc-George Bundy and Mortimer Caplan [commissioner of the Internal Revenue Service] had been on the Normandy beaches on D-day plus 1 . . . Lieutenant Nicholas Katzenbach [assistant attorney general, then deputy attorney general], a B-25 navigator, had been shot down in the Mediterranean and spent two years in Italian and German prison camps; he twice escaped and was twice recaptured. Lieutenant Commander Douglas Dillon had been under Kamikaze attack in Lingayen Gulf and had flown a dozen combat patrol missions . . . Lieutenant Byron White [deputy attorney general] had fought in the Solomons. Ensign Pierre Salinger had been decorated for a dangerous rescue in the midst of a typhoon from his sub-chaser off Okinawa. Major Dean Rusk [secretary of state] had been a staff officer in the China-Burma-India theater. Major Arthur Goldberg had organized labor espionage for the OSS in Europe. Lieutenant Stewart Udall [secretary of the interior] had served in the Air Force.[22]

Having assembled and appointed this group, Kennedy now faced the task of coordinating their actions. He was not yet in office, so he lacked the executive power. So again he turned to a power that he did have, the ability to write and deliver a speech. In two important addresses — one lesser known, and a second that is regarded as one of the best in American history — Kennedy explained to his new executive branch staff and to the nation what he hoped they would accomplish.

The first speech was a kind of farewell to the state he had represented in the U.S. Senate. It was an address to a joint convention of the General Court of the Commonwealth of Massachusetts — the formal name for the state's House of Representatives and Senate — delivered on January 9, 1961. As he had done in his election-eve televised address from Faneuil Hall, Kennedy reached back for inspiration to the Puritan founders of the Massachusetts Bay Colony, and he asked for God's help:

For forty-three years — whether I was in London, Washington, the South Pacific, or elsewhere — this has been my home; and, God willing, wherever I serve this shall remain my home . . . The enduring qualities of Massachusetts — the common threads woven by the Pilgrim and the Puritan, the fisherman and the farmer, the Yankee and the immigrant — will not be and could not be forgotten in this nation's executive mansion.

They are an indelible part of my life, my convictions, my view of the past, and my hopes for the future . . . Allow me to illustrate: During the last sixty days, I have been at the task of constructing an administration. It has been a long and deliberate process. Some have counseled greater speed. Others have counseled more expedient tests.

But I have been guided by the standard John Winthrop set before his shipmates on the flagship *Arbella* three hundred and thirty-one years ago, as they, too, faced the task of building a new government on a perilous frontier.

"We must always consider," he said, "that we shall be as a city upon a hill — the eyes of all people are upon us."

Today the eyes of all people are truly upon us — and our governments, in every branch, at every level, national, state and local, must be as a city upon a hill — constructed and inhabited by men aware of their great trust and their great responsibilities . . . These are the qualities which, with God's help, this son of Massachusetts hopes will characterize our government's conduct in the four stormy years that lie ahead.

Humbly I ask His help in that undertaking — but aware that on earth His will is worked by men. I ask for your help and your prayers, as I embark on this new and solemn journey.[23]

Kennedy's mother writes in her memoir that "because the speech was delivered to a state audience, it is not as widely remembered as it deserves to be." It was her favorite speech of John F. Kennedy's other than his inaugural address. She particularly liked the line in it where he said, "Of those to whom much is given, much is required." It was a passage from Luke that Rose Kennedy had often repeated to her son.[24]

The speech to the Massachusetts legislature laid out the general expectations Kennedy had of his administration — "courage, judgment, integrity, dedication." And it revived the "city upon a hill" phrase that would reemerge after Kennedy's death in the voice of a different president.

Declaring the broad goals of the new administration, and of the country, to the American people and to the rest of the world, though, would take a different speech, Kennedy's inaugural address.

Two other leaders on the world stage had already had their say in the preceding days. The outgoing president, Dwight Eisenhower, was a five-star general who had once held the title of Supreme Allied Commander, Europe. He had gone on national television on January 17, 1961, to deliver a farewell address that warned of "unwarranted influence" by "the military-industrial complex." Implicitly defending his administration's record against the criticism in the 1960 campaign that military spending had been insufficient, the president observed, "We annually spend on military security more than the net income of all United States corporations."

Eisenhower recognized that the Communist threat was genuine. "We face a hostile ideology — global in scope, atheistic in character, ruthless in purpose, and insidious in method," he said. But he also called disarmament an "imperative" and expressed disappointment that he had not accomplished more on that front. He feared that excessive spending could threaten America's security in the long term.

On January 17, the West began to get word of a speech Nikita Khrushchev had delivered on January 6 in which the Soviet premier promised to support "wars of national liberation." "Communists are revolutionaries," he said, "and it would be a bad thing if they did not exploit new opportunities."[25] An Associated Press dispatch from Moscow that appeared in the next day's *New York Times* began, "In a speech published today, Premier Khrushchev declared that victory 'is no longer far off' for world communism." The article went on to report that Khrushchev had said war is not necessary, "but it will come, he warned, if capitalist nations try to resist the communist victory — 'inevitable by the laws of historical development.'"

If Kennedy and other Americans perceived this as menacing, it fit with what they knew of Khrushchev. The Soviet leader was twenty-three years older than Kennedy. He was also nine inches shorter, and his bald head contrasted with Kennedy's thick hair. Though Khrushchev had distanced himself somewhat from Stalin following Stalin's death in 1953, Kennedy knew that the Russian leader had spent more than a decade as the Stalin-appointed ruler of Ukraine. He knew that Khrushchev had seized power by arresting and executing the fearsome leader of Stalin's secret police, Lavrentiy Beria. No one could forget that in 1956 Khrushchev had told Western diplomats, "We will bury you," and that in 1960 he had furiously banged his shoe on a desk at the United Nations.

It was the threat of Khrushchev and of his Soviet empire that Eisenhower and Kennedy had in mind when, on January 19, 1961, the two men met. The outgoing president demonstrated to the incoming one how to use the "football" briefcase that was carried at all times by a military aide accompanying the president and that contained the commands and codes to launch a nuclear strike. Eisenhower showed Kennedy how to summon a Marine helicopter that would immediately whisk the president away to safety in the event of an attack on the White House.[26]

Kennedy's response to ruthless, hostile, and atheistic global communism began on his inauguration day, Friday, January 20, with his first stop upon leaving his home at 3307 N Street in Georgetown. Nearly eight inches of snow had fallen the evening and night before on Washington, a city, then as now, northern enough to be socked with a good snowstorm almost every winter, but southern enough not to have invested in the plowing equipment required to remove it with any efficiency. Shovels scraped against brick sidewalks, boots crunched against snow, and Kennedy made his way the two blocks from his house to Holy Trinity Church, which was soon filled with the music of the same Latin words that had been used for Mass since 1570.

Rose Kennedy, age seventy, who had walked half a mile through the snow to the same church not knowing her son would also be there, wrote later, "I realized he was there of his own volition: that he wanted to start his presidency by offering his mind and heart, and expressing his hopes and fears, to Almighty God, and asking His blessing as he began his great duties."[27]

It was just the beginning of the day's worship. There were more prayers outdoors at the inaugural ceremony, at the east front of the

Capitol, in which Kennedy had served as a congressman and senator. First, an invocation from Richard Cardinal Cushing of Boston, during which smoke rose from the podium, the result of a short circuit in an electrical mechanism used to lower and raise the lectern. As Cushing concluded, Kennedy made the sign of the cross. Then, a blessing from the leader of the Greek Orthodox Church in America, Archbishop Iakovos. Kennedy crossed himself again, as Richard J. Tofel has written in his book on Kennedy's inaugural, *Sounding the Trumpet.* Finally, prayers from a Protestant, Reverend John Barclay of Central Christian Church in Austin, Texas, and from a Jew, Rabbi Nelson Glueck, the president of Hebrew Union College. Kennedy later wrote to the author John Steinbeck: "No President was ever prayed over with such fervor. Evidently they felt that the country or I needed it — probably both!"[28]

The day's most important religious references, though, came not from a member of the clergy but from John Kennedy himself. Just as he had promised in the televised address to the voters of West Virginia before the Democratic primary, and as he had promised the Houston ministers in the segment taped and rebroadcast as part of the program from Faneuil Hall on election eve, Kennedy put his hand on the Bible and swore the oath of office. It was the Fitzgerald family Bible, originally brought to America from Ireland, a leather-bound Catholic translation the size of an unabridged dictionary. Two Secret Service agents had retrieved it for the occasion from Boston's Dorchester neighborhood, where it had been in the possession of an uncle of the president-elect. At the end of the constitutionally prescribed oath to "preserve, protect and defend the Constitution," the president, following tradition, added the words "so help me God."[29]

John F. Kennedy was now president of the United States, and his first official act was to deliver an inaugural address. He began with a greeting — "Vice President Johnson, Mr. Speaker, Mr. Chief Justice, President Eisenhower, Vice President Nixon, President Truman, reverend clergy, fellow citizens" — that singled out the "reverend clergy," but not members of the Senate or the House of Representatives, the foreign diplomatic corps, or his own wife or parents, all of whom were present, for special mention.

Then, he called attention to what he had just done: "I have sworn before you and almighty God the same solemn oath our forebears prescribed nearly a century and three quarters ago."

And as he had in his speech on July 4, 1946, and consistently since then, he linked Americans today with their Revolutionary predecessors through the idea of God-given rights. "The same revolutionary beliefs for which our forebears fought are still at issue around the globe — the belief that the rights of man come not from the generosity of the state but from the hand of God."

Twice in his speech, Kennedy referred to the Bible: "Let both sides unite to heed in all corners of the earth the command of Isaiah — to 'undo the heavy burdens . . . [and] let the oppressed go free.'" Later, he quoted the Bible again, this time from Romans: "rejoicing in hope, patient in tribulation."

As Kennedy had during the campaign and earlier in his career, he moved from the concept of God-given rights to the Cold War and the importance of American victory. The speech struck a balance between a hard-line defense of freedom against the Soviet threat and a more conciliatory approach. One of the best-remembered lines was: "Let every nation know, whether it wishes us well or ill, that we shall pay any price, bear any burden, meet any hardship, support any friend, oppose any foe to assure the survival and success of liberty." There was also this: "We dare not tempt them with weakness. For only when our arms are sufficient beyond doubt can we be certain beyond doubt that they will never be employed." And this: "In the long history of the world, only a few generations have been granted the role of defending freedom in its hour of maximum danger. I do not shrink from this responsibility — I welcome it." The liberal *New York Times* reporter Tom Wicker later characterized the speech as "bellicose."[30]

Yet there were also passages that spoke of arms control and cooperation:

> Let us never negotiate out of fear. But let us never fear to negotiate.
> Let both sides explore what problems unite us instead of belaboring those problems which divide us.
> Let both sides, for the first time, formulate serious and precise proposals for the inspection and control of arms — and bring the abso-

lute power to destroy other nations under the absolute control of all nations.

And there was the most famous line of the whole speech: "And so, my fellow Americans: ask not what your country can do for you — ask what you can do for your country."

Ted Sorensen later wrote that the "ask not" line "resonated" with "conservatives who were weary of government handouts."[31] The Democratic congressional aide, journalist, and author Chris Matthews later called it "a hard Republican-sounding slap at the welfare state."[32] The libertarian economist Milton Friedman began his 1962 book *Capitalism and Freedom* by agreeing with Kennedy that asking "what your country can do for you" was, in Friedman's view, "at odds with the free man's belief in his own responsibility for his own destiny." But he also rejected the "ask what you can do for your country" alternative, complaining that it "implies that government is the master or the deity, the citizen, the servant or the votary." Friedman wrote, "The free man will ask neither what his country can do for him nor what he can do for his country."

Kennedy's own earlier speeches, such as his 1950 Notre Dame speech ("Catholics can never adhere to any political theory which holds that the state is a separate, distinct organization to which allegiance must be paid rather than a representative institution which derives its powers from the consent of the governed"), made clear he understood Friedman's point about the dangers of substituting the state for God.

But almost as if Kennedy were attempting to prevent any confusion on the point, the concluding paragraph of the inaugural address, the part known in classical rhetoric as the peroration, returned to the God with whom he had begun the speech by reminding his audience he had sworn an oath before: "With a good conscience our only sure reward, with history the final judge of our deeds, let us go forth to lead the land we love, asking His blessing and His help, but knowing that here on earth God's work must truly be our own."

Historians have debated who wrote the address. One book on the speech, Thurston Clarke's *Ask Not*, says the words were primarily Kennedy's own; another, Richard Tofel's *Sounding the Trumpet*, says, "Of the fifty-one sentences in the inaugural address, John Kennedy might be said to have been the principal original author of no more than fourteen." Theodore Sorensen, in his own 2008 book *Counselor*, calls both Clarke's book and Tofel's "excellent," and says he destroyed his own handwritten first draft after a conversation with Jacqueline Kennedy in 1965. But Sorensen did attribute some of the key sentences of the speech to Kennedy himself. The line about rights coming "not from the generosity of the state but from the hand of God," Sorensen, in a 2004 interview with Tofel, called Kennedy's favorite "shorthand way to describe the difference between our system and totalitarian systems." And even Tofel traces the line about "only when our arms are sufficient beyond doubt" — what Sorensen called "the most important sentence in the speech" — back to *Why England Slept*, which Kennedy had written in 1940, a dozen years before he met Sorensen.[33]

If one accepts the distinction between lines originating with JFK and those originating with Sorensen or with others — a big "if" to begin with, since Kennedy was the one who had hired Sorensen and who had the final editorial control — Kennedy was the "principal author" of the "pay any price, bear any burden" line, the "maximum danger" line, and the "not from the generosity of the state but from the hand of God" line. The more dovish passages of the speech were the ones for which Sorensen or others would, by this distinction, receive principal credit.

No matter who wrote its particular lines, the inaugural address won attention not only for the ideas behind the words but for the delivery. Kennedy had worked with a coach on slowing down his speaking style, and he loved poetry. (Robert Frost, after all, read a poem at the inauguration.) At its best, the inaugural address was poetry, complete with rhyme and rhythm, or music, played on the instrument of Kennedy's own Boston accent, with its long, broad "ahs": "the belief that the rights of m*a*n come not from the generosity of the state but from the h*a*nd of God."

And so the torch was passed, as Kennedy put it in his speech, "to a new generation of Americans — born in this century, tempered by war, disciplined by a hard and bitter peace, proud of our ancient heritage — and unwilling to witness or permit the slow undoing of those human rights to which this nation has always been committed, and to which we are committed today at home and around the world."

In the years ahead, that commitment, and the new president, would be put to the test.

CHAPTER 6

The New Frontier: Domestic Policy

January 20, 1961–November 1963

> Everything that we do ought to really be tied into getting onto the moon and ahead of the Russians . . . Otherwise we shouldn't be spending this kind of money, because I'm not that interested in space.
>
> — JOHN F. KENNEDY, in a meeting on the NASA budget,
>   November 21, 1962[1]

Washington

KENNEDY'S INAUGURAL MESSAGE of "ask not what your country can do for you" flowed logically from his speech at the 1960 Democratic Convention accepting the nomination. There, he had spoken of a "New Frontier" that both followed FDR's New Deal and differed from it: "Franklin Roosevelt's New Deal promised security and succor to those in need. But the New Frontier of which I speak is not a set of promises — it is a set of challenges. It sums up not what I intend to offer the American people, but what I intend to ask of them. It appeals to their pride, not to their pocketbook — it holds out the promise of more sacrifice instead of more security . . . Beyond that frontier are the uncharted areas of science and space, unsolved problems of peace and war, unconquered pockets of ignorance and prejudice, unanswered questions of poverty and surplus."

Those who have seen Kennedy as a liberal have focused on these New Frontier issues — space, poverty, prejudice — and remembered the president who launched the effort to put a man on the moon, in whose administration can be traced the origins of Medicare and the War on Poverty, and who took on prejudice by introducing a civil rights bill and by using federal power to force the racial integration of southern universities.

So, for example, in their book *The Liberal Hour: Washington and the Politics of Change in the 1960s,* two professors at Colby College, G. Calvin Mackenzie and Robert Weisbrot, acknowledge that Kennedy "may not have been much of a liberal in 1956 and only a tepid one early in 1960." But they credit him with undergoing a kind of conversion in office: "While Kennedy made limited headway in Congress, he did much to educate the public on the need for active government."[2]

Kennedy's special assistant for congressional relations, Lawrence O'Brien, rejected the notion that Kennedy was unsuccessful with Congress. O'Brien's memoir reports that Kennedy got passed, among other legislation, "a $435-million Manpower Development and Training Act to provide job training for the unemployed, $400 million in special accelerated public works funds, a record budget of $5.4 billion to expand space exploration, a drug-labeling act, the air-pollution-control study, the poll-tax constitutional amendment, a 32-million-dollar program of assistance to educational television . . ." O'Brien also credits Kennedy for laying the groundwork for laws eventually signed by President Johnson: "We could not pass Medicare in 1961–63, but we raised the issue, we forced our opponents to go on record against it, and we paved the way for its eventual passage in 1965 . . . I believe that, had Kennedy lived, his record in his second term would have been comparable to the record Johnson established."[3]

Yet a careful examination of Kennedy's domestic policy record shows a president who kept a tight rein on federal spending and who chose to make Medicare, fighting poverty, and even civil rights lower priorities than other issues, such as free trade and tax cuts.

The biggest-ticket item by far on O'Brien's list, the space program, is a perfect example. The appropriation for the National Aeronautics and Space Administration, which had been created during the Eisenhower years, was less than the agency had requested. NASA's director, James Webb, met with President Kennedy to ask for $400 million in supplemental funding for scientific space research "to understand the environment" and "the laws of nature." Kennedy rejected the request and set Webb straight: "This is important for political reasons, international political reasons. This is, whether we like it or not, in a sense a race. If we get second to the Moon, it's nice, but it's like being second any time . . . Everything that we do ought to really be tied into getting onto the Moon ahead of the Russians . . . Otherwise we shouldn't be spending this kind of money because I'm not that interested in space. I think it's good; I think we ought to know about it; we're ready to spend reasonable amounts of money. But we're talking about these *fantastic* expenditures which wreck our budget and all these other domestic programs and the only justification for it, in my opinion, to do it in this time or fashion, is because we hope to beat them."[4]

This spending restraint applied to everything except defense-related programs or those directly linked to the Cold War was characteristic of Kennedy, and it defined his administration from the start. Kennedy took office, like many other recent first-term presidents from a different party than the incumbent, in the midst of what felt like an economic downturn. The unemployment rate in January 1961 was 6.6 percent — not terrible, but up sharply from the recent low of 4.8 percent in February 1960. The gross domestic product, adjusted for inflation and for seasonal variations, was not growing, but had shrunk in the fourth quarter of 1960 at an annualized rate of 5 percent.[5]

Some voices in the Democratic Party urged Kennedy to follow a path of economic stimulus or "pump-priming" via government spending of the sort that had been advocated by the British economist John Maynard Keynes and pursued by Franklin Roosevelt to combat the Great Depression. The Harvard economist John Kenneth Galbraith suggested grants and loans to unemployed families, "to buy materials and paint to fix up or improve their houses," along with a Youth Conservation Corps for unemployed teenagers.[6] The president did not rush to embrace either idea; he appointed Galbraith as ambassador to India, not exactly a pivotal post in making American economic policy. Senator Gore, in the same Georgetown session where he made the case against Douglas Dillon, cited Roosevelt's "activist programs" and "projects" to provide jobs. Gore suggested that Kennedy raise taxes to pay for a new set of such programs.[7] The president rejected Gore's economic advice, just as he had rejected Gore's opposition to Dillon. Kennedy's secretary of labor, Arthur Goldberg, who had been the top in-house lawyer for the Congress of Industrial Organizations, also urged increased government antipoverty spending, to be paid for by a tax increase on the rich, advice JFK rejected.[8]

Sorensen later explained Kennedy's thinking: "Make-work public works, in his view, were not likely to create many full-time jobs until too late to fight the recession, and they would, with considerable waste, add to the published Budget deficit during the very spring and summer he was requesting more defense funds. That extra defense spending, he ruled, would have to serve as a substitute stimulant."[9]

Instead, Kennedy's economic recovery plan involved reducing tariffs and taxes, keeping a tight rein on nonmilitary government spending, cutting back regulation on domestic energy production, advocating a strong dollar backed by gold, and taking a hard line against inflation.

In an April 13, 1961, letter to Congress on regulation, Kennedy urged lawmakers to be careful not to overregulate: "If it is in the public interest to maintain an industry, it is clearly not in the public interest by the impact of regulatory authority to destroy its otherwise viable way of life." In the same letter, he spoke of the job-creating value of natural gas pipelines, and called on Congress to revise the law to exempt more gas producers from the regulations and permit requirements of the Federal Power Commission. "More prompt handling of these matters would release hundreds of millions of dollars for construction, giving substantial employment throughout the country," Kennedy wrote. "The Commission should be authorized to exempt from rate regulation up to 100% of the small individual producers of natural gas . . . With respect to the processing of pipeline construction permits, the Commission should be authorized to exempt from all or part of its procedures up to 100% of those applications by interstate pipeline companies which seek merely to enlarge, extend or replace existing facilities . . . The formulation of these standards will require creative imagination; but the alternative is to defend bureaucracy for bureaucracy's sake."

Defending bureaucracy for bureaucracy's sake was the last thing Kennedy wanted to do. The director of the Bureau of the Budget in 1961 and 1962, David Bell, recalled Kennedy's "own innate fiscal conservatism."[10]

"The President's strong personal views on the desirability of holding down expenditures and [government] employment were made plain in a series of questions to me as Budget Director both orally and in writing," Bell said in a 1964 oral history interview. "The President kept reverting to this point. He had a strong feeling that federal employment was rising when it should not rise. I remember his using as an illustration to me one day the shock and indeed horror he felt when he found that it took (I don't recall the figures) 'X' number of gardeners to maintain the White House grounds. 'Why,' he said, 'the man we have handling our grounds at Hyannis Port could do this whole thing with the assistance of maybe a boy.' I think there were six gardeners on the White House payroll, and the President didn't see the use for more than a man and a half. And he said (I don't know whether he ever did this) he was going to bring that gardener down from Hyannis Port and have him look over the White House grounds and tell him what the proper staffing pattern would be. This is just one illustration of many occasions and many ways in which the President hammered at the problem of rising federal employment."[11]

"I don't want to be tagged as a big spender early in this administration," Schlesinger recalls the president telling his staff.[12] Schlesinger, a liberal who would have preferred more spending, lamented that "even Kennedy, to meet his congressional problems, used occasionally to talk about frugality in government as if the reduction of public spending were per se a good thing."[13]

But Kennedy spoke this way not only to congressional conservatives but to liberals on his own staff, suggesting that the position was sincerely held, not merely adopted in response to legislative obstacles. The economist Paul Samuelson recalls flying back from Cape Cod with Kennedy. "I'm for economy in expenditure," the president told him. "After all, I'm a taxpayer myself. I don't believe in big expenditure for its own sake. In fact, one of the things that I've tried hardest to do is spend less on the White House staff than Eisenhower. Up until now I've succeeded in doing so, but it's a hard battle."[14] As a first step, Kennedy reduced the salaries of top White House staffers to $21,000 a year from the $22,500 that Eisenhower's closest aides had been paid.[15]

Sorensen recalled, "His success with the Congress and the country depended, he felt, on weakening the traditional Republican charge that Democrats were spendthrifts and wastrels who would drown the nation in debt . . . He personally scrutinized every agency request with a cold eye and encouraged his budget director to say 'no.'"[16]

Carl Kaysen, a National Security Council staff member, recalled that for the White House ceremony granting Winston Churchill honorary American citizenship, Kennedy declared, "Hell, let's get New York State champagne, not French champagne. It's good enough for them." Kaysen observed, "I thought that was, in a certain respect, a very characteristic attitude about spending public money."[17]

This approach to the federal budget was outlined in the Program for Economic Recovery and Growth that the president released on February 2, 1961. "This Administration is pledged to a Federal revenue system that balances the budget over the years of the economic cycle — yielding surpluses for debt retirement in times of high employment that more than offset the deficits which accompany — and indeed help overcome — low levels of economic activity in poor years," Kennedy said. "Debt retirement at high employment contributes to economic growth by releasing savings for productive investment by private enterprise and State and local governments." This last sentence implied that private enterprise or state or local governments could use money more productively than could the federal government.

Comparing the spending records of presidential administrations is complicated because the lengths of time in office vary and because adjusting for inflation can skew the results. But the historical figures kept by what is now known as the Office of Management and Budget show that Kennedy, by the standard of the administrations that followed, exercised restraint. Federal outlays rose to $111.3 billion in 1963, the final year of the Kennedy presidency, from $97.7 billion in 1961, the first year. Of the $13.6 billion increase, $3.8 billion was for defense spending and $2.1 billion was for international affairs, which left room for barely any real growth in spending for domestic programs. The annual deficits — $3.3 billion in 1961, $7.1 billion in 1962, and $4.8 billion in 1963 — were modest by modern standards and as a percentage of gross domestic product. Eisenhower's deficit for 1959 had been $12.8 billion, larger than any of Kennedy's both in absolute terms and as a percentage of GDP, though the Eisenhower budget in 1960 had been essentially balanced.

In a December 11, 1961, Oval Office meeting with Vermont Royster of the *Wall Street Journal,* Kennedy emphasized the importance of a balanced budget. Royster reported afterward to his publisher, "On the budget, he said again that it will be balanced . . . He took some time to explain that there were many of his advisers who argued that even this spending budget was not big enough and who contended that there ought to be a deficit to keep the boom going. But he was being firm on this point. My impression here was that he was trying to convey the idea that while he might be spending more than the WSJ thought wise he was still being more conservative than some of his advisers. I suspect that's right."[18]

Kennedy's spending did not always appear restrained to his political opponents. A December 1962 memo to the president from the undersecretary of the Treasury, Henry Fowler, noted a speech by Governor Nelson Rockefeller to the National Association of Manufacturers in which Rockefeller complained, "In the course of the first two fiscal years of this administration, non-defense spending will be up 20 percent." Such criticism, however, only bolstered efforts within the administration for further spending restraint.

When the Yale economist James Tobin, a member of the president's Council of Economic Advisers, met with Kennedy in early 1961 to propose aiming for a larger budget deficit, of $10 billion, as a "fiscal stimulus" to boost employment, the president, Tobin recalled, "showed himself very much scared of the financial conservatives in Congress and a good deal more conservative himself, and less sophisticated, than I had expected." Kennedy's reaction was that if he proposed such a deficit spending binge, Congress "would kick us in the balls and we'd lose everything."[19]

Kennedy conducted his administration accordingly. While he proposed a health insurance program for seniors along the lines of what became Medicare, he made it a lower priority than tariff reduction. In his February 9, 1961, message to Congress on health, the president described the plan for the elderly as "a very modest proposal cut to meet absolutely essential needs, and with sufficient 'deductible' requirements to discourage any malingering or unnecessary overcrowding of our hospitals." He went on, "This program is not a program of socialized medicine. It is a program of prepayment of health costs with absolute freedom of choice guaranteed. Every person will choose his own doctor and hospital . . . The program is a sound one and entirely in accordance with the traditional American system of placing responsibility on the employee and the employer, rather than on the general taxpayers, to help finance retirement and health costs."

The reference to "malingering" signaled Kennedy's awareness that welfare programs tend to create perverse incentives. In the same February 2, 1961, Program for Economic Recovery and Growth that called for a balanced budget over the course of an economic cycle, Kennedy called for reforming the welfare system so that it did not encourage absent fathers. He said, "Under the Aid to Dependent Children program, needy children are eligible for assistance if their fathers are deceased, disabled, or family deserters. In logic and humanity, a child should also be eligible for assistance if his father is a needy unemployed worker — for example, a person who has exhausted unemployment benefits and is not receiving adequate local assistance. Too many fathers, unable to support their families, have resorted to real or pretended desertion to qualify their children for help." He also called for states to put welfare recipients to work: "I am recommending a change in the law to permit States to maintain with Federal financial help community work and training projects for unemployed people receiving welfare payments. Under such a program, unemployed people on welfare would be helped to retain their work skills or learn new ones; and the local community would obtain additional manpower on public projects." In signing into law the Public Welfare Amendments of 1962, Kennedy spoke of a "new approach — stressing services in addition to support, rehabilitation instead of relief, and training for useful work instead of prolonged dependency."

Kennedy's Program for Economic Recovery and Growth also called for moving ahead with "pilot Food-Stamp programs" that had been authorized by a law enacted in the final year of the Eisenhower-Nixon administration. Here even some of Kennedy's most liberal advisers urged caution. "We should have another look at it," Galbraith wrote to Kennedy. "It could be a liberal cliché."[20]

Kennedy did sign into law the Area Redevelopment Act of 1961, which gave the Commerce Department authority to approve federal grants and loans for projects in poor areas. He also, surely with his sister Rosemary in mind, signed the Mental Retardation Planning Act of 1963 and the Mental Retardation Facilities and Community Mental Health Centers Act of 1963. And he sought additional federal aid for education, though that effort stalled amid conflicts over whether and how to include religious schools.[21] Larger antipoverty programs were still at the tentative stage. In the fall of 1963, Kennedy told his economic adviser Walter Heller that he would be in favor of doing something about poverty "if we can get a good program, but I also think it's important to make clear that we're doing something for the middle income man in the suburbs."[22] He also is said to have told Heller, "First we'll have your tax cut, then we'll have my expenditures program," but that sentence can be read as saying more about Kennedy's faith in the revenue-generating effects of cutting tax rates than about his eagerness for expenditures.[23]

The Program for Economic Recovery and Growth also did call for an increase in the minimum wage, to $1.25 an hour from $1, over two years. A free-market purist would have questioned the need for the government to set a minimum wage to begin with. But Kennedy's proposed 25 percent increase was modest compared to the 1956 minimum-wage hike of the previous administration — 33 percent, to $1 an hour from 75 cents. And Richard Nixon in his memoir recalls an Oval Office meeting after the Bay of Pigs invasion in which Kennedy said to him, "Who gives a shit if the minimum wage is $1.15 or $1.25, in comparison to something like this?"[24]

Kennedy wanted neither a rapid rise in wages nor in prices. As president he followed through on the "sound dollar" policy he had outlined in his October 1960 speech about how "inflation robs every man."

Schlesinger recalls that Kennedy "had acquired somewhere, perhaps from his father, the belief that a nation was only as strong as the value of its currency," and the president once went so far as to suggest that money was more important than nuclear weapons to national prestige: "What really matters is the strength of the currency . . . Britain has nuclear weapons, but the pound is weak, so everyone pushes it around. Why are people so nice to Spain today? Not because Spain has nuclear weapons but because of all those lovely gold reserves."[25]

In a January 30, 1961, address to a joint session of Congress, Kennedy said, "We have some $22 billion in total gold stocks and other international monetary reserves available — and I now pledge that their full strength stands behind the value of the dollar for use if needed . . . In short, we need not — and we shall not — take any action to increase the dollar price of gold from $35 an ounce — to impose exchange controls — to reduce our anti-recession efforts — to fall back on restrictive trade policies — or to weaken our commitments around the world. This Administration will not distort the value of the dollar in any fashion. And this is a commitment."

In his February 6, 1961, Special Message to the Congress on Gold and the Balance of Payments Deficit, Kennedy emphasized the point again: "This growth in foreign dollar holdings placed upon the United States a special responsibility — that of maintaining the dollar as the principal reserve currency of the free world. This required that the dollar be considered by many countries to be as good as gold. It is our responsibility to sustain this confidence . . . The United States official dollar price of gold can and will be maintained at $35 an ounce. Exchange controls over trade and investment will not be invoked . . . Those who fear weakness in the dollar will find their fears unfounded. Those who hope for speculative reasons for an increase in the price of gold will find their hopes in vain."

Kennedy reiterated this position in a July 23, 1962, press conference in which he vowed to keep the dollar convertible to gold, but also spoke against scrapping the dollar altogether for a gold standard:

If the United States refused to cash in dollars for gold, then everyone would go to the gold standard and the United States, which is the reserve currency of the whole free world — we would all be dependent upon the available supply of gold, which is quite limited.

Obviously, it isn't enough to finance the great movements of trade today and it would be the most backward step that the United States has taken since the end of the Second World War . . .

Those who speculate against the dollar are going to lose. The United States will not devalue its dollar . . . I feel it requires a cooperative effort by all those involved in order to maintain this free currency, the dollar, upon which so much of Western prosperity is built.

I have confidence in it, and I think that if others examine the wealth of this country and its determination to bring its balance of payments into order, which it will do, I think that they will feel that the dollar is a good investment and as good as gold.

In a press conference nearly a year later, Kennedy used the term "gold standard" to describe the current system under which paper dollars were convertible to gold on demand at a fixed rate of $35 an ounce. "I think we can still continue on the gold standard," the president said.

Privately, Kennedy expressed frustration over the gold issue. "The trouble is that the problems are so complicated and technical that only a handful of people really understand them, and so the average man discussing these problems falls back on a bunch of outdated, if not meaningless slogans like 'sound dollar,' and 'fiscal integrity,' and these old slogans are losing their value," he said in a May 30, 1962, phone call with his friend the journalist Ben Bradlee. He neglected to mention that he himself used the "sound dollar" phrase — said to originate from the sound that a metal coin, but not paper currency, makes when plunked down on a counter — in his 1960 campaign.[26] The economist James Tobin recalls a session in the fall of 1962 in which Kennedy asked him, in essence, "We could, if we wanted to, run the world without gold? And wouldn't that be more sensible? Wasn't it just the irrational prejudices of bankers that kept us tied to gold? We don't have any real national, or international, interest in it, do we?" Tobin allows, however, for the possibility that "he was just showing that he understood my points, without indicating that he agreed with them."[27]

The president's concerns about inflation, price stability, and the value of the dollar provided the context for the coming clash between the administration and the steel industry. So, too, did the steel strike of 1959, which had involved 519,000 workers, shut steel mills for months, and was the largest strike in American history. Arthur Goldberg, Kennedy's secretary of labor, had firsthand experience with the 1959 strike as the lawyer for both the Congress of Industrial Organizations and the United Steelworkers of America. The stress of that conflict, along with the related legal work that had gone all the way to the Supreme Court, left Goldberg exhausted and hospitalized afterward. With the master contract that had resolved the 1959 strike due to expire in July 1962, Goldberg got involved early to try to mediate a renewal, inviting the president of the steelworkers' union, David McDonald, and the chairman of United States Steel, Roger Blough, to a January 23, 1962, White House meeting with the president. Kennedy asked them to negotiate a new contract that would cost between 2.5 and 3 percent more than the old one, a small enough increase to prevent an inflationary hike in steel prices. Blough was noncommittal, but under pressure from Goldberg, the union and eleven steelmakers, including U.S. Steel, eventually reached an agreement on a new contract that would increase labor compensation the next year about 2.2 percent, mostly through increases in benefits rather than hourly wages.[28]

The labor-management deal was announced on March 31. Ten days later, Roger Blough visited Kennedy again to hand him a copy of a press release in which U.S. Steel announced it was raising its prices by $6 a ton, or 3.5 percent. The president was furious, and aired his feelings in an April 11 press conference. First, Kennedy described the problem:

> Simultaneous and identical actions of United States Steel and other leading steel corporations increasing steel prices by some $6 a ton constitute a wholly unjustifiable and irresponsible defiance of the public interest . . . The American people will find it hard, as I do, to accept a situation in which a tiny handful of steel executives whose

pursuit of private power and profit exceeds their sense of public responsibility can show such utter contempt for the interests of 185 million Americans.

If this rise in the cost of steel is imitated by the rest of the industry, instead of rescinded, it would increase the cost of homes, autos, appliances, and most other items for every American family. It would increase the cost of machinery and tools to every American businessman and farmer. It would seriously handicap our efforts to prevent an inflationary spiral from eating up the pensions of our older citizens, and our new gains in purchasing power.

It would add, Secretary McNamara informed me this morning, an estimated $1 billion to the cost of our defenses, at a time when every dollar is needed for national security and other purposes. It would make it more difficult for American goods to compete in foreign markets, more difficult to withstand competition from foreign imports, and thus more difficult to improve our balance of payments position, and stem the flow of gold. And it is necessary to stem it for our national security, if we're going to pay for our security commitments abroad. And it would surely handicap our efforts to induce other industries and unions to adopt responsible price and wage policies.

Then Kennedy announced what he planned to do about it:

The Steelworkers Union can be proud that it abided by its responsibilities in this agreement, and this Government also has responsibilities which we intend to meet. The Department of Justice and the Federal Trade Commission are examining the significance of this action in a free, competitive economy. The Department of Defense and other agencies are reviewing its impact on their policies of procurement. And I am informed that steps are under way by those members of the Congress who plan appropriate inquiries into how these price decisions are so quickly made and reached and what legislative safeguards may be needed to protect the public interest.

Price and wage decisions in this country, except for a very limited restriction in the case of monopolies and national emergency strikes, are and ought to be freely and privately made. But the American people have a right to expect, in return for that freedom, a higher sense of business responsibility for the welfare of their country than has been shown in the last 2 days.

Some time ago I asked each American to consider what he would do for his country and I asked the steel companies. In the last 24 hours we had their answer.

When some other steel companies quickly followed U.S. Steel's price increase, Kennedy complained further, in an April 13 phone call to Ben Bradlee: "Is this the way the private enterprise system is really supposed to work? When U.S. Steel says, 'Go,' the boys go? How could they all raise their prices almost to a penny within six hours of each other?" Bradlee suggested that the Democrats could benefit politically by running against U.S. Steel in November. Kennedy replied, "But I don't want that. Everything that we have tried is in the other direction. We want the support of business on trade. We want them on the tax bill."[29]

Either taking direction from the president or following his leadership with excessive zeal, executive branch personnel carried the campaign against the steel companies and executives further than appropriate in a free-market economy, tapping telephone conversations and auditing tax returns. The attorney general later explained to Ben Bradlee, in what Bradlee described as "mock seriousness," "They were mean to my brother."[30]

The steel companies eventually backed down on the price increase, but the conflict left tensions between the Kennedy administration and the broader business community that the president tried to ease.

In an April 30, 1962, speech to the U.S. Chamber of Commerce, Kennedy said, "We have many burdens in Washington — we do not want the added burden of determining individual prices for individual products . . . While Government economists can point out the necessity of increasing the rates of investment, of modernizing plant and productivity, while Washington officials may urge responsible collective bargaining and responsible wage-price decisions, we also recognize that beneath all the laws and guidelines and tax policies and stimulants we can provide, these matters all come down, quite properly in the last analysis, to private decisions by private individuals."

The president went on, "We want prosperity and in a free enterprise system there can be no prosperity without profit. We want a growing economy, and there can be no growth without the investment that is inspired and financed by profit. We want to maintain our national security and other essential programs and we will have little revenue to finance them unless there is profit. We want to improve our balance of payments without reducing our commitments abroad, and we cannot increase our export surplus, which we must, without modernizing our plants through profit . . . In short, our primary challenge is not how to divide the economic pie, but how to enlarge it."

The public, and the markets, put more weight on the president's actions than on his speech, however. On May 28, the Dow Jones Industrial Average, which had risen 27 percent in 1961, plunged 5.7 percent in a single day; some called it Blue Monday, a reference to the Black Friday crash that started the Great Depression. The Federal Reserve, at the White House's request, lowered margin requirements on stocks to 50 percent from 70 percent, meaning that fewer investors would be forced to liquidate their positions at fire-sale prices because of margin calls from their brokerage firms.[31]

Schlesinger reports a poll of six thousand business executives released on June 30, 1962, by the Research Institute of America: 52 percent of respondents described the administration as "strongly anti-business," 36 percent as "moderately anti-business," and just 9 percent as "neutral" or "pro-business."[32] Jokes circulated: "Kennedy cocktail? Stocks on the rocks."[33] Another featured the president trying to reassure a visiting businessman: "The economic outlook is good, no matter what the market says. If I weren't president, I'd be buying stock myself." The businessman replies, "If you weren't president, so would I."[34]

A "widely repeated" story had it that the president, in the midst of the steel price battle, had quoted his father as saying "all businessmen" were sons-of-bitches. Kennedy, in a press conference, clarified that his father — "a businessman himself" — had been talking only about steel men. "But that's past, that's past. Now we are working together, I hope."[35]

In April 1963, a year after the big fight with the White House, a steel company raised prices again, and the president, as Sorensen puts it, "confined himself" to "releasing a low-key statement" observing that "selective price adjustments" are "characteristic of any healthy economy."[36]

Kennedy can reasonably be faulted for overstepping the appropriate bounds of government involvement on the steel price question. In assessing the whole episode, it is worth remembering, first, that the government's activism was motivated largely by a conservative desire to fight inflation, and second, that Kennedy, unlike the wartime Roosevelt presidency or the early 1970s under Nixon, did not seek price controls over huge areas of the American economy. Third, the administration backed down the following year. And fourth, part of what set the dispute in motion had been the Kennedy administration's original success in seeking restraint in the *union's* contract demands. None of this makes the president's behavior toward the steel manufacturers admirable from a conservative, free-market perspective, but at least it makes it less egregious than it would otherwise be.

The call for restraint in union demands was consistent with the administration's overall approach toward labor-management relations. Sorensen recalls that Secretary Goldberg set the tone from the start: "Labor and management will both be making a mistake if they believe that the Kennedy administration is going to be prolabor."[37]

One Kennedy action sometimes cited as a significant pro-union step was Executive Order 10988,[38] which clarified that federal employees had the right to organize labor unions. Critics say it opened the door to the vast expansion of public employee unions in state and local governments. These unions became powerful forces in the Democratic Party and in public policy, sometimes to the disadvantage of private-sector taxpayers. And yet the executive order itself did not include the term "collective bargaining." Indeed, it emphasized that the government would refuse to recognize any employee organization "which asserts the right to strike against the Government of the United States or any agency thereof, or to assist or participate in any such strike, or which imposes a duty or obligation to conduct, assist or participate in any such strike, or . . . which advocates the overthrow of the constitutional form of Government in the United States." The reference to "overthrow" was a slap at Communists, who, as Kennedy well knew, had often tried to infiltrate and influence the labor movement. Even in expanding recognition of public employee unions, Kennedy managed to take a hard line against the Communists. He also exempted both the FBI and the CIA from the executive order's provisions concerning the recognition of employee organizations.

But the administration did not always side with organized labor. Twice at press conferences in 1963, Kennedy was asked about labor-backed efforts to reduce the standard American workweek to thirty-five hours from forty. Both times, Kennedy rejected the idea, warning that it could "make it more difficult for us to compete abroad, if it was going to launch an inflationary spiral of wages and prices in the United States." At the first of those press conferences, on February 21, Kennedy opened with a statement about the New York newspaper strike, urging the typographical union to back down. "It is clear in the case of the New York newspaper strike that the Local of the International Typographical Union and its president, Bertram Powers, insofar as anyone can understand his position, are attempting to impose a settlement which could shut down several newspapers in New York and throw thousands out of work. Collective bargaining has failed. The most intensive mediation has failed. This is a situation which is bad for the union movement all over the country, bad for the newspaper managements and bad for the New York citizens, more than five million of them, who are newspaper readers," Kennedy said. "I think the best solution is for the union to demonstrate a sense of responsibility and not merely try to carry this to its final ultimate of cracking the publishers, because if they do it they will close down some papers and I think will hurt their employment possibilities themselves."[39]

Another instance in which Kennedy sided with business was the decision "to put the communications satellite system under private ownership."[40] That decision, Sorensen reports, "was filibustered by Senate liberals as a giveaway to big business."[41] The opponents included Senator Gore and his fellow Democrat from Tennessee, Estes Kefauver.[42] But Kennedy eventually got his way and signed the Communications Satellite Act into law.

Kennedy's description of his tax bill as "the most urgent task confronting the Congress in 1963" and as the most important legislation of the year raises questions about his commitment to other priorities, such as civil rights legislation. Schlesinger later wrote that Kennedy saw the tax cut itself as a remedy to the problems of black Americans: "He knew that a slow rate of economic growth made every problem of equal rights more intractable, as a faster rate would make every such problem easier of solution. In 1963 he counted on his tax cut to reduce Negro unemployment."[43] Douglas Dillon expanded on this point in a 1964 interview: "Certainly the basic reason for the tax bill was to make our economy move better. And when our economy moved better those who were least favored, which would be the Negroes, would naturally be helped."[44]

The race problem, however, was deep-rooted enough that many leaders in the black community thought it required solutions well beyond a tax cut. Kennedy's record on race is worth a careful look, in part because it is sometimes cited as an area in which the president was a liberal. Sorensen, for example, in the same 1981 JFK Library session where he described Kennedy as "extremely conservative" on fiscal matters, states flatly that on civil rights "he was a liberal."[45]

At the time, a liberal on race was someone who favored vigorous federal action to speed integration in states with segregated public and private institutions, while conservatives favored a slower approach that left decisions up to state and local governments and business owners rather than the federal government. The Supreme Court, in its 1954 decision in *Brown v. Board of Education of Topeka,* had ruled that segregated public schools violated the Fourteenth Amendment's guarantee of equal protection under the law, and, in a follow-up decision the next year, had ordered that the integration begin "with all deliberate speed." In September 1957, President Eisenhower sent paratroopers from the 101st Airborne Division into Little Rock, Arkansas, and he federalized the National Guard there to protect nine black students entering a previously all-white high school. (Kennedy had told southern Democrats in the 1960 campaign that he was never convinced the Little Rock police could not have handled the trouble.[46]) But many southern buses, hotels, restaurants, universities, swimming pools, toilets, and water fountains were still segregated when Kennedy took office, and voting rights for blacks were not secure.

Kennedy certainly had a personal commitment to civil rights. Just hours after Kennedy took the oath of office, following the inaugural parade, he had changed out of his formal attire into a business suit and gone to look at his new office in the West Wing. In a White House hallway Kennedy saw his aide Richard Goodwin, who had come to work following the parade. "Did you see the Coast Guard detachment?" Kennedy asked Goodwin, who recalled the episode later in his memoir. "There wasn't a black face in the entire group. That's not acceptable. Something ought to be done about it."

Goodwin remembers calling the Treasury secretary, who oversaw the Coast Guard at the time. Goodwin writes: "That summer the first black professor was hired at the Coast Guard Academy and the following year four black cadets entered."[47] In 1966, Ensign Merle Smith Jr. became the first black graduate of the Coast Guard Academy.[48]

The president's children, Caroline and John, attended an integrated school on the White House grounds that had been organized by Jacqueline Kennedy. *Jet* magazine reported that "the kindergarten class attended by Caroline Kennedy enrolled five-year-old Avery Hatcher," the son of the associate White House press secretary, Andrew Hatcher.[49]

Another example of Kennedy's personal attitudes on race and civil rights came in 1963. Medgar Evers, the field secretary of the Mississippi NAACP, was working late one night. Evers's wife had let their three children stay up past midnight to wait for their father, who was returning from a strategy meeting. At about 12:20, they heard the sound of his car, which they recognized. Next, they heard the car door open, and then the sound of a rifle shot.

The children kept crying, "Daddy, get up, please get up," as their father bled to death in the driveway.[50]

The morning after Evers was buried at Arlington National Cemetery, a limousine took his widow and the two oldest children to the White House. President Kennedy showed the children the coconut shell that got him rescued in the Solomon Islands, and the secret door in his Oval Office desk, and, as Myrlie Evers later wrote, he "told them they should be very proud of their father." Kennedy arranged to have the family given a tour of the executive mansion, and young Rena Evers sat down on a bed in which Queen Elizabeth had slept. Myrlie Evers later wrote that in the midst of her grief, she was "pleased at the warmth and gentleness and what seemed like the genuineness of President Kennedy's reception of us."[51]

For all those apparently genuine personal feelings, when it came to government action on civil rights, or presidential support for the actions of civil rights groups, Kennedy often was cautious, hesitant, even discouraging. He seemed to consider civil rights an issue less important than tax cuts, free trade, or the Cold War. The politics were complicated; the Democratic Party of the late 1950s and early 1960s included southern white conservatives who favored racial segregation. Some of them, such as Governor John Patterson of Alabama, had supported Kennedy's presidential candidacy.[52] In 1960 Kennedy had carried the electoral votes of Georgia, Louisiana, and of North and South Carolina.

When, in May 1961, interracial groups from the Congress of Racial Equality set out on "Freedom Rides" to dramatize and challenge the segregated facilities in southern public bus stations, they were brutally beaten by racist mobs. Kennedy called his special assistant for civil rights, Harris Wofford, and in a tone that Wofford later described as "angry . . . urgent and sharp," demanded, "Tell them to call it off! Stop them!" The president was talking not about the white mobs, but about the Freedom Riders. Robert Kennedy publicly called for a "cooling-off" period, which Freedom Rider James Farmer rejected: blacks had "been cooling off for a hundred years." Robert Kennedy warned Martin Luther King Jr. in a phone call: "Don't make statements that sound like a threat. That's not the way to deal with us." The attorney general later complained to Wofford, "This is too much! I wonder whether they have the best interest of their country at heart. Do you know that one of them is against the atom bomb — yes, he even picketed against it in jail! The President is going abroad and this is all embarrassing him."[53]

The Kennedy administration did not send a civil rights bill to Congress until 1962, and did not mount a major push for civil rights legislation until 1963. Even in 1963, Kennedy asked the liberal New York Democrat who took the lead on the legislation, the chairman of the House Judiciary Committee, Emanuel Celler, to delay the civil rights bill so as not to anger Wilbur Mills, a southerner, who might stall the tax bill in retaliation.[54] Similarly, Arthur Schlesinger Jr., who wrote that Kennedy had "a terrible ambivalence" about civil rights, reports that Kennedy delayed issuing an executive order integrating federally financed housing at least in part "because he sought southern votes for the trade expansion bill in 1962." The president was criticized for this by Martin Luther King Jr., who called the administration's civil rights record "essentially cautious and defensive."[55]

Privately, Kennedy argued against the August 1963 March on Washington, telling civil rights leaders, including King, "It seemed to me a great mistake to announce a march on Washington before the bill was even in committee. The only effect is to create an atmosphere of intimidation."[56] Publicly, the president eventually expressed support.[57] His brother the attorney general nonetheless referred to the march as "that old black fairy's anti-Kennedy demonstration," a derisive reference to Bayard Rustin, the organizer of the march, who was gay.[58]

After the march, President Kennedy met with its organizers, who asked the government to do more to help black Americans. Kennedy turned the question back on them: "Now, isn't it possible for the Negro community to take the lead in committing major emphasis upon the responsibility of these families, even if they're split and all the rest of the problems they have, on educating their children? Now, in my opinion, the Jewish community, which suffered a good deal under discrimination, and what a great effort they made, which I think has made their role influential, was in education: education of their children. And therefore they've been able to establish a pretty strong position for themselves . . . With all the influence that all you gentlemen have in the Negro community . . . [you] really have to concentrate on what I think the Jewish community has done on educating their children, on making them stay in school, and all the rest."[59]

After the meeting, the president took Martin Luther King Jr. aside and told him that two of his associates were Communists: "You've got to get rid of them."[60]

In September 1963, just days after four black girls were killed in the bombing of the 16th Street Baptist Church in Birmingham, Alabama, Kennedy told civil rights leaders, including King, "I can't do much. Congress can't do very much unless we keep the support of the white community." The same president who was promising to put a man on the moon and committing American troops to defend South Vietnam was insisting that on civil rights, "I can't do much."

With that statement, Kennedy was probably trying to manage expectations more than accurately describing his own power. After all, when the situation demanded it, his administration had deployed the power of the federal government to enforce the Fourteenth Amendment's guarantee of equal protection under the law, as it had been interpreted by the Supreme Court and other federal judges who ordered integration. James Meredith, an Air Force veteran, had written to the registrar at the University of Mississippi on January 21, 1961, the day after Kennedy's inauguration, asking for an application for admission. He had been encouraged by Medgar Evers and by Thurgood Marshall, the chief counsel of the NAACP, who had been the lawyer for Oliver Brown and his daughter Linda in the *Brown v. Board of Education of Topeka* case, and who himself had been rejected for admission to the University of Maryland's law school because of his race. Meredith pursued admission in the courts and, ultimately, in person. The state's Democratic governor, Ross Barnett, the son of a Confederate veteran of the Civil War, resisted, as did a violent mob on the Oxford, Mississippi, campus. Kennedy sent in the Army to reinforce the hundreds of U.S. marshals and Border Patrol agents on the scene, and on October 1, 1962, James Meredith registered as a student at the University of Mississippi.[61] On June 11, 1963, U.S. marshals, Deputy Attorney General Nicholas Katzenbach, and the federalized Alabama National Guard accompanied two other black students, Vivian Malone and James Hood, who enrolled for the summer session at the University of Alabama, Tuscaloosa. They, too, did so despite the resistance of a segregationist Democratic governor, in this case George Wallace. This time around, there was no violence.[62]

Kennedy seized the occasion of the Alabama integration for a prime-time television and radio "report to the American People on civil rights," delivered from the Oval Office. "New laws are needed at every level," the president said, "but law alone cannot make men see right. We are confronted primarily with a moral issue. It is as old as the scriptures and is as clear as the American Constitution." Kennedy announced his intention to send Congress legislation desegregating public accommodations such as theaters, hotels, restaurants, and retail stores, and also adding protection for voting rights. Yet he reiterated that "legislation, I repeat, cannot solve this problem alone. It must be solved in the homes of every American in every community across our country."

This skepticism about the power of legislation alone to solve the problems of black Americans, together with his comments after the March on Washington asking the black leaders whether it was "possible for the Negro community to take the lead" on education, go to the heart of Kennedy's attitude toward America's race problem. Schlesinger recalls that on civil rights, "Kennedy used to quote Jefferson: 'Great innovations should not be forced on slender majorities.'"[63]

It was not only Martin Luther King Jr. who found Kennedy's approach unsatisfactory in some respects. On college campuses, student political activism was beginning to stir. From June 11 to June 15, 1962, a group called Students for a Democratic Society gathered at Port Huron, Michigan. Led by Tom Hayden, SDS issued a statement that faulted Kennedy. "He fraternizes with racist scoundrels," it asserted, criticizing the president for having "appointed at least four segregationist judges in areas where voter registration is a desperate need."

Kennedy's judicial appointments did indeed include some segregationists, most notably William Harold Cox, whose nomination was opposed by the NAACP. In comments from the bench, Judge Cox called black plaintiffs in a voting rights case "a bunch of niggers . . . acting like a bunch of chimpanzees."[64] But Kennedy also named Thurgood Marshall — who had won twenty-nine of the thirty-two cases he had argued before the Supreme Court — to the U.S. Court of Appeals for the Second Circuit. For eight months, Marshall's nomination languished before the Senate Judiciary Committee, and, as an interim appointee, he was treated a bit like a visitor in a courthouse that was already short of space; he helped his staff carry their files from office to office. Once, the other judges on the circuit were gathered for a group photograph, and the photographer's flash equipment blew a fuse in the courthouse at 40 Foley Square in New York, where the Second Circuit sits. Then Marshall arrived for the photo, and a secretary for one of the other judges mistook him for the electrician called to fix the blown fuse. Marshall took no offense. Instead, when he returned to his chambers, he used the event to remark to his clerk on how certain of the trade unions were still not open to black Americans: "Boy, that woman must be crazy if she thinks I could become an electrician."[65] The stereotype is that black progress was blocked by southern conservatives, and there is some truth to that story. Yet as Marshall's comment shows, racial discrimination extended to the North, and in the North to groups, such as labor unions, usually thought of as progressive.

Another litmus test for presidential politics is the Supreme Court. The Republican Eisenhower had chosen a liberal chief justice, Earl Warren. Kennedy had two nominations. He used them to elevate first Byron White, who had been deputy attorney general, and then Arthur Goldberg, who had been secretary of labor. Goldberg stepped down in 1965 to become the U.S. ambassador to the United Nations. White, however, served until 1993, and sided with conservatives on a number of high-profile cases. In the 1965 case *United States v. Brown,* the Supreme Court struck down as unconstitutional a provision of the 1959 Landrum-Griffin Act that made it a crime for Communist Party members or those who had been party members in the past five years to serve on the executive boards of labor unions. Goldberg was among the five justices who overturned the law, but White wrote the dissenting opinion, contending, "The Communist Party's illegal purpose and its domination by a foreign power have already been adjudicated, both administratively and judicially." White dissented in the 1966 case *Miranda v. Arizona,* which required police to warn detainees about their right to remain silent and their right to a lawyer. He was one of only two justices who dissented against the 1973 decision in *Roe v. Wade,* which found that women had the constitutional right to an abortion. White's dissent accused the *Roe* majority of "interposing a constitutional barrier to state efforts to protect human life." He also wrote the majority opinion in *Bowers v. Hardwick,* refusing to rescind a Georgia law against sodomy, writing, "The Court is most vulnerable and comes nearest to illegitimacy when it deals with judge-made constitutional law having little or no cognizable roots in the language or design of the Constitution."

Kennedy could not have predicted how Justice White would rule in each of those cases, but the president's own views of the wedge issues that tend to rise to the level of the Supreme Court were sometimes more conservative than those of his friends and colleagues. Ben Bradlee reports on a dinner party at which "it turned out we were all against capital punishment except the president."[66] An assistant special counsel to President Kennedy, Lee White, recalls a federal death penalty case in which White recommended that "this fellow's life shouldn't be taken." The president responded, "Is there any circumstances, in your view, under which somebody's life should be taken?" White said no. Kennedy replied, "Well, what does the law say?" White later recalled, "I told him. He said, 'Okay. Let's don't have you advising me then that I shouldn't take people's lives.' And that guy was put to death."[67]

Asked at a June 27, 1962, press conference about the Supreme Court's decision in *Engel v. Vitale*, which struck down government-written prayers in public schools as an unconstitutional violation of the Establishment clause of the First Amendment, Kennedy replied:

> The Supreme Court has made its judgment, and a good many people obviously will disagree with it. Others will agree with it. But I think that it is important for us if we are going to maintain our constitutional principle that we support the Supreme Court decisions even when we may not agree with them.
>
> In addition, we have in this case a very easy remedy and that is to pray ourselves. And I would think that it would be a welcome reminder to every American family that we can pray a good deal more at home, we can attend our churches with a good deal more fidelity, and we can make the true meaning of prayer much more important in the lives of all of our children.

When Kennedy talked about praying at home and attending church regularly, he did so from personal experience.

"He was just as good a Catholic as I am," Cardinal Cushing said. "He spent more time in private prayer than many people know. Time and again, he would drop into the Archbishop's House in Boston when I would be broadcasting the evening rosary and participate in that prayer." Cushing was in a position to know, in part because he was with Kennedy in some of the most trying moments, including on August 10, 1963, for the funeral of his son Patrick Bouvier Kennedy, who had died at Children's Hospital in Boston two days after being born prematurely on Cape Cod. The president was the last to leave the funeral in the private chapel of Cushing's residence; the archbishop said to him, "Come on, Jack. Let's go. God is good."[68]

"Kennedy was a more deeply religious man than he appeared to be, or wanted to appear to be," his longtime aides Kenneth O'Donnell and David Powers wrote in their book about JFK. The same book relates that as part of the president's regular bedtime routine, he would "kneel beside his bed and say his prayers." It also reports that Kennedy's regular breakfast was freshly squeezed orange juice, two four-and-a-half-minute boiled eggs, toast, coffee, and four strips of bacon — except that "on Fridays, the bacon was omitted," in keeping with the Catholic tradition of "meatless Fridays," to remember the day of Jesus' death.[69]

Kennedy's own faith meant that he was able to use language like that of his inaugural address — "the rights of man come not from the generosity of the state but from the hand of God" — without embarrassment, and without a lot of worry about philosophical objections posed by critics who might point out that such a conception is not much help either to atheists or when there is a disagreement over the definition of a right.[70]

Tucked into the frame of his dresser mirror in the White House, Kennedy kept a handwritten schedule of Washington Masses: "St. Stephen's 8, 9, 10, 11 high, 12 noon; Holy Trinity 8, 9, 10 high, 11:15, 12:05; St. Matthew's 10 high, 11:30, 12:30."[71]

Sorensen reports that Kennedy "faithfully attended Mass each Sunday, even in the midst of fatiguing out-of-state travels when no voter would know whether he attended services or not."[72] And indeed Kennedy not only attended Mass on the morning of his Friday inauguration, he also did so, according to Sorensen, on the Sunday that followed.[73]

"If we were working at Cape Cod he usually asked me to meet him at his house after church," Sorensen wrote.[74]

On August 12, 1962, while at Dark Harbor, Maine, visiting the heavyweight boxing champion Gene Tunney and Watson K. Blair, who was the chairman of Morgan Guaranty, and cruising in the presidential yacht *Manitou* off the Maine coast, Kennedy shuttled via a Navy radar picket ship to an early Mass at Our Lady Queen of Peace Church in Boothbay Harbor.[75] He had made the same trip on a different Navy boat as a lieutenant in the Solomon Islands, traveling to Sesape Island from Tulagi every Sunday for Mass.[76]

Barbara Sinatra, the wife of the singer Frank Sinatra, recalled a visit by President Kennedy to Palm Springs, California, in 1962: "Jack was a devout Catholic and went to church to pray for his family almost every day in between hitting on all the girls, which I thought strange."[77]

Any depiction of Kennedy as a religious conservative must reckon with the reports of his sex life. "Strange" is probably as apt a description as any, even discounting heavily, as one should, the lurid exaggerations by sensationalist biographers and their enablers in the press, emboldened by the fact that under American law it is impossible to libel a dead person. In Kennedy's defense it has been said that the president's father had set an example of inappropriately close relations with attractive women other than his spouse, or that medications the president was taking for his health problems increased his libido.[78]

The Catholic Church of Kennedy's era had announced its views on Christian marriage in Pope Pius XI's 1930 encyclical *Casti Connubii*, which cited "the counsel of virginity given by Jesus Christ." It held that when conception is prevented through birth control or withdrawal, intercourse even "with one's legitimate wife" is a "horrible crime" at times punished with death, as in the case of the biblical character Onan. And it quoted Jesus' words from Matthew: "Whosoever shall look on a woman to lust after her hath already committed adultery with her in his heart." If Kennedy found these standards unrealistically strict or hopelessly difficult to live by, he had plenty of company.

The least charitable interpretation — that Kennedy's religiosity was a hypocritical pose designed to put a guise of godliness over a crude adulterer — is undercut by the fact that JFK observed religious rituals even in private, away from the public eye. Perhaps he was so diligent about Mass and confession and daily prayers and meatless Fridays because he knew he was sinning and felt a need to compensate for it or confess.

If there was an area in which Kennedy, as president, would most need to draw on his faith to sustain him, though, it was not in restraining federal spending or navigating the issue of civil rights. Rather, it was the nuclear-fused Cold War conflict with the Soviet Union. We will turn to that part of his presidency soon enough. But first, let us take a closer look at the true centerpiece of Kennedy's domestic policy agenda, his tax cuts.

CHAPTER 7

Tax Cutter

1960–1963

This philosophy of the free market — the wider economic choice
for men and nations — is as old as freedom itself.

— JOHN F. KENNEDY, Special Message to the Congress on
Foreign Trade Policy, January 25, 1962

R EDUCING TARIFFS — taxes on imported goods similar in
some respects to the American Revolution–inspiring levy
on tea — was a focus for President Kennedy from the transition forward.

The idea's origin was somewhat unlikely. George Ball was the Iowa-
born son of a Standard Oil executive, a graduate of Northwestern University and Northwestern University Law School who had practiced
law in Chicago at the firm that is now Sidley Austin, where he became
friends with a junior partner named Adlai Stevenson. After a civilian
World War II stint that included interrogating the head of the Nazi
war production machine, Albert Speer, Ball settled in Washington as a
trade lawyer and founding partner at the firm that is now Cleary Got-
tlieb Steen & Hamilton. There his clients included the French government, Venezuelans fighting restrictions on exporting their oil to the
United States, and pre-Castro Cuban sugar producers seeking access
to the American market. In 1953, Ball, who described himself as an "ar-
dent advocate" of free trade against the "protectionist lobbies," helped
create an organization to promote lower tariffs and more open mar-

kets, the Committee for a National Trade Policy, with participation by executives from General Mills, Gillette, and the Chase Manhattan Bank.[1]

During the 1960 transition, Ball wrote a report recommending a new law giving the president authority to reduce tariffs by 50 percent over five years. Ball had his law firm colleague John Sharon, who was closer to Kennedy, present the document to the president-elect at Palm Beach. When JFK finished reading the briefing book that included the proposal, he said, "Very good. Terrific. This is excellent. Just what I needed."[2]

Kennedy appointed Ball undersecretary of state and later named a Republican former governor of Massachusetts and secretary of state under Eisenhower, Christian Herter, as special representative for trade negotiations. Important as both of those men were, though, Kennedy himself played a leading role in articulating to the nation and the Congress the case for free trade. The president first outlined his position in the Special Message to the Congress on Gold and the Balance of Payments Deficit, issued less than a month after the inauguration. "A return to protectionism is not a solution. Such a course would provoke retaliation," he said. "In the tariff negotiations now going forward under GATT [the General Agreement on Tariffs and Trade] we shall seek the fullest possible measure of tariff reduction by foreign countries to the benefit of our exports."

In a December 11, 1961, Oval Office meeting with the editor of the *Wall Street Journal*, Vermont Royster, Kennedy, according to a report Royster sent three days later to his publisher, "expressed his appreciation of our editorial support of the general idea of liberalizing trade." In the same meeting, Kennedy voiced disappointment that on *Meet the Press* the preceding Sunday, George Ball, along with Royster, "didn't get more chance to discuss the trade program" because the conversation kept veering off in other directions.[3]

In 1962, Kennedy made trade his foremost legislative priority, reacting in part to the efforts by European nations to eliminate tariffs within Western Europe by establishing what they called the Common Market. He concluded his January 11, 1962, State of the Union address with a long section on trade:

We need a new law—a wholly new approach—a bold new instrument of American trade policy. Our decision could well affect the unity of the West, the course of the Cold War, and the economic growth of our Nation for a generation to come.

If we move decisively, our factories and farms can increase their sales to their richest, fastest-growing market. Our exports will increase. Our balance of payments position will improve. And we will have forged across the Atlantic a trading partnership with vast resources for freedom.

If, on the other hand, we hang back in deference to local economic pressures, we will find ourselves cut off from our major allies. Industries—and I believe this is most vital—industries will move their plants and jobs and capital inside the walls of the Common Market, and jobs, therefore, will be lost here in the United States . . .

To seize that initiative, I shall shortly send to the Congress a new five-year Trade Expansion Action, far-reaching in scope but designed with great care to make certain that its benefits to our people far outweigh any risks. The bill will permit the gradual elimination of tariffs here in the United States and in the Common Market on those items in which we together supply 80 percent of the world's trade — mostly items in which our own ability to compete is demonstrated by the fact that we sell abroad, in these items, substantially more than we import. This step will make it possible for our major industries to compete with their counterparts in Western Europe for access to European consumers.

On other goods the bill will permit a gradual reduction of duties up to 50 percent — permitting bargaining by major categories — and provide for appropriate and tested forms of assistance to firms and employees adjusting to import competition . . . For together we face a common challenge: to enlarge the prosperity of free men everywhere — to build in partnership a new trading community in which all free nations may gain from the productive energy of free competitive effort.

The trade initiative met with resistance from liberals within the administration as well as from some domestic manufacturing interests. The liberals faulted Kennedy for using his political capital on trade expansion rather than for spending on schools or health care. Arthur Schlesinger Jr. recalled, "We thought him mistaken in 1962 in making the entirely respectable, safe, and overrated trade expansion bill his top legislative priority instead of staging a knockdown-dragout fight over federal aid to education or Medicare. To the president I would cite the Roosevelts, Wilson, Jackson and so on in arguing the inevitability and superiority of the politics of combat as against the politics of consensus."[4] American textile manufacturers also balked at proposals that would subject them to more competition from lower-priced or higher-quality foreign competitors. Ball recalls in his memoir that he had a series of "acrimonious and unpleasant" meetings with textile trade groups: "For my private and secret gratification, I appeared before each textile group dressed in a British-made suit, a British-made shirt, shoes made for me in Hong Kong, and a French necktie."[5]

The president pressed ahead with a series of messages and speeches on the topic. In a January 25, 1962, Special Message to the Congress on Foreign Trade Policy, he linked lowering trade barriers to "the need to accelerate our own economic growth." The president explained that "to try to shield American industry from the discipline of foreign competition would isolate our domestic price level from world prices, encourage domestic inflation, reduce our exports still further and invite less desirable Governmental solutions." He said, "The American consumer benefits most of all from an increase in foreign trade. Imports give him a wider choice of products at competitive prices. They introduce new ideas and new tastes, which often lead to new demands for American production." He insisted, "The warnings against increased imports based upon the lower level of wages paid in other countries are not telling the whole story." And he concluded, "This philosophy of the free market — the wider economic choice for men and nations — is as old as freedom itself. It is not a partisan philosophy. For many years our trade legislation has enjoyed bi-partisan backing from those members of both parties who recognized how essential trade is to our basic security abroad and our economic health at home. This is even more true today. The Trade Expansion Act of 1962 is designed as the expression of a nation, not of any single faction or section. It is in that spirit that I recommend it to the Congress for prompt and favorable action."

The Kennedy bill included some adjustment assistance to help employees and producers adversely affected by new foreign competition, but the president's message in explaining that program was stern: "This cannot be and will not be a subsidy program of government paternalism. It is instead a program to afford time for American initiative, American adaptability and American resiliency to assert themselves . . . The accent is on 'adjustment' more than 'assistance.'"

In a May 17, 1962, speech on trade, Kennedy linked his own tariff-lowering efforts to those of the nation's revolutionaries: "When the people of Boston in 1773 threw cargoes of tea into the harbor, the American Revolution was in effect underway, symbolized by this revolution against a tariff — a tariff which meant taxation without representation." Kennedy spoke of the link between trade and growth: "Today we wish to step up our growth — and trade expansion, by increasing exports as well as imports, and providing new outlets and new jobs will help expand that growth." He explained what economists call the law of comparative advantage: "We will be producing more of what we produce best, and others will be producing more of what they produce best."

The Trade Expansion Act of 1962 passed the House by a vote of 298 to 125, the Senate by 78 to 8. When Kennedy signed it into law on October 11, he said, "This act recognizes, fully and completely, that we cannot protect our economy by stagnating behind tariff walls, but that the best protection possible is a mutual lowering of tariff barriers among friendly nations so that all may benefit from a free flow of goods . . . The results can bring a dynamic new era of growth." The Kennedy round of trade negotiations that followed, from January 1963 to June 1967, cut tariffs on 6,300 items by an average of 35 percent.[6] While Kennedy's record on free trade was strong, it was not perfect; on July 19, 1963, he proposed an "interest equalization tax" that made it more expensive for Americans to buy stocks and bonds from Europe, Japan, Australia, South Africa, and New Zealand. The tax was enacted in 1964, effective retroactively to the date on which it had been proposed.[7]

Tariffs were hardly the only taxes that President Kennedy favored cutting. Sorensen points out that the tax credit for business investment in machinery and equipment, combined with accelerated depreciation, passed in 1962, provided a "reduction in business taxes of some $2.5 billion, an 11 percent tax cut for corporations."[8]

The economic issue for which Kennedy would become best known, however, was not the relatively more obscure tariff reductions, but the reductions he proposed in personal and corporate income tax rates. When he took office, the income tax rate at the highest bracket was 91 percent, though deductions and shelters meant few actually paid such a high rate. The lowest rate was 20 percent. The corporate tax rate was 52 percent, and the capital gains rate was 25 percent. Kennedy wanted to lower them all, arguing that the growth that resulted would more than make up the revenue loss to the government. It was the same argument Ronald Reagan would make in 1980, but with precisely the opposite partisan reaction: many Republicans (and some Democrats) thought Kennedy's plan was reckless, but centrist Democrats and a few farsighted Republicans agreed with their president.

While Kennedy thought tax rates were too high, he also thought that administration officials must obey the law and pay what was required. One former campaign aide, Frank Reeves, had a job in the White House until it emerged that he had failed to pay income taxes. Kennedy announced he would leave immediately. As Bradlee tells it, "I spoke to the president on the telephone a day later and asked him when Reeves was in fact going to leave. 'He's left,' Kennedy said, sure of himself. I told him how I'd seen him twenty-four hours ago. There was a pause and I could hear the president ask O'Donnell, 'Is Frank Reeves still around here?' Another pause, then Kennedy back to O'Donnell: 'Get his ass out of here, *tonight.*'"[9]

There was a debate within the administration over the tax cut issue that required a judgment to be made, in the end, by President Kennedy himself. That judgment was hastened by the desire to respond to the stock market downturn and the overall climate of tension between the White House and business that remained in the air following the initial clash over the steel price increase. The day after the Blue Monday stock market plunge of May 28, 1962, the liberal economist John Kenneth Galbraith, back from his post in India for a visit to his country home in Newfane, Vermont, dictated a memo to the president, "Subject: The

Stock Market." Galbraith advised, "As usual, I would be against a tax cut," and concluded, on a note that could hardly have inspired confidence, "I am sending you a copy of my history of the 1929 episode."[10]

Even the advisers who favored a tax cut were divided over whether the best medicine was an immediate, if temporary, tax cut or a permanent one connected with a broader tax reform later on. Walter Heller, the economist who had become chairman of Kennedy's Council of Economic Advisers, sent the president a May 28, 1962, memo, "Subject: The Market": "We have been talking to a market trader we know who also happens to be a well-trained economist . . . We pass on his impressions to you, because we think they are well-informed and make a lot of sense. As to what would help the market, our friend believes . . . for the longer term, a cut in taxes to add vigor to the recovery is the market's main hope. (We have heard this from a dozen sources in finance and business.)"

The *Washington Post,* owned by Kennedy's friend Philip Graham, suggested in a May 30, 1962, editorial, which was clipped and forwarded to Kennedy by Walter Heller, that Kennedy could "take several actions that are inherently desirable and that, proposed at this time, would help rebuild confidence . . . The President could announce now the principal constructive features of the tax reform proposal which the Treasury is readying for later in the year. It is expected to include a tax cut in the upper brackets, and perhaps in the corporate tax rate."

Heller commented on the *Washington Post* editorial in a June 2 memo to the president: "We surely can score with the public when we announce that a net tax reduction is forthcoming. But the package will contain some bitter (loophole closing) along with the sweet (rate reduction) . . . There is a strong case for Presidential announcement of the program in the near future."

Heller also forwarded to the president a June 5 memo from the undersecretary of commerce, Edward Gudeman, reporting on "several phone calls to business acquaintances located primarily in New York, Chicago, and Los Angeles." Gudeman wrote, "The hostility toward the President and the Administration seems to be greater than it ever has been. It is highly emotional . . . Every businessman to whom I talked believed that taxes should be reduced and immediate action taken —

this applies to both corporate and individual income taxes . . . None of the men to whom I talked were in favor of the Public Works proposal, either the $600 million or the $2 billion proposal. Most of them said that it would be better to reduce taxes by this amount." (The Public Works Acceleration Act, authorizing $900 million for federal and local public works projects aimed at relieving unemployment and spurring economic expansion, was nonetheless signed into law by Kennedy on September 14, 1962.) A section of the Gudeman memo on the attitude of businessmen toward a budget deficit observed, "A few mentioned that with lower taxes but with the economy running at a rapid rate revenue would be sufficient to cause either a surplus or only a small deficit."

A June 6 memo to the president from the economists Paul Samuelson and Robert Solow, who were working with Heller's Council of Economic Advisers, warned, "There is right now a substantial possibility that you will go into the 1964 election with the highest average unemployment rate of any postwar administration . . . More can be done for confidence by expansionary policies — early tax cuts — than by any feasible alternatives . . . Under present circumstances only an early tax cut appears to be capable of giving the economy the stimulus it needs in time to be really effective."[11]

The best insights into Kennedy's tax policy, though, come not from the memos of his advisers, but from the words of the president himself. "Our tax structure as presently weighted exerts too heavy a drain on a prospering economy," Kennedy said at a June 7 news conference. He spoke of accelerated depreciation and an investment tax credit for businesses. He recommended repealing the 10 percent transportation tax on train and bus travel, resulting in a tax saving for travelers of $90 million a year, and reducing it to 5 percent on airlines. The centerpiece of the tax agenda, however, was to be what the president called "a comprehensive tax reform bill." He said it "will be offered for action by the next Congress, making effective as of January 1 of next year an across-the-board reduction in personal and corporate income tax rates which will not be wholly offset by other reforms — in other words, a net tax reduction."

Kennedy still had to decide whether to go for an immediate "early" or "quickie" tax cut of the sort that Samuelson and Solow recommended. He invited Wilbur Mills, the chairman of the tax-writing House Ways and Means Committee, to an Oval Office meeting. Kennedy pressed the button in his desk to activate a newly installed system that tape-recorded the session. He did not record all his meetings, so his action suggested he thought the tax cut would be part of his historic legacy. Mills indicated that an early tax cut would be hard to get through Congress. Kennedy responded that he did not trust the ability of his Council of Economic Advisers to measure the performance of the economy in real time with enough precision to calibrate the tax cuts. "I don't have any confidence in these fellows," Kennedy said. "They can't tell. They can't tell."[12] If the MIT economics professors failed to recognize the limits of their ability to fine-tune the performance of the vast and complex American economy with the tools of fiscal policy, the president certainly did.

Kennedy's next big tax move came in an August 13, 1962, "Radio and Television Report to the American People on the State of the National Economy." He began, as he often did when approaching economic issues, with a reference to inflation, which he called "the archenemy of consumers and housewives." Kennedy said, "I think it will be obvious in the next 12 to 18 months, as I believe it is today, that the dollar is as good as gold." The president then moved on to the tax issue: "The single most important fiscal weapon available to strengthen the national economy is the federal tax policy. The right kind of tax cut at the right time is the most effective measure that this Government could take to spur our economy forward. For the facts of the matter are that our present tax system is a drag on economic recovery and economic growth, biting heavily into the purchasing power of every taxpayer and every consumer."

The president elaborated on the "growth" theme that had been an important element of his 1960 campaign:

> This administration intends to cut taxes in order to build the fundamental strength of our economy, to remove a serious barrier to long-term growth, to increase incentives by routing out inequities and complexities and to prevent the even greater budget deficit that a

lagging economy would otherwise surely produce. The worst deficit comes from a recession, and if we can take the proper action in the proper time, this can be the most important step we could take to prevent another recession. That is the right kind of a tax cut both for your family budget and the national budget resulting from a permanent basic reform and reduction in our rate structure, a creative tax cut creating more jobs and income and eventually more revenue. And the right time for that kind of bill, it now appears in the absence of an economic crisis today — and if the job is to be done in a responsible way — is January 1963.

Such a bill will be presented to the Congress for action next year. It will include an across the board, top to bottom cut in both corporate and personal income taxes. It will include long-needed tax reform that logic and equity demand. And it will date that cut in taxes to take effect as of the start of next year, January 1963.

. . . Every dollar released from taxation that is spent or invested will help create a new job and a new salary. And these new jobs and new salaries can create other jobs and other salaries and more customers and more growth for an expanding American economy.

For skeptical balanced-budget advocates or deficit hawks who might have been watching on television, Kennedy made the case that the tax cut would "eventually" pay for itself. "By removing tax roadblocks to new jobs and new growth," he said, "the enactment of this measure next year will eventually more than make up in new revenue all that it will initially cost."

The president took pains to distinguish the "permanent" tax cut he proposed from the immediate or early cut that was being pressed on him by some of his more pessimistic economic advisers, but which he had decided against "in the absence of an economic crisis today." Kennedy said, "Let me emphasize, however, that I have not been talking about a different kind of tax cut, a quick, temporary tax cut, to prevent a new recession. Under the right circumstances that is also a sound and effective weapon, but like many weapons it should be fired only at a period of maximum advantage."

Sorensen later called this August speech, delivered from the Oval Office at 7 p.m., "the worst" that Kennedy ever gave, "without qualification." "A speech announcing you're not going to do something," Sorensen said, "cannot be a very exciting speech."[13] With the passage of years, though, Kennedy's announcement that he was going to skip the "quick, temporary tax cut" — the "not going to do something" part — seems less important than the parts of the speech that laid the growth-oriented groundwork for the permanent tax cuts ahead.

Kennedy continued turning over the tax cut idea in his own mind, accepting advice and testing his thoughts about it privately against those of others.

Philip Graham, who owned *Newsweek* as well as the *Washington Post,* sent Kennedy a letter on October 17, 1962, stressing "the need for Western economic strength and growth as the greatest anti-Communist weapon" and recommending "a $10 billion tax cut — simple, across-the-board, reducing maximum rates to 65% and reducing all other rates a flat percentage; while also reducing corporate rates a flat percentage."[14]

Senator Gore recounts in his 1972 memoir that at Eleanor Roosevelt's funeral on November 10, 1962, Kennedy approached him in the living room of a cottage at Roosevelt's Hyde Park estate.

"What do you think I should do about a tax cut?" Kennedy asked.

"Forget it," Gore replied.

The two men launched into a lengthy debate on the matter, with Gore arguing that the best way to get the economy going was to increase government spending, and Kennedy making the case for a tax cut. Kennedy was so immersed in the conversation that he ignored a line of people waiting to shake his hand, including President Eisenhower. Gore explained later, "I thought the real needs of our society lay in the inadequacy of health, education, transportation. These were largely in the public sector. Not in the private sector." Kennedy was so keen to persuade Gore that, as Air Force One waited on the tarmac at the West Point airfield to return to Washington from the funeral, he had his military aides fetch the senator from another aircraft and bring him aboard the presidential plane to continue the conversation on the flight home. Gore warned, "Once taxes are cut, they are not likely to be reimposed."[15]

Kennedy's arguments did not win over Gore, who, on economic matters, was a liberal by the standards of his fellow Senate Democrats. But neither did Gore's arguments win over Kennedy. The president next made the case for a tax cut to a more receptive audience, the Economic Club of New York, in a December 14, 1962, address. Like the televised speech in August, it made a growth-oriented case for permanent tax reductions. Kennedy began by rejecting the increased-spending approach advocated by Gore and by Galbraith, although he did not name them. "Increasing Federal expenditures more rapidly than necessary," Kennedy said, "would soon demoralize both the Government and our economy. If Government is to retain the confidence of the people, it must not spend more than can be justified on grounds of national need or spent with maximum efficiency."

Instead, the president proposed "to reduce the burden on private income and the deterrents to private initiative which are imposed by our present tax system." He made reference to his August televised speech: "This administration pledged itself last summer to an across-the-board, top-to-bottom cut in personal and corporate income taxes to be enacted and become effective in 1963."

As he had in August, Kennedy drew a distinction between the permanent tax reductions he was proposing and "a 'quickie' or a temporary tax cut, which would be more appropriate if a recession were imminent":

> I am talking about the accumulated evidence of the last 5 years that our present tax system, developed as it was, in good part, during World War II to restrain growth, exerts too heavy a drag on growth in peace time; that it siphons out of the private economy too large a share of personal and business purchasing power; that it reduces the financial incentives for personal effort, investment, and risk-taking.
>
> In short, to increase demand and lift the economy, the Federal Government's most useful role is not to rush into a program of excessive increases in public expenditures, but to expand the incentives and opportunities for private expenditures . . . Too large a tax cut, of course, could result in inflation and insufficient future revenues — but the greatest danger is a tax cut too little or too late to be effective.

In the Economic Club speech, Kennedy also pushed back against those, such as labor leaders, who argued that the tax cuts should be concentrated in the lower brackets. "Next year's tax bill should reduce personal as well as corporate income taxes, for those in the lower brackets, who are certain to spend their additional take-home pay, and for those in the middle and upper brackets, who can thereby be encouraged to undertake additional efforts and enabled to invest more capital," the president said. He linked the tax rate reductions to tax reform and simplification. "The new tax bill should improve both the equity and the simplicity of our present tax system. This means the enactment of long-needed tax reforms, a broadening of the tax base and the elimination or modification of many special tax privileges. These steps are not only needed to recover lost revenue and thus make possible a larger cut in present rates; they are also tied directly to our goal of greater growth. For the present patchwork of special provisions and preferences lightens the tax load of some only at the cost of placing a heavier burden on others. It distorts economic judgments and channels an undue amount of energy into efforts to avoid tax liabilities. It makes certain types of less productive activity more profitable than other more valuable undertakings. All this inhibits our growth and efficiency, as well as considerably complicating the work of both the taxpayer and the Internal Revenue Service."

Finally, as he had in August, Kennedy again tried to reassure those worried about deficits. He said that his tax reductions would pay for themselves. "Our true choice is not between tax reduction, on the one hand, and the avoidance of large Federal deficits on the other," Kennedy said. "An economy hampered by restrictive tax rates will never produce enough revenue to balance our budget just as it will never produce enough jobs or enough profits . . . In short, it is a paradoxical truth that tax rates are too high today and tax revenues are too low and the soundest way to raise the revenues in the long run is to cut the rates now . . . The reason is that only full employment can balance the budget, and tax reduction can pave the way to that employment. The purpose of cutting taxes now is not to incur a budget deficit, but to achieve the more prosperous, expanding economy which can bring a budget surplus."

Galbraith, visiting from India, called Kennedy's New York Economic Club address "the most Republican speech since McKinley." Sorensen wrote that "it sounded like Hoover."[16] Sorensen also later recalled that Galbraith and "his economics student," Arthur Schlesinger Jr., thought the talk was "the worst speech the President had ever given and that it was full of Republican dogma and McKinley-like phrases."[17] The Kennedy speech may have been Republicanism of the past (or of the future), but it was not Republicanism of the Eisenhower-Nixon variety. Eisenhower denounced Kennedy's proposed "huge tax cut" as "fiscal recklessness."[18] The *Wall Street Journal* likewise was skeptical, greeting the Economic Club speech with an editorial fretting that "the economic impact of lower taxes is a guess at best," and calling Kennedy's "refusal to base tax cuts on lower spending" a "drastic error."[19] One voice on the right, *National Review,* did support Kennedy, editorially predicting that "the increased economic energy released by increasing economic incentives would shortly amplify the economic flow enough to supplant the tax revenues lost initially, and then some."[20]

Nor was Kennedy's approach to corporate and individual tax reduction merely the stuff of a speech or two to selected audiences of prosperous New York businessmen. It was, as JFK himself described it, the centerpiece of his 1963 pre-election agenda, and he repeatedly took the argument to Congress and, on television, to the American people.

Here was Kennedy again making the case for tax reductions as the path to jobs and growth, this time in his State of the Union address on January 14, 1963. "We must move along the path to a higher rate of growth and full employment," the president said. "To achieve these greater gains, one step, above all, is essential — the enactment this year of a substantial reduction and revision in Federal income taxes. For it is increasingly clear — to those in government, business, and labor who are responsible for our economy's success — that our obsolete tax system exerts too heavy a drag on private purchasing power, profits, and employment. Designed to check inflation in earlier years, it now checks growth instead. It discourages extra effort and risk. It distorts the use of resources. It invites recurrent recessions, depresses our Federal revenues, and causes chronic budget deficits."

In this speech, for the first time, Kennedy gave details of his proposed rate reductions. "I shall propose a permanent reduction in tax rates which will lower liabilities by $13.5 billion. Of this, $11 billion results from reducing individual tax rates, which now range between 20 and 91 percent, to a more sensible range of 14 to 65 percent, with a split in the present first bracket. Two and one-half billion dollars results from reducing corporate tax rates, from 52 percent — which gives the Government today a majority interest in profits — to the permanent pre–Korean [War] level of 47 percent." He said the tax cut would "encourage the initiative and risk-taking on which our free system depends" and would "reinforce the American principle of additional reward for additional effort."

As was Kennedy's habit, he said a tax cut was preferable to the liberal alternative of more government spending: "No doubt a massive increase in Federal spending could also create jobs and growth — but, in today's setting, private consumers, employers, and investors should be given a full opportunity first."

And again, as was his custom, he said that the tax rate cut, far from adding to the budget deficit, would eventually increase federal tax revenues by expanding the size of the overall economy. "This combined program, by increasing the amount of our national income, will in time result in still higher Federal revenues. It is a fiscally responsible program," he insisted.

Finally, Kennedy made it unmistakably clear that the tax cut was his top domestic legislative priority. "This is the most urgent task confronting the Congress in 1963. I am convinced that the enactment this year of tax reduction and tax reform overshadows all other domestic problems in this Congress."

The president's January 24, 1963, Special Message to the Congress on Tax Reduction and Reform offered further details of the rate reductions, including the proposal to lower the maximum rate on long-term capital gains to 19.5 percent from the 25 percent rate that was then in place. This message, too, contained an explanation of why tax reduction was a better stimulus than government spending: "I do not favor raising demand by a massive increase in Government expenditures. In today's circumstances, it is desirable to seek expansion through our free market processes — to place increased spending power in the hands of private consumers and investors and offer more encouragement to private initiative. The most effective policy, therefore, is to expand demand and unleash incentives through a program of tax reduction and reform." Once again, he emphasized that lowering the tax rates would, through growth, eventually help balance the federal budget by increasing tax receipts: "Within a few years of the enactment of this program, Federal revenues will be larger than if present tax rates continue to prevail."

Though Galbraith fought a rear-guard action against the tax cut well into 1963, Kennedy eventually lost patience with it and told Galbraith to stop. Walter Heller, a tax-cut advocate, joked about establishing a "Galbraith Early Warning System" to alert the president's economic advisers when the big-spending Harvard economist was away from his ambassadorial post in New Delhi and in danger of pleading with the president. Finally, one day in 1963, Galbraith entered the White House mess and said, "Heller, you've won. The president told me to shut up about my opposition to tax cuts."[21]

When congressmen asked whether more federal spending would achieve the same goals as the tax cuts, Kennedy administration representatives said there was a difference. Senator William Proxmire, a Democrat of Wisconsin, who was an advocate of balanced budgets, said, "What you are asking for, then, is an increased deficit rather than a tax cut, and it makes little difference if we spend more or reduce taxes . . . Increased government spending would provide a greater multiplier effect." Walter Heller responded at a January 1963 hearing of the Joint Economic Committee, "It isn't the deficit we seek," explaining that tax cuts had a certain "effect on incentives" that spending did not have. Arthur Burns, who had chaired the Council of Economic Advisers for President Eisenhower and who had been appointed by Kennedy to his Advisory Committee on Labor-Management Policy, testified in favor of the tax cut, telling Senator Proxmire that a $10 billion cut would be "more stimulative" than $10 billion in government spending because, with the tax cut, "individuals and businessmen will begin thinking very differently about the future. They will be in a position not merely to use the larger cash income which is at their disposal, but they may well be in a mood also to dip into their accumulated assets and to use their credit."[22]

As Congress took its time, Kennedy pressed for the tax cut. At a September 10, 1963, speech in Washington to the Business Committee for Tax Reduction, the president called the tax cut "the most important domestic economic measure to come before the Congress in the past 15 years."

Kennedy plugged away at the tax issue again and again. "No more important legislation will come before the Congress this year than the bill before the House next week to reduce Federal taxes . . ." he told the nation in a radio and television address on September 18 from the Oval Office. "It is urgently needed and I hope you will support it in the national interest." The existing high rates, the president said, "do not leave enough money in private hands to keep this country's economy growing and healthy."

In this speech especially, Kennedy tried to explain in concrete terms what the tax cut would mean for individual citizens. "Every taxpayer and his family will have more money left over after taxes for a new car, a new home, new conveniences, education, and investment," the president said. "A factory earner with three dependents earning $90 a week will have his taxes reduced by a third. The typical American family, a father, mother, and two children, earning about $6,000 a year, now pays an annual tax of $600. This bill will cut that tax by 25 percent. A salaried employee with a wife and two children who earns $8,000 a year will receive a tax cut of more than 20 percent that will enable him perhaps to pay the installments on a car or a dishwasher or some other necessary expense, thereby creating work for others."

In contrast with Reagan-era debates over "supply-side" economics, Kennedy met resistance from congressional Republicans. "Frankly, we find Mr. Kennedy's economic theories mystifying," the Republican leader in the House of Representatives, Charles Halleck, said in a September 18 statement on the tax cut proposal. The Republican Senate leader, Everett Dirksen, rejected the idea that the tax cut would reduce the deficit. "We will be borrowing nearly $11 billion from our children so we can make it easier on ourselves," Dirksen said. "The American people do not favor a tax cut based on this kind of fiscal juggling."[23] Senator Barry Goldwater, too, warned that the Kennedy tax cut would lead to deficits, inflation, and even bankruptcy.[24]

Liberal Democrats also voiced opposition, complaining that too much of the tax cut would benefit the rich. "Gore Rips Bonanza for 'Fat Cats'" was the headline of one column, and Gore's biographer reports that the Tennessean's opposition to the tax cut led the president, in a meeting with economic advisers, to repeatedly denounce the senator as a "son of a bitch."[25] Secretary Dillon responded to Gore's line of criticism by observing, "Obviously, taxpayers who have higher incomes and pay higher taxes will get greater dollar reductions in any tax cutting bill than people who pay very little taxes."[26]

The House finally approved the tax cut bill on September 25, 1963, on a 271–155 vote. Favoring the bill were 223 Democrats and 48 Republicans, and opposing it were 29 Democrats and 126 Republicans.[27] Now all Kennedy needed was for the Senate to pass the tax cut into law. He planned to spur it to action in part by speaking publicly about the tax cut and economic growth during a trip to Texas that was scheduled for November.

CHAPTER 8

The Cold War and the Freedom Doctrine

January 20, 1961–November 1963

There are some who say in Europe and elsewhere we can work with the Communists. Let them come to Berlin.

— JOHN F. KENNEDY, June 26, 1963

Washington

WHEN KENNEDY SAID IN HIS inaugural address that "only a few generations have been granted the role of defending freedom in its hour of maximum danger," the line accurately conveyed his view of the world at the moment he took office.

Theodore Sorensen, the conscientious objector and son of two peace activists who, in the array of Kennedy advisers, was among the liberals, gave this tour of the strategic horizon in his 1965 book *Kennedy:*

> The freedom of West Berlin had been threatened by a Soviet ultimatum, backed by boasts of medium-range ballistic missiles targeted on Western Europe. The existence of South Vietnam had been menaced by a campaign of guerrilla tactics and terror planned and supplied by the Communist regime in Hanoi. The independence of Laos had been endangered by pro-Communist insurgent forces . . . The Russian and Chinese Communists had competed for a Central African base in Ghana, in Guinea, in Mali and particularly in the chaotic Congo. The

Russians had obtained a base in the Western Hemisphere through Fidel Castro's takeover in Cuba and his campaign to subvert Latin America. Red China was busy building its own Afro-Asian collection of client states and its own atomic bomb.[1]

The president himself summed it up in his January 30, 1961, State of the Union message to Congress. Speaking of the Soviet Union and China, he said, "We must never be lulled into believing that either power has yielded its ambitions for world domination."

Kennedy and his advisers, in other words, felt encircled, embattled, under siege by a menacing, expansionist, subversive Communist empire. Fighting back was the top priority. "I had no doubt that his number one issue was foreign policy, his number one interest," Kennedy's domestic civil rights adviser, Harris Wofford, later recalled.[2]

Geographically, the closest front in the struggle with communism was Cuba, ninety miles from the coast of Florida. During the campaign, Kennedy had advocated "encouraging those liberty-loving Cubans who are leading the resistance to Castro." Now, as president, he was in a position to do so with more than just words.

Notwithstanding Vice President Nixon's contention in the 1960 presidential debates that American backing of the Cuban opposition would violate the United Nations charter,[3] Eisenhower's staff had left Kennedy plans for precisely such an operation against Castro. Liberals within the Kennedy administration and outside it argued against going through with the plans. "It'll be a massacre . . . an American Hungary," Richard Goodwin told national security adviser McGeorge Bundy over breakfast in the White House mess.[4] Chester Bowles wrote a memo to the secretary of state, Dean Rusk, warning that the covert operation would be "a grave mistake."[5] Senator William Fulbright, the Democrat from Arkansas who chaired the Senate Foreign Relations Committee, wrote to Kennedy that the plans were "ill-considered" and that Castro was a mere "thorn in the flesh . . . not a dagger in the heart."[6] Schlesinger told the president in person that he was against any such plan and wrote two memos to him explaining why.[7]

Yet Kennedy ignored or overrode the warnings and instead allowed the operation, an invasion of Cuba by a force of anti-Castro exiles who had been trained by the CIA in Guatemala, to go ahead. It was a flop from start to finish. First, an advance air strike by eight B-26 bombers piloted by the Cuban exiles failed to disable Castro's air force. Then, one of the seven boats carrying the exiles — the boat with most of the communications equipment and ammunition on board — was sunk by one of Castro's planes. When the 1,400 exiles landed at the Bay of Pigs on April 17, 1961, they were soon outnumbered by tens of thousands of Castro's troops. Kennedy eventually approved the use of carrier-based U.S. Navy fighter planes to provide cover for the B-26s flown by Cuban exiles and CIA contractors, but even that failed; the jet fighters, off by a time zone, arrived an hour late. Rather than fading into the Escambray Mountains, the backup in the CIA contingency plans, the American-backed exile fighters were captured or killed.[8]

Kennedy has been faulted by some critics on the right for contributing to the defeat by not acting more aggressively to order American naval, air, or ground support for the Cuban opposition. But his restraint, such as it was, was not motivated by a lack of hostility toward Castro or by illusions about the nature of his rule. Instead it was a judgment — and probably a prudent one — that the chance of dislodging Castro through a hastily assembled follow-up American invasion of Cuba would be more than offset by the risk of a precipitous Soviet retaliation against Berlin, which in turn could trigger a world war whose only certain outcome would be massive casualties on all sides.

Schlesinger's *A Thousand Days* gives a detailed account of the protests that erupted against Kennedy from left-wing intellectuals following the Bay of Pigs:

> The Harvard historian H. Stuart Hughes led seventy academicians in an open letter to Kennedy, imprudently endorsing the thesis that the United States had driven Castro into the arms of the Soviet Union, calling for a restoration of diplomatic and economic relations with Castro and demanding that the government "reverse the present drift towards American military intervention in Cuba." . . . Protest meetings erupted on a dozen campuses. [The Columbia University sociology professor] C. Wright Mills wired a Fair Play for Cuba rally in San Francisco: KENNEDY AND COMPANY HAVE RETURNED US TO BARBARISM . . . I FEEL A DESPERATE SHAME FOR MY COUN-

TRY. SORRY I CANNOT BE WITH YOU. WERE I PHYSICALLY
ABLE TO DO SO, I WOULD AT THIS MOMENT BE FIGHTING
ALONGSIDE FIDEL CASTRO.[9]

Those who wished the failure at the Bay of Pigs to be the beginning
of a new, friendlier American policy toward Castro would be disappointed, however, as Kennedy made clear in an address on April 20,
1961, to the American Society of Newspaper Editors. "Let the record
show that our restraint is not inexhaustible," Kennedy said. "I want it
clearly understood that this Government will not hesitate in meeting
its primary obligations which are to the security of our Nation!" The
president went on:

> Should that time ever come, we do not intend to be lectured on "in-
> tervention" by those whose character was stamped for all time on the
> bloody streets of Budapest! Nor would we expect or accept the same
> outcome which this small band of gallant Cuban refugees must have
> known that they were chancing, determined as they were against
> heavy odds to pursue their courageous attempts to regain their is-
> land's freedom.
> But Cuba is not an island unto itself; and our concern is not ended
> by mere expressions of nonintervention or regret. This is not the first
> time in either ancient or recent history that a small band of freedom
> fighters has engaged the armor of totalitarianism.
> It is not the first time that Communist tanks have rolled over gal-
> lant men and women fighting to redeem the independence of their
> homeland. Nor is it by any means the final episode in the eternal
> struggle of liberty against tyranny, anywhere on the face of the globe,
> including Cuba itself.
> Mr. Castro has said that these were mercenaries. According to press
> reports, the final message to be relayed from the refugee forces on the
> beach came from the rebel commander when asked if he wished to
> be evacuated. His answer was: "I will never leave this country." That
> is not the reply of a mercenary. He has gone now to join in the moun-
> tains countless other guerrilla fighters, who are equally determined
> that the dedication of those who gave their lives shall not be forgotten,
> and that Cuba must not be abandoned to the Communists. And we
> do not intend to abandon it either!

Nor did they. When Secretary of State Rusk flew to Uruguay in January 1962 for the Punta del Este conference of the Organization of American States, isolating Cuba topped the agenda.[10] President Kennedy followed up on February 3 with a proclamation imposing an embargo on all trade with the island "in light of the subversive offensive of Sino-Soviet Communism with which the Government of Cuba is publicly aligned." (Some restrictions on trade had already been imposed by Eisenhower in October 1960.) Even privately, some White House officials defended the Bay of Pigs invasion against criticism from left-leaning intellectuals. In a May 7, 1962, letter to the author and literary critic Alfred Kazin, for example, Kennedy policy adviser Richard Goodwin faulted Kazin for "blithely" calling the Cuba invasion "immoral."[11]

The climax of the tension between Kennedy and Cuba came in October of 1962, with the thirteen days of the Cuban Missile Crisis. The president had been getting reports in September of a Soviet military buildup in Cuba, and he issued two public warnings. On September 4, Kennedy, through his press secretary, said, "There is no evidence of any organized combat force in Cuba from any Soviet bloc country; of military bases provided to Russia; of a violation of the 1934 treaty relating to Guantanamo; of the presence of offensive ground-to-ground missiles; or of other significant offensive capability either in Cuban hands or under Soviet direction and guidance. Were it to be otherwise, the gravest issues would arise."

On September 13, Kennedy himself opened a news conference with a preliminary statement along the same lines: "Let me make this clear once again: If at any time the Communist buildup in Cuba were to endanger or interfere with our security in any way, including our base at Guantanamo, our passage to the Panama Canal, our missile and space activities at Cape Canaveral, or the lives of American citizens in this country, or if Cuba should ever attempt to export its aggressive purposes by force or the threat of force against any nation in this hemisphere, or become an offensive military base of significant capacity for the Soviet Union, then this country will do whatever must be done to protect its own security and that of its allies."

These statements had been based on direct public and private assurances from top Soviet officials. As Robert Kennedy wrote in his memoir of the Cuban Missile Crisis, *Thirteen Days,* "During this same period of time, an important official in the Soviet Embassy, returning from Moscow, brought me a personal message from Khrushchev to President Kennedy, stating that he wanted the President to be assured that under no circumstances would surface-to-surface missiles be sent to Cuba." On September 11, the official Soviet news agency, TASS, had reported that "there is no need for the Soviet Union to shift its weapons for the repulsion of aggression for a retaliatory blow to any other country, for instance, Cuba. Our nuclear weapons are so powerful in their explosive force, the Soviet Union has so powerful rockets to carry these nuclear warheads, that there is no need to search for sites for them beyond the boundaries of the Soviet Union."[12]

Kennedy's statements in September had also been based on extensive analysis and assurances from U.S. intelligence experts. Four formal National Intelligence Estimates in 1962 alone had reached the assessment that Russia would not try to turn Cuba into a base for offensive weapons. The most recent such estimate, dated September 19, 1962, Robert Kennedy recalled, "advised the President that without reservation the United States Intelligence Board, after considerable discussion and examination, had concluded that the Soviet Union would not make Cuba a strategic base. It pointed out that the Soviet Union had not taken this kind of step with any of its satellites in the past and would feel the risk of retaliation from the United States to be too great to take the risk in this case."

So, Robert Kennedy wrote, when, on October 16, the CIA briefed the president on new photographs from U-2 spy planes that showed offensive-missile sites under construction in Cuba, the president and his advisers were shocked as they realized that the Russian assurances "had all been lies, one gigantic fabric of lies."[13]

One of President Kennedy's first reactions, on October 16, the first day of the crisis, was to muse aloud that the news proved that his support the year before for the expedition to overthrow Castro had been fundamentally correct, even if the execution had been flawed: "It shows the Bay of Pigs was really right, if we had done it right."[14]

It was nearly a week before Kennedy told the American public what was happening. The precautions taken by cabinet members and other administration officials to avoid arousing suspicion among the press or the public during this period were sometimes comical. Robert Kennedy writes that he, the chairman of the Joint Chiefs of Staff, and eight others all piled into one car; George Ball remembers nine high-ranking officials in his car, sitting on each other's laps, for a trip from the State Department. Instead of going straight to the White House, they went to the less watched Treasury Department, "then by a set of secret passages through the White House bomb shelter" into the basement of the executive mansion.[15]

Kennedy had the time to consider recommendations from a number of advisers about how to deal with the Soviet missiles in Cuba. Some historians, looking back at Kennedy's handling of the crisis, have emphasized his restraint. Tony Judt wrote, for example, "At each turn in the proceedings, Kennedy chose the most moderate available option, sometimes against the specialized advice pressing in on him. Instead of an invasion he favored an air strike on missile bases; instead of a blanket air strike he favored selective strikes only; he insisted that no strikes, however selective, should happen until warning had been given. He opted for a naval blockade over immediate military action, and a partial naval quarantine over a blanket blockade on all shipping."[16]

That analysis and other similar ones ignore two important points, however. The first is that there were those inside and outside the administration who counseled that even the quarantine was too hard-line a step. The president himself, dictating an account into the Oval Office taping system, said that Robert Lovett, who had been defense secretary under President Truman, "was not convinced that any action was desirable," and that McGeorge Bundy, Kennedy's own national security adviser, "continued to argue against any action."[17]

Bundy's contention was that the Cuban missiles did not materially change the strategic equation. In a Soviet nuclear attack, an American would be equally dead whether hit by a medium-range missile fired from Cuba or by an intercontinental ballistic missile fired from Russia. Sorensen went so far as to attempt to draft a letter to Khrushchev explaining that the United States would deal with the missiles entirely through "the quiet diplomatic route," which Sorensen described as "my own natural inclination from start to finish."[18] Adlai Stevenson suggested that the president offer to close the American naval base at Guantánamo Bay and withdraw American missiles from Turkey. The president rejected that advice, which prompted Robert Kennedy to complain about Stevenson after the meeting: "He's not strong enough or tough enough to be representing us at the UN at a time like this."[19]

The second point about the Cuban Missile Crisis is that, as with the Bay of Pigs, what restraint was displayed by Kennedy was not a sign of cowardice or pacifism, but rather a calculation about the risk of triggering a Soviet attack on West Berlin. In an October 26 telephone call, the British prime minister, Harold Macmillan, told Kennedy, "At this stage any movement . . . by you may produce a result in Berlin which would be very bad for us all. That's the danger." Kennedy replied, "That's correct, and that is really why we have not done more than we've done up until now."

When, on October 22, President Kennedy finally did report to the American people what was occurring in Cuba, it was in a televised address whose audience was not only Americans but also the world. First, Kennedy explained the threat to American cities: "Each of these missiles, in short, is capable of striking Washington, D.C., the Panama Canal, Cape Canaveral, Mexico City, or any other city in the southeastern part of the United States, in Central America, or in the Caribbean area . . . In addition, jet bombers, capable of carrying nuclear weapons, are now being uncrated and assembled in Cuba, while the necessary air bases are being prepared."

Then, Kennedy returned to the lessons of World War II, in which he had served and whose origins he had studied in his 1940 book *Why England Slept.* "The 1930's taught us a clear lesson: aggressive conduct, if allowed to go unchecked and unchallenged, ultimately leads to war. This nation is opposed to war. We are also true to our word. Our unswerving objective, therefore, must be to prevent the use of these missiles against this or any other country, and to secure their withdrawal or elimination from the Western Hemisphere." Because the Soviet Union had also fought against Nazi aggression, and taken massive casualties in the process, the line likening Moscow's "aggressive conduct" to that of Nazi Germany was calculated to resonate in the Kremlin.

Kennedy's speech announced the quarantine that would turn back any ships carrying cargoes of offensive weapons to Cuba. He called for an emergency meeting of the United Nations Security Council to consider a resolution "for the prompt dismantling and withdrawal of all offensive weapons in Cuba, under the supervision of U.N. observers." To Khrushchev, Kennedy offered, as he had in his inaugural address, an invitation to peace but also a declaration of American determination. "We will not prematurely or unnecessarily risk the costs of world-wide nuclear war in which even the fruits of victory would be ashes in our mouth — but neither will we shrink from that risk at any time it must be faced," the president said. "I call upon him further to abandon this course of world domination, and to join in an historic effort to end the perilous arms race and to transform the history of man."

> We have no wish to war with the Soviet Union — for we are a peaceful people who desire to live in peace with all other peoples. But it is difficult to settle or even discuss these problems in an atmosphere of intimidation. That is why this latest Soviet threat — or any other threat which is made either independently or in response to our actions this week — must and will be met with determination. Any hostile move anywhere in the world against the safety and freedom of peoples to whom we are committed — including in particular the brave people of West Berlin — will be met by whatever action is needed . . . The greatest danger of all would be to do nothing.
>
> The path we have chosen for the present is full of hazards, as all paths are — but it is the one most consistent with our character and courage as a nation and our commitments around the world. The cost of freedom is always high — but Americans have always paid it. And one path we shall never choose, and that is the path of surrender or submission.
>
> Our goal is not the victory of might, but the vindication of right — not peace at the expense of freedom, but both peace and freedom, here in this hemisphere, and, we hope, around the world. God willing, that goal will be achieved.

The president made clear that his final objective was not solely removal of the missiles from Cuba, but the ouster of Castro and the replacement of his Communist rule by one characterized by freedom and democracy:

> I want to say a few words to the captive people of Cuba, to whom this speech is being directly carried by special radio facilities. I speak to you as a friend, as one who knows of your deep attachment to your fatherland, as one who shares your aspirations for liberty and justice for all. And I have watched and the American people have watched with deep sorrow how your nationalist revolution was betrayed — and how your fatherland fell under foreign domination. Now your leaders are no longer Cuban leaders inspired by Cuban ideals. They are puppets and agents of an international conspiracy which has turned Cuba against your friends and neighbors in the Americas — and turned it into the first Latin American country to become a target for nuclear war — the first Latin American country to have these weapons on its soil.
>
> . . . Your lives and land are being used as pawns by those who deny your freedom.
>
> Many times in the past, the Cuban people have risen to throw out tyrants who destroyed their liberty. And I have no doubt that most Cubans today look forward to the time when they will be truly free — free from foreign domination, free to choose their own leaders, free to select their own system, free to own their own land, free to speak and write and worship without fear or degradation. And then shall Cuba be welcomed back to the society of free nations and to the associations of this hemisphere.

One of Kennedy adviser Robert Lovett's concerns about a quarantine or blockade had been that, as he later recalled, "we would be under pressure from the bleeding hearts, the unilateral disarmament groups and the peace-at-any-price units that were always ready to spring to the battlements, to relax or withdraw the blockade."[20]

They did not disappoint. The day after Kennedy's speech, the *New York Times* carried on its front page a report that the Student Peace Union had decided to organize a march on Washington to protest the quarantine as an American provocation that increased the risk of war.

Arthur Schlesinger Jr. recounts that the British intellectuals A. J. Ayer and A.J.P. Taylor also criticized the quarantine. The British philosopher and Nobel laureate Bertrand Russell, who had already called Kennedy "much more wicked than Hitler," sent a telegram to him: "YOUR ACTION DESPERATE . . . NO CONCEIVABLE JUSTIFICATION. WE WILL NOT HAVE MASS MURDER . . . END THIS MADNESS."[21]

The secretary-general of the United Nations, U Thant, called on the United States to suspend the quarantine for two or three weeks if the Soviet Union would suspend its arms shipments to Cuba. That would do nothing about the Soviet missiles already on the island. If anything, it would lessen the pressure to dismantle them. George Ball describes the proposal as "anything but helpful."[22]

The Air Force's strategic bombers were ordered into the air, loaded with nuclear weapons. "As one came down to land, another immediately took its place," Robert Kennedy writes in *Thirteen Days*.[23]

Plans called for administration officials to be whisked away to a secret command center in the event of a Soviet attack. Their spouses and children were to be left to fend for themselves; the Secret Service was authorized to shoot anyone trying to get on a helicopter who was not on the approved evacuation list.[24] George Ball's wife, Ruth, moved some canned food and flashlights into their home's basement in case she had to use it as a bomb shelter.[25]

Tensions flared between civilian and military personnel. The secretary of defense, Robert McNamara, quizzed the chief of naval operations, Admiral George Anderson, on the details of the blockade. Would the Soviet ships be hailed in English or in Russian? What if they do not stop? Anderson shot back, "This is none of your goddamn business. We've been doing this ever since the days of John Paul Jones."[26]

What did Kennedy do to keep himself calm during this period? He prayed.

On Wednesday, October 17, the day after he first got news of the missiles, Kennedy, traveling from the White House to a luncheon at the Libyan embassy, stopped in at the almost empty St. Matthew's Cathedral. To his perplexed personal aide David Powers, who did not yet know about the missiles, the president explained, "We're going in here to say a prayer . . . Right now we need all the prayers we can get." On

Sunday, October 21, President Kennedy went to Mass at St. Stephen's. On Saturday, October 28, he learned that Soviet surface-to-air missiles had downed Major Rudolf Anderson Jr., an American pilot who had originally photographed the sites in Cuba and who was on a return mission. At bedtime that night, with plans advancing for American air strikes on the Cuban missile sites, the president told Powers, "We'll be going to the ten o'clock mass at Saint Stephen's, Dave, and we'll have plenty of hard praying to do, so don't be late."[27]

One recent account of the missile crisis praised Kennedy for becoming a hero "not by winning a war, but by averting one far more horrible than any leader in the past could have imagined."[28] Kennedy does deserve credit for his handling of the crisis. His great achievement, though, was not merely averting a war. That, after all, could have been done simply by following the suggestions of some of his advisers to do nothing. If averting war had been Kennedy's only goal, he unnecessarily put a lot of lives at risk to achieve it. But it was not his only goal. The real reason Kennedy was a hero is that, through skillful use of American military power — the quarantine — and both public and private diplomacy, he got the USSR to dismantle and remove the missiles. Kennedy faced down the Soviet Communists and *won*. The Soviets backed down.

Others have faulted Kennedy for providing the Russians private assurances that, in exchange for dismantling the missiles in Cuba, the United States would not invade the island and would withdraw some Jupiter nuclear missiles from Turkey.[29] But administration officials later described the Jupiters as obsolete, said Kennedy wanted them out even before the Cuban crisis, and said their role was superseded by Polaris nuclear-armed submarines in the Mediterranean.[30] In any event, as Peter Rodman, who served in the administrations of Presidents Nixon, Ford, Reagan, and both Presidents Bush, and who has been critical of Kennedy on some issues, wrote twenty years after the crisis, "It was universally perceived even in the Communist world that the removal of the missiles was a humiliation for the Soviet Union: the Chinese denounced Khrushchev for 'capitulationism.'"[31]

Kennedy, to his credit, realized that a full victory for America and for freedom in Cuba would require the removal not only of the missiles, but also of Castro. Any joy that Kennedy took in the resolution of the missile crisis was dampened by the realization that more than one thousand anti-Castro Cubans captured in the Bay of Pigs invasion were languishing in Communist prisons. The president and the attorney general launched a new effort to get the prisoners home to America by Christmas. Castro demanded tens of millions of dollars in American milk, baby food, and medicine in return. Robert Kennedy met with pharmaceutical company executives to encourage them to donate the medicine, and the Internal Revenue Service worked to make sure the contributions would be tax deductible, citing, among other factors, a passage of the Talmud that describes paying a ransom to redeem captives as a great commandment.[32] When, just days before Christmas, Castro demanded a cash payment in addition to the humanitarian aid, Robert Kennedy called Cardinal Cushing and asked the archbishop of Boston if he could somehow come up with $1 million by the end of the day. Cushing called back three hours later with a promise to deliver the money to the White House by 6 p.m., which he did. "There was to be no publicity . . . Some are skeptical, but these are the facts," Cushing insisted later.[33]

When the prisoners were finally released, Kennedy invited some of their leaders to visit him at Palm Beach.[34] Two days later, on December 29, 1962, Kennedy met the entire group at a rally in Miami's Orange Bowl football stadium. There, Jacqueline Kennedy told them in Spanish that though her son was still too young to realize what had happened, "I will make it my business to tell him the story of your courage as he grows up. It is my wish and my hope that some day he may be a man at least half as brave."[35] Members of the freed brigade presented their flag to the president, who responded:

> I can assure you that this flag will be returned to this brigade in a free Havana . . . Cuba is today, as Marti described it many years ago, as beautiful as Greece, and stretched out in chains — a prison, moated by water . . . Your small brigade is a tangible reaffirmation that the human desire for freedom and independence is essentially unconquerable. Your conduct and valor are proof that although Castro and his fellow dictators may rule nations, they do not rule people; that they may imprison bodies, but they do not imprison spirits; that they

may destroy the exercise of liberty, but they cannot eliminate the determination to be free. And by helping to free you, the United States has been given the opportunity to demonstrate once again that all men who fight for freedom are our brothers, and shall be until your country and others are free.

The Cuban people were promised by the revolution political liberty, social justice, intellectual freedom, land for the campesinos, and an end to economic exploitation. They have received a police state, the elimination of the dignity of land ownership, the destruction of free speech and of free press, and the complete subjugation of individual human welfare to the service of the state and of foreign states . . . I can assure you that it is the strongest wish of the people of this country, as well as the people of this hemisphere, that Cuba shall one day be free again, and when it is, this brigade will deserve to march at the head of the free column.

Richard Goodwin, who was involved in Latin American policy, later told the author David Talbot that Kennedy, "carried away by the moment," had gone "off script." "That line about bringing back the flag to a free Cuba was not in the text," Goodwin said.[36]

Kennedy returned to the theme of a free Cuba yet again on April 19, 1963, in a question-and-answer session with the American Society of Newspaper Editors:

It is really a struggle against the Communist infiltration in this hemisphere . . . It is quite obvious now to the hemisphere and, in fact, to the world that Castro is only a Soviet satellite . . . He's generally regarded in the hemisphere as having sold out to the Communist movement and having now become a spearhead for the Soviet advance . . . I don't accept the view that Mr. Castro is going to be in power in 5 years. I can't indicate the roads by which there will be a change, but I've seen enough — as we all have — enough change in the last 15 years to make me feel that time will see Cuba free again.

When Kennedy said "I can't indicate the roads by which there will be a change," he could have meant that he did not know, or he could have meant that he did know, or at least hoped he knew, but could not say for fear of exposing a secret. A congressional investigation in the mid-1970s disclosed Operation Mongoose, a covert operation against Castro's government that involved 400 CIA officers and the expenditure of between $50 million and $100 million.[37] Richard Helms, the CIA's deputy director of operations under Kennedy, later recalled, "He was *wild* with Castro, and the whole government was pushed hard to see if there wasn't some way to unseat him. The fact that the agency was not able to get the results was something that did not please him."[38]

To this day, how closely Kennedy supervised the CIA is cloaked in mystery. Some accounts say either the agency or an American diplomat provided information to assist the white South African officials who, in August 1962, arrested the anti-apartheid activist Nelson Mandela, who would remain in jail for twenty-seven years.[39] Mandela, who was elected president of South Africa after the end of apartheid and his release from prison, is now widely recognized as a hero, but in the 1960s relations among his African National Congress, the South African Communist Party, and the Soviet Union were a concern of some American cold warriors. There is no indication that Kennedy approved such American assistance in Mandela's arrest, but if that assistance was indeed given, it occurred during his presidency.

Cuba and South Africa were fronts in the Cold War, which stretched from Berlin to Southeast Asia and even into outer space.

The president himself inserted his own ideology of freedom, of the individual versus the state, and references to the competition with the Soviet Union into remarks about the arts, sports, and space exploration.

The performance of the Spanish cellist Pablo Casals at the White House, for example, has long been remembered as one of the most glittering evenings of the Kennedy administration. Jacqueline Kennedy wore a silk top by Oleg Cassini embroidered with crystal beads and sequins. The plaintive chords of Casals's cello were followed by vigorous applause from the president and his honored guests, who included Alice Roosevelt Longworth, Henry Ford II, the composers Aaron Copland and Leonard Bernstein, and the governor of Puerto Rico.[40]

In his brief remarks introducing the concert, Kennedy said that "artistic achievement and action" are "an integral part of our free society. We believe that an artist, in order to be true to himself and his work, must be a free man or woman." Kennedy repeated the comment for emphasis at the end of his speech: "an artist must be a free man."[41]

Kennedy spoke of freedom not only for artists but also for athletes. If there were an evening that could compete with the Casals performance for sheer glamour, it might have been the dinner that the Australian ambassador gave in Newport, Rhode Island, at the Breakers, the seventy-room oceanfront villa constructed in the 1890s for Cornelius Vanderbilt II. The occasion was the America's Cup yacht race, which was dear to the heart of the president, a lifelong sailor who loved the sea. Kennedy told the assembled crew members and guests: "I am particularly glad to be here because this Cup is being challenged by our friends from Australia . . . who have demonstrated on many occasions, on many fields, in many countries, that they are the most extraordinary athletic group in the world today, and that this extraordinary demonstration of physical vigor and skill has come not by the dictates of the State, because the Australians are among the freest citizens in the world, but because of their choice."[42]

To a listener unfamiliar with Kennedy's history, this language contrasting "the dictates of the State" with the "choice" of free citizens might sound like a bit much for a speech about a boat race. But those who remembered Kennedy's July 4, 1946, speech at Faneuil Hall, his 1950 speech at Notre Dame, his 1955 Assumption College speech, and the line from his inaugural address about how "the rights of man come not from the generosity of the state but from the hand of God," those who knew that on the shelves of the president's Boston apartment were the books *Our Enemy, the State* and *The Man Versus the State,* would recognize the line for what it was — a classic example of core John F. Kennedy ideology.

Kennedy also placed space exploration in the context of the Cold War. He announced the goal of putting a man on the moon in a May 25, 1961, speech to a joint session of Congress. It was not so much a speech about space exploration as it was about foreign policy and national security. "I am here to promote the freedom doctrine," he began, asking Congress for an additional $100 million in the defense budget for "new helicopters, new armored personnel carriers, and new howitzers." The president announced that he wanted to increase the size of the Marine Corps while also increasing special forces and the ability of the military to conduct "para-military operations and sub-limited or unconventional wars." He said he would triple spending on civil defense — fallout shelters to "protect millions of people against the hazards of radioactive fallout in the event of large-scale nuclear attack." Only after all of this did JFK introduce "the goal, before this decade is out, of landing a man on the moon and returning him safely to the earth." And even that space section of the speech was introduced with language about how "if we are to win the battle that is now going on around the world between freedom and tyranny," American space achievements would help to impress those choosing between communism and freedom.

Kennedy returned to the connection between space and the Cold War six months later, in a November 18 speech in Los Angeles to a dinner of the Democratic Party of California. There, too, he first stressed the military buildup. "When we came into office, of the 14 divisions of the United States, three of them were training divisions, and we have turned them into combat divisions, and we have called up two of our National Guard. We have developed five additional combat divisions, therefore, for the United States in the last 9 months. Now 50 percent of the strategic Air Force in the United States is on a 15-minute alert — we will have a substantially increased number of Polaris submarines by 1963 and 1964 than we would have had," Kennedy said. Then, immediately following this section of the speech, he pivoted to the space race: "While many may think that it is foolish to go to the moon, I do not believe that a powerful country like the United States, which wishes to demonstrate to a watching world that it is first in the field of technology and science, which represents so basic an aspiration of so many people, I do not believe that we want to permit the Soviet Union to dominate space, with all that it might mean to our peace and security in the coming years."

The May and November 1961 speeches mentioning a military

buildup were follow-ups to Kennedy's March 28 Special Message to the Congress on the Defense Budget, which had called for a $650 million increase in military spending for fiscal year 1962. "Our arms must be adequate to meet our commitments and ensure our security, without being bound by arbitrary budget ceilings. This nation can afford to be strong — it cannot afford to be weak. We shall do what is needed to make and to keep us strong," he said in the March 28 message, itself a follow-up to Kennedy's promises in the 1960 campaign. The message called for increasing the number of Polaris nuclear-powered submarines to twenty-nine from the nineteen under the present program, and for completing their construction two years faster than planned. It also asked for $230 million "for increased procurement of such items as helicopters, rifles, modern non-nuclear weapons, electronics and communications equipment, improved ammunition for artillery and infantry weapons, and torpedoes."

All of this was just the beginning. Shortly after the May 25 speech about the military buildup and the goal of placing a man on the moon, Kennedy left for Europe. The first stop on the trip, Paris, is remembered for the dinner at Versailles, the crowds lining the streets shouting "Vive Jacqui!" and the president's quip that "I am the man who accompanied Jacqueline Kennedy to Paris." Less well remembered is that Kennedy's relations with France so deteriorated over the course of his administration that Jacqueline Kennedy told Schlesinger in 1964 that "basically, he didn't like the French, and I loathe the French."[43] The main purpose of Kennedy's 1961 trip to Europe, though, was not the visit to Paris, but a summit meeting at Vienna with Khrushchev. It was Kennedy's chance to see, face to face, only four months into his presidency, the man he was up against. On Sunday, June 4, the president had taken a break from the negotiations and gone to Mass at St. Stephen's Cathedral, a fact Khrushchev recognized in toasting Kennedy later that day, after lunch at the Soviet embassy: "You are a religious man and would say that God should help us in this endeavor."[44]

The summit did not go well. On the plane trip home, when Kennedy's secretary was putting away some papers, she uncovered one on which the president had written words similar to those he had attributed to Abraham Lincoln in the 1960 campaign: "I know there is a God — and I see a storm coming; If he has a place for me, I believe that I am ready."[45]

Kennedy reported to the American people upon his return, in a radio and television address:

> We have wholly different views of right and wrong, of what is an internal affair and what is aggression, and, above all, we have wholly different concepts of where the world is and where it is going . . .
>
> He was certain that the tide there was moving his way, that the revolution of rising peoples would eventually be a Communist revolution, and that the so-called wars of liberation, supported by the Kremlin, would replace the old methods of direct aggression and invasion.
>
> In the 1940's and early fifties, the great danger was from Communist armies marching across free borders, which we saw in Korea. Our nuclear monopoly helped to prevent this in other areas. Now we face a new and different threat. We no longer have a nuclear monopoly. Their missiles, they believe, will hold off our missiles, and their troops can match our troops should we intervene in these so-called wars of liberation. Thus, the local conflict they support can turn in their favor through guerrillas or insurgents or subversion. A small group of disciplined Communists could exploit discontent and misery in a country where the average income may be $60 or $70 a year, and seize control, therefore, of an entire country without Communist troops ever crossing any international frontier. This is the Communist theory.
>
> But I believe just as strongly that time will prove it wrong, that liberty and independence and self-determination — not communism — is the future of man, and that free men have the will and the resources to win the struggle for freedom.

In a July 25, 1961, speech, Kennedy announced an additional $207 million in civil defense spending for identifying fallout shelters for use in case of a nuclear attack, and for stocking them with food, water, and first-aid kits. He said that amounted to "an increase in the defense budget of $6 billion since January."

The details of the Kennedy military buildup are subject to some variation. Sorensen's book *Kennedy* said the president increased the strength of the armed forces by as much as 300,000 and increased defense spending by "some eight billion dollars."[46] Current statistics show the active-duty military growing to 2,695,240 at the end of September 1963 from 2,492,037 in September 1960, an increase of about 200,000. The Office of Management and Budget also records that Kennedy increased national defense spending to $53.4 billion in 1963 from $48.1 billion in 1960. Those levels put defense spending at about 50 percent of total federal outlays, and at about 9 percent of GDP. For comparison's sake, in 2010 defense spending was about 20 percent of federal outlays and about 4.8 percent of GDP, and the uniformed active-duty military numbered about 1.4 million.

Kennedy was able to reject some weapons programs. He canceled the $2.5 billion effort to build Skybolt, a nuclear missile that would have been launched from the wings of American and British bombers.[47] He also structured the military buildup so that America's friends shared the benefits. Kennedy's sale to Israel of sophisticated surface-to-air missiles known as Hawks — short for "Homing All the Way Killer" — has been described by one historian, Warren Bass, as "perhaps the most underappreciated milestone in the U.S.-Israel special relationship."[48]

Of all the places the president was adding troops and spending, his favorite may have been the Green Berets. These were the elite Army Special Forces whose distinctive headwear was ordered by the president, Sorensen reports, "over the opposition of top generals."[49] Kennedy told Brigadier General William Yarborough, the head of the Special Warfare Center at Fort Bragg, North Carolina, to make sure his troops wore the berets on October 12, 1961, when JFK and the White House press corps would be visiting for a demonstration that included what one reporter described as "a Buck Rogers show: a soldier with a rocket on his back who flew over water to land on the other side."[50] Sorensen writes that Kennedy wanted the Green Berets "to be a dedicated, high-quality elite corps of specialists, trained to train local partisans in guerrilla warfare, prepared to perform a wide range of civilian as well as military tasks, able to live off the bush, in a village or behind enemy lines. He personally supervised the selection of new equipment — the replacement of heavy, noisy combat boots with sneakers, for example, and when the sneakers proved vulnerable to bamboo spikes, their reinforcement with flexible steel inner soles."[51]

With all of these troops and military hardware on hand, Kennedy found a way to use them — and not only in Cuba. In Laos, in Berlin, and in Vietnam, he sent in the armed forces and explained his actions to the American people in terms of the global struggle for freedom against communism.

On March 23, 1961, Kennedy devoted a televised evening press conference to Communist incursions in the Southeast Asian nation of Laos, describing them as a "grave problem." He came equipped with maps showing the Communist-dominated areas as an expanding red-colored blot. "My fellow Americans, Laos is far away from America, but the world is small," the president said. "The security of all Southeast Asia will be endangered if Laos loses its neutral independence. Its own safety runs with the safety of us all . . . It's quite obvious that if the Communists were able to move in and dominate this country, it would endanger the security of all, and the peace of all, of Southeast Asia."

Veterans of the Kennedy administration recall the deployment of forces to the region in both 1961 and 1962. "More than five thousand marines and Army combat personnel were put ashore in Thailand and moved up to the Laos border," Sorensen wrote.[52] Schlesinger noted that the Seventh Fleet moved into the South China Sea, and that the American military advisers in Laos were upgraded from a plainclothes force to a uniformed Military Assistance and Advisory Group. Schlesinger credited the actions with bringing to a "halt" the "imminent communization of Laos."[53]

Some historians have portrayed Laos as an exercise in presidential restraint because Kennedy did stop short of bombing or an invasion. A footnote about Laos by Michael Beschloss in a collection of Jacqueline Kennedy's interviews with Arthur Schlesinger Jr., for example, says, in its entirety, "In 1961, Kennedy resisted pressures to deploy the U.S. military against pro-Communist forces in Laos. Instead he authorized negotiation, which resulted, the following year, in the country's neutrality."[54] It is indeed true that Kennedy authorized negotiation, but it is also true that once the five thousand American troops appeared on the Laotian border, as Sorensen put it, "the negotiating atmosphere quickly improved."[55] Somewhat similarly, the historian Mark Moyar faults Kennedy for failing to send American troops into Laos in 1962 to force out the North Vietnamese Communists who had infiltrated there. "It was a disastrous concession to the enemy, a concession that would haunt South Vietnam and the United States" for the next fourteen years, Moyar writes, though he does concede that Kennedy "did authorize limited air strikes."[56] A CIA report of a 1963 planning meeting about Laos records, "The President commented that we are not likely to receive Congressional or public support of U.S. intervention in Laos and we should not kid ourselves about this too much."

Berlin was another place Kennedy deployed troops to block Communist advances. In August 1961, he ordered the 18th Infantry's 1st Battle Group up the autobahn, through Soviet-controlled East Germany, to reinforce West Berlin. The 1,500 American troops would have been no match for the 250,000 Soviet soldiers, but it was the symbolism that mattered. So, too, in October 1961, when an American diplomat in a Volkswagen sedan, accompanied by four M48 Patton tanks, crossed into East Berlin to prove America's access rights there. And again later in October, when ten American tanks faced off overnight against ten Soviet T-54 tanks. The Soviet tanks retreated first.[57]

Kennedy had braced the American people for a Berlin crisis in the same July 25, 1961, speech in which he had announced the increased levels of civil defense spending. "I hear it said that West Berlin is militarily untenable. And so was Bastogne. And so, in fact, was Stalingrad. Any dangerous spot is tenable if men — brave men — will make it so," he said.

"We do not want to fight — but we have fought before. And others in earlier times have made the same dangerous mistake of assuming that the West was too selfish and too soft and too divided to resist invasions of freedom in other lands," he said. "We cannot and will not permit the Communists to drive us out of Berlin, either gradually or by force. For the fulfillment of our pledge to that city is essential to the morale and security of Western Germany, to the unity of Western Europe, and to the faith of the entire Free World."

Some commentators, both at the time and since, have faulted Kennedy for actions that were less resolute than his rhetoric. Frederick Kempe, in a 2011 book on the Berlin crisis, writes of Kennedy's "missing backbone" and of "Kennedy's greater comfort at appearing tough than at actually being so." Kempe quotes *New York Times* columnist James Reston likening Kennedy to British appeasers before World War II: "talked like Churchill but acted like Chamberlain."[58] At the core of the criticism is that while JFK did successfully defend West Berlin, he also, in August 1961, stood by as the Soviet-backed East German government divided Berlin by erecting a wall that imprisoned the population of East Berlin.

Kennedy's defenders dismiss that criticism. Douglas Dillon, asked about it in an oral history interview in 1964, said, "To prevent its being built would have required western forces to forcefully move into the Soviet sector where they had no right to be . . . I, for one, find it very difficult to see what else we could have done without putting ourselves into the position of being an aggressor. In fact, this wall was merely a continuation of the wall which the Soviets had constructed along the whole boundary between east and west all the way from the Baltic down through Germany, Czechoslovakia and Hungary around Austria."

As we shall see, Kennedy would return to Berlin and the question of German reunification. For the moment, though, it is sufficient to note it as a place where, during his administration, American tanks retreated only after Soviet tanks had backed down first.

Victory and defeat were less easily measured in the villages and jungles of Vietnam, where the American-allied South was fighting off an assault from the Communist North. There, too, Kennedy sent troops. Sorensen reports that Kennedy increased the size of the U.S. military presence in South Vietnam to 15,500 at the end of 1963 from 2,000 at the end of 1961, including 600 Green Berets.[59] Another Kennedy biographer, Michael O'Brien, puts the strength under Kennedy at the end of his presidency at 16,900, up from 685 at the beginning of the administration.[60] A Reston column in early 1962 in the *New York Times* declared, "The United States is now involved in an undeclared war in South Vietnam." The Vietnam Veterans Memorial in Washington lists the names of American casualties on its black granite wall, organized by year as a measure of the conflict's escalation: 16 dead in 1961, 53 in 1962, 118 in 1963.

With Vietnam, as with Cuba and Laos and Berlin, Kennedy was resolute and direct in publicly explaining his approach. In a March 6, 1963, letter to Bobbie Lou Pendergrass of Santa Ana, California, whose brother had been killed in action in January, the president wrote, "Americans are in Viet Nam because we have determined that this country must not fall under Communist domination . . . Your brother was in Viet Nam because the threat to the Viet Namese people is, in the long run, a threat to the Free World community, and ultimately a threat to us also. For when freedom is destroyed in one country, it is threatened throughout the world."[61]

In a July 17, 1963, news conference, Kennedy said, "We are not going to withdraw from that effort. In my opinion, for us to withdraw from that effort would mean a collapse not only of South Viet-Nam, but Southeast Asia. So we are going to stay there." In an interview with Walter Cronkite, broadcast on CBS News on September 2, Kennedy said, "I don't agree with those who say we should withdraw. That would be a great mistake. I know people don't like Americans to be engaged in this kind of an effort. Forty-seven Americans have been killed in combat with the enemy, but this is a very important struggle even though it is far away. We took all this — made this effort to defend Europe. Now Europe is quite secure. We also have to participate — we may not like it — in the defense of Asia." In an interview with Chet Huntley and David Brinkley, broadcast on NBC News on September 9, the president said, "What I am concerned about is that Americans will get impatient and say because they don't like events in southeast Asia or they don't like the government in Saigon, that we should withdraw. That only makes it easy for the Communists. I think we should stay. We should use our influence in as effective a way as we can, but we should not withdraw." In a September 12 press conference, Kennedy said, "We have a very simple policy in that area, I think. In some ways I think the Vietnamese people and ourselves agree: we want the war to be won, the Communists to be contained, and the Americans to go home."

That simple policy was succeeding in Vietnam until Kennedy allowed himself to be outmaneuvered by his old political opponent Henry Cabot Lodge Jr. Kennedy had appointed Lodge ambassador to Saigon. The president of South Vietnam, Ngo Dinh Diem, and his brother, Ngo Dinh Nhu, who were Catholics, were unpopular with some elements of the American press corps in Vietnam, in part because their regime, while effective, fell short of American ideals of transparency and civil liberties, a flaw dramatized by protesting Buddhist monks. A photograph of one such monk, setting himself on fire in June 1963, helped to undermine support for Diem in both the press and the State Department, notwithstanding that, as it later emerged, some of the monks were, in fact, agents of the North Vietnamese Communists.

Lodge, disregarding orders from Washington, encouraged a coup that, by November 2, 1963, had forced Diem and Nhu out of the presidential palace and into a Saigon church, where they had taken refuge. After Diem and Nhu surrendered to their opponents in exchange for a promise of safe passage to the airport, two soldiers participating in the coup, one armed with a submachine gun and the other with a Colt .45, shot them repeatedly in the back, then stabbed them with knives.[62]

The coup was greeted with glee by Lodge and his allies in the press and the State Department. Kennedy, though, was horrified. His chairman of the Joint Chiefs of Staff, Maxwell Taylor, later described the president's reaction on hearing the news: "Kennedy leaped to his feet and rushed from the room with a look of shock and dismay on his face which I had never seen before. He had always insisted that Diem must never suffer more than exile and had been led to believe or had persuaded himself that a change in government could be carried out without bloodshed."[63]

Schlesinger writes: "The Saigon generals were claiming that he had killed himself; but the President, shaking his head, doubted that, as a Catholic, he would have taken this way out. He said that Diem had fought for his country for twenty years and that it should not have ended like this."[64]

On November 4 the president dictated notes about the coup into his Oval Office taping system. "I was shocked by the deaths of Diem and Nhu," Kennedy said, calling Diem "an extraordinary character" who had "held his country together" over a decade and "maintained its independence under very adverse conditions.

"The way he was killed made it particularly abhorrent."[65]

The president said the coup had culminated months of division within his administration. Opposed to a coup, the president reported, had been General Taylor, the attorney general, Secretary McNamara, and the CIA director, John McCone; "in favor of the coup was State."

The State Department was a perennial thorn in the president's side, and, along with the press and some peace groups and professors, it was among the places where Kennedy's policies met resistance.

Schlesinger writes, "The President used to divert himself with the dream of establishing a secret office of thirty people or so to run foreign policy while maintaining the state department as a façade in which people might contentedly carry papers from bureau to bureau . . . One almost concluded that the definition of a Foreign Service officer was a man for whom the risks always outweighed the opportunities."[66] Chester Bowles recalled that Kennedy "looked on the State Department as a huge bureaucratic roadblock to all the things he would like to do."[67] And Joseph Alsop remembered, "At the beginning of his administration he had the conviction that the State Department was a hopeless swamp in any case and that this was a natural state of affairs and that you shouldn't expect to get anything out of the State Department."[68] The president himself said, "It's got all those people over there who are constantly smiling. I think we need to smile less and be tougher."[69]

Still, Kennedy tried to wring what he could from the bureaucracy. Schlesinger reports Kennedy as having said, in the face of State Department resistance, "They ought to read the Constitution over there and find out who was responsible for foreign affairs and whose government it was anyway."[70]

Though Kennedy had friends in the press and was sometimes able to use them, and particularly television, to his advantage, the press was also at times one of the forces arrayed against him. It was during the Kennedy administration that some influential reporters started to write critically about the American war effort in Vietnam. Among the most influential was the *New York Times* correspondent in South Vietnam, David Halberstam. In certain respects Kennedy and Halberstam had similar profiles. Both had followed older brothers to Harvard, both had worked on the *Crimson,* and both had family homes growing up in New York's Westchester County.[71] Halberstam was seventeen years younger than the president — in his late twenties when he was covering Vietnam during the JFK years. Kennedy did not believe what Halberstam was writing, and worse, he thought the *Times* reporter was naïve about the Communists.

At a September 3, 1963, meeting with about fifteen of his top officials, including Secretaries Rusk, Dillon, and McNamara, Attorney General Kennedy, CIA Director McCone, and General Taylor, the president commented that Halberstam was not an accurate reporter. In a September 23 White House meeting with McNamara, Taylor, George Ball, and McGeorge Bundy, the president mentioned a column by his friend Joseph Alsop likening Halberstam to the American reporters of the 1940s who had criticized Chiang Kai-shek and praised the Communist Mao Tse-tung, and also to Herbert Matthews, a *Times* reporter who had helped to elevate Castro in Cuba.[72] Kennedy said there was a great deal of truth in Alsop's column.[73] A September 26 CIA memo prepared for McCone titled "David Halberstam's Reporting on South Vietnam" concluded, "In his almost invariably pessimistic reports, Halberstam makes liberal use of phrases 'some Americans,' 'informed Vietnamese,' or 'lower (or higher) ranking Americans,' etc. Such sourcing is impossible to refute. However, other observers writing from South Vietnam indicate that large segments of the American military community have been and still remain optimistic about the course of the war. Such optimistic sources are almost never quoted by Mr. Halberstam."[74]

Kennedy's press secretary, Pierre Salinger, later said of Halberstam and other like-minded American correspondents, among them Neil Sheehan, "If they wanted to bring down the government of President Diem, they should have gotten outside of the press and gone about it as lobbyists or activists."[75] The exasperation was shared by the president himself, who, according to the minutes of one meeting, "observed that Mr. Halberstam of the New York Times is actually running a political campaign; that he is wholly unobjective" and "stated that it was essential that we not permit Halberstam to influence our actions."[76]

The Halberstam situation was unfolding at a time of already icy relations between Kennedy and the *Times*. The newspaper had endorsed JFK in the 1960 campaign, but only tepidly, asserting that when it came to the choice between Kennedy and Nixon, "there are points of strength and points of weakness on both sides." The endorsement editorial had faulted the Democratic platform for promising "no increase in present tax rates" and also faulted Kennedy for his "blunder suggesting intervention in Cuba."[77] Speaking of the *Times*'s editorial page editor, John Oakes, Kennedy told a friend, "If I tried to run the country the way Oakes writes those editorials . . . we'd all be in a ditch." The *Times*'s criticism of nepotism in President Kennedy's appointment of his brother as attorney general was seen by the Kennedys as hypocritical: the newspaper itself had been run by the Ochs-Sulzberger family for generations.[78] A climax of sorts came at an October 22, 1963, meeting between the president and the *Times*'s newly installed publisher, Arthur Ochs Sulzberger, during which Kennedy suggested that Halberstam might be transferred to Paris or Rome.[79] Sulzberger refused, going so far as to tell Halberstam to cancel a scheduled vacation so that it would not look as if the *Times* were caving in to Kennedy.[80]

If the *New York Times* was a headache for Kennedy, so too was the brewing peace movement, with its roots on college campuses. The large antiwar demonstrations would come later in the decade, but Kennedy and his policies — not only Vietnam, but also nuclear testing and Cuba — drew pickets and protests. On February 26, 1962, the *Times* carried a front-page article from London reporting on Bertrand Russell's protest of the president's plan to resume nuclear testing. "Unless the governments are resisted and stopped, the chances of human survival are slight," Russell said. At the same London rally, an actor read aloud a letter from Professor Linus Pauling of the California Institute of Technology, who, like Russell, was a Nobel laureate. The letter described the resumption of nuclear weapons testing as "premeditated murder of millions of people." The same day's *New York Times* carried a letter to the editor from Corliss Lamont, an author and activist who had taught philosophy at Columbia University and who was a son of Thomas W. Lamont, who had been the chairman of J. P. Morgan. The letter ran under the headline "Vietnam Aid Protested;

U.S. Intervention to Prop Up Diem Dictatorship Charged." Lamont's letter described Diem's South Vietnam as "one of the most cruel and backward governments on the face of the earth" and said the Kennedy administration "is guilty of outright intervention to prop up the Diem dictatorship." The U.S. government, Lamont wrote, was "showing a reckless disregard for international law" and also was "unconstitutionally involving us in a real, though undeclared, war in which there are 1,000 casualties a month and which may develop into a major conflict, without sufficiently informing either Congress or the American people." Lamont declared that this approach "is likely to be self-defeating in the long run."

On March 3, 1962, the *Times* carried a report of a telegram from Linus Pauling to Kennedy. The cable warned the president that an American resumption of atmospheric nuclear testing would be a "monstrous immorality" that would cause Kennedy "to go down in history as one of the most immoral men of all times and one of the greatest enemies of the human race."

Pauling and Lamont returned to the pages of the *Times* on April 11. Together with seven current and former Yale professors, they published, as an advertisement, "An Open Letter to President John F. Kennedy against U.S. military intervention in South Vietnam." The ad repeated many of the points that had been raised by Lamont in his February letter to the editor, but in somewhat stronger terms. "We wish to ask you why at present the United States is sending its Army, Navy, and Air Force to bring death and bloodshed to South Vietnam, a small Asian country approximately 10,000 miles from our Pacific coast," the letter began. "U.S. casualties are piling up, including the 93 Army men who lost their lives when a Super Constellation [a troop transport plane] crashed on March 16 while flying them from San Francisco to Saigon."

On May 8, 1963, the *Times* ran a story on a group called Women Strike for Peace, which had brought two thousand women to Capitol Hill to press for a nuclear test ban. The *Times* dispatch quoted the group's founder, Dagmar Wilson, criticizing Kennedy. "We're not able to get the straight word from the President on what his disarmament policy is," she said. "He's obviously trying to be popular with everyone by not offending anyone." The next day, the *Times* reported on an hourlong vigil in Times Square by picketers calling for a "General Strike for Peace."

On July 14, 1963, Lamont and Pauling returned to the *Times* with a full-page ad in the Sunday magazine section, "An Open Letter to President John F. Kennedy for ending the war and making peace in South Vietnam." The ad called on the president to halt the American military intervention in Vietnam, which it described as a "dirty, cruel war" being fought to bolster Diem's "brutal dictatorship."

In October, Lamont's pamphlet-publishing firm, assisted by the American Civil Liberties Union, sued the federal government to challenge a Kennedy-signed law that gave the U.S. Post Office permission to withhold delivery of Communist political propaganda mailed from abroad.[81] (The constitutional challenge eventually prevailed in the 1965 Supreme Court case *Lamont v. Postmaster General*, with Justice White not participating.)

At this juncture, readers only casually familiar with the Kennedy foreign policy record, or familiar only with certain slanted accounts of it, will be entitled to pause in disbelief. John F. Kennedy — the founder of the Peace Corps, the man who gave a dovish speech at American University ushering in a new era of détente, the man whose proudest accomplishment was his treaty with the Soviet Union banning nuclear weapons testing — the peace activists were protesting against *him*? Were the activists just misguided, or were they correct to perceive that Kennedy's agenda was significantly different from their own?

For an answer, let us turn away from the words of Kennedy's critics and return instead to the words of the president himself.

The Peace Corps? Notwithstanding the appearance of the word "peace" in the name of the agency, Kennedy intended the American volunteers to advance American goals in the Cold War by winning the friendship of developing countries that had not yet taken sides between the United States and the Soviet Union. In a November 2, 1960, campaign speech in San Francisco elaborating the idea, he had put it this way:

We need a stronger free world . . . a stronger United States foreign policy speaking for a stronger America, and that is what we are going to get . . . To be peace loving is not enough . . .

The fact of the matter is that out of Moscow and Peiping [Beijing] and Czechoslovakia and Eastern Germany are hundreds of men and women, scientists, physicists, teachers, engineers, doctors, nurses, studying in those institutes, prepared to spend their lives abroad in the service of world communism. A friend of mine visiting the Soviet Union last summer met a young Russian couple studying Swahili and African customs at the Moscow Institute of Languages. They were not language teachers. He was a sanitation engineer and she was a nurse, and they were being prepared to live their lives in Africa as missionaries for world communism . . . This can only be countered by skill and dedication of Americans who are willing to spend their lives serving the cause of freedom . . . We in the sixties are going to move the world again in the direction of freedom.

In his March 1, 1961, message to Congress announcing that he had established the Peace Corps as a pilot program by executive order, Kennedy linked the project to "our own freedom, and the future of freedom around the world." It seems clear enough that Kennedy was not talking exclusively, FDR-style, about freedom from poverty; he was talking also about political and economic and religious freedom of the sort available in America but not under communism. Otherwise, why not stand back and let the Moscow-trained missionaries do the work in Africa and in other newly independent colonies?

As for the American University speech, it is true that it came amid a period, after the Cuban Missile Crisis, when relations between Washington and Moscow warmed somewhat, at least rhetorically. In March 1963, Kennedy had said in a speech marking the fiftieth anniversary of the Department of Labor: "I don't know why it is that expenditures which deal with enforcement of the minimum wage, that deal with the problem of school dropouts, of retraining of workers, of unskilled labor, all the problems that are so much with us in the sixties, why they are always regarded as the waste in the budget and expenditures for defense are always regarded as the untouchable item in the budget."[82]

As the growth in the defense budget during his own administration showed, however, it was primarily a rhetorical question.

The American University speech was delivered on June 10, 1963, at the commencement exercises of the university, which is in Washington, D.C. The speech is remembered for Kennedy's reflections about the arms race in the nuclear age. He called world peace "the most important topic on earth," and said, "Let us reexamine our attitude toward the Soviet Union." He said, "We can help make the world safe for diversity. For, in the final analysis, our most basic common link is that we all inhabit this small planet. We all breathe the same air. We all cherish our children's future. And we are all mortal." (Consciously or not, it was an echo of Ambassador Joseph Kennedy's November 1938 Trafalgar Day speech, which had said, "It is true that the democratic and dictator countries have important and fundamental divergences of outlook, which in certain areas go deeper than politics. But there is simply no sense, common or otherwise, in letting these differences grow into unrelenting antagonisms. After all, we have to live together in the same world, whether we like it or not."[83])

Less well remembered are these lines of the speech: "As Americans, we find communism profoundly repugnant as a negation of personal freedom and dignity," and "The Communist drive to impose their political and economic system on others is the primary cause of world tension today."

The American University speech approached its conclusion with a religious reference, a quotation from the biblical book of Proverbs. Kennedy said, "'When a man's ways please the Lord,' the Scriptures tell us, 'he maketh even his enemies to be at peace with him.'"

It is intriguing that Kennedy connected his peace message to religious values, because just two months before the American University speech, on April 11, 1963, Pope John XXIII had issued an encyclical, *Pacem in Terris,* on the subject of peace on earth. The message from the pope defended Western freedom against the Communist system, just as Kennedy had over his career. *Pacem in Terris* listed a series of rights that Americans would easily recognize, among them "being able to worship God in accordance with the right dictates of his own conscience," "the right to the private ownership of property, including that of productive goods," and "the right to emigrate and immigrate." As Kennedy had said in his inaugural address and in so many speeches before that, the encyclical claimed that the ultimate source of these rights was not the state, but God: "authority comes from God." Without naming the Soviet Union directly, the encyclical criticized it harshly: "In defining the scope of a just freedom within which individual citizens may live lives worthy of their human dignity, the rulers of some nations have been far too restrictive. Sometimes in States of this kind the very right to freedom is called in question, and even flatly denied."

The pope paired this ideological criticism of the Communist side of the Cold War, however, with language warning against the arms race and calling for disarmament. "We are deeply distressed to see the enormous stocks of armaments that have been, and continue to be, manufactured in the economically more developed countries," the encyclical said, speaking of the "terrifying destructive force of modern weapons" and "fear of the ghastly and catastrophic consequences of their use." The pope went on to speak out against nuclear testing: "There is reason to fear that the very testing of nuclear devices for war purposes can, if continued, lead to serious danger for various forms of life on earth."

Kennedy seems to have read the papal document and to have been favorably impressed. In an April 20 speech at Boston College, a Catholic university, Kennedy said, "I am much encouraged by a reading in this last week of the remarkable encyclical, *Pacem in Terris*. In its penetrating analysis of today's great problems, of social welfare and human rights, of disarmament and international order and peace, that document surely shows that on the basis of one great faith and its traditions there can be developed counsel on public affairs that is of value to all men and women of good will. As a Catholic I am proud of it; and as an American I have learned from it." A May 7 private telegram from Kennedy to the pope, a copy of which is in the president's files, congratulated the pontiff on winning the Balzan peace prize and said, "The award is particularly appropriate now following Your Holiness's encyclical, *Pacem in Terris*." In early July, when Kennedy visited the Vatican, Cardinal Cushing presented him with one of only three signed copies of the encyclical.[84]

In the American University speech, Kennedy declared an American moratorium on atmospheric nuclear tests. U.S. and Soviet negotiators reached an agreement on a limited nuclear test ban treaty soon thereafter. The Senate ratified it on September 23, 1963, by a vote of 80 to 19. Kennedy signed it on October 7 with somewhat tepid remarks, observing, "If this treaty fails, it will not be our doing, and even if it fails, we shall not regret that we have made this clear and honorable national commitment to the cause of man's survival. For under this treaty we can and must still keep our vigil in defense of freedom."

Several facts about the treaty and about Kennedy's record on nuclear weapons testing are crucial to understanding the test ban. First is that the treaty applied only to tests underwater, in the air, and in outer space. Underground tests of atomic bombs — tests that served the same purpose of assuring military readiness and improving lethality — were still allowed. Second, a moratorium on nuclear testing had been imposed by Eisenhower in 1958. Kennedy broke that moratorium and ordered the resumption of weapons testing, first underground, beginning September 5, 1961, and then in the atmosphere, beginning April 25, 1962.[85] The president used a March 2, 1962, television and radio address to explain the decision to resume American testing in the atmosphere:

> On September first of last year, while the United States and the United Kingdom were negotiating in good faith at Geneva, the Soviet Union callously broke its moratorium with a two month series of tests of more than 40 nuclear weapons. Preparations for these tests had been secretly underway for many months. Accompanied by new threats and new tactics of terror, these tests — conducted mostly in the atmosphere — represented a major Soviet effort to put nuclear weapons back into the arms race . . . I must report to you in all candor that further Soviet tests, in the absence of further Western progress, could well provide the Soviet Union with a nuclear attack and defense capability so powerful as to encourage aggressive designs. Were we to

stand still while the Soviets surpassed us — or even appeared to sur-
pass us — the free World's ability to deter, to survive and to respond to
an all-out attack would be seriously weakened.

The fact of the matter is that we cannot make similar strides without testing in the atmosphere as well as underground . . . The leaders
of the Soviet Union are also watching this decision. Should we fail
to follow the dictates of our own security, they will chalk it up, not
to goodwill, but to a failure of will — not to our confidence in Western superiority, but to our fear of world opinion . . . If they persist in
rejecting all means of true inspection, then we shall be left with no
choice but to keep our own defensive arsenal adequate for the security
of all free men.

Carl Kaysen remembers joining another Kennedy national security
official, Jerome Wiesner, in reacting to the news of a Soviet nuclear
test:

> "Great! This is the occasion for the president to make a stirring speech
> about how the Soviets are going to resume testing but we were too
> good to do that." And we went over with this great idea, and promptly
> got our sort of heads bashed in. Kennedy's response was, "That's all
> very well for you peaceniks, but how would I look if my response to
> this Soviet aggressive gesture were to say, 'You go ahead, and we're
> going to do nothing.'" He then used one of his elegant expressions,
> and said that, "You know, I've been kicked someplace, and I've got
> to contemplate about how I respond. And so the response is not, 'It's
> OK, go ahead.'" So Jerry and I hung our heads, and walked across
> West Avenue again.[86]

Finally, it is worth remembering that during this same period, from
the June 1963 American University speech to the October 1963 signing
of the limited test ban treaty, Kennedy went to Berlin and gave one of
his most famous speeches, an unequivocal statement about the impos-
sibility of working with the Soviets.

Kennedy had discussed his position on Germany after the Berlin
crisis had passed during a November 25, 1961, interview at Hyannis
Port with the editor of *Izvestia*, the state-controlled Russian newspaper. "We do not recognize the division of Germany," Kennedy said. "In

our opinion the German people wish to have one united country. If the Soviet Union had lost the war, the Soviet people themselves would object to a line being drawn through Moscow and the entire country. If we had been defeated in war, we wouldn't like to have a line drawn down the Mississippi River. The Germans want to be united. I think it should be possible to provide for that under conditions which will protect the interests of all concerned. But the Soviet Union believes that it is more in their interest to keep Germany divided."

Just sixteen days after his American University speech, when he had said, "Let us reexamine our attitude toward the Soviet Union," on June 26, 1963, Kennedy spoke in Berlin. His reception showed that whatever resentment the people of West Berlin had toward Kennedy for allowing the construction of the Berlin Wall was far outweighed by their appreciation for his defense of their city. One million of them lined the route from the airport to see the president, and 300,000 gathered in the plaza in front of the City Hall to hear him speak.[87] Kennedy said:

There are many people in the world who really don't understand, or say they don't, what is the great issue between the free world and the Communist world. Let them come to Berlin. There are some who say that communism is the wave of the future. Let them come to Berlin. And there are some who say in Europe and elsewhere we can work with the Communists. Let them come to Berlin. And there are even a few who say that it is true that communism is an evil system, but it permits us to make economic progress. *Lass' sie nach Berlin kommen.* Let them come to Berlin.

Freedom has many difficulties and democracy is not perfect, but we have never had to put a wall up to keep our people in, to prevent them from leaving us . . . Freedom is indivisible, and when one man is enslaved, all are not free. When all are free, then we can look forward to that day when this city will be joined as one and this country and this great Continent of Europe in a peaceful and hopeful globe. When that day finally comes, as it will, the people of West Berlin can take sober satisfaction in the fact that they were in the front lines for almost two decades.

All free men, wherever they may live, are citizens of Berlin, and, therefore, as a free man, I take pride in the words *"Ich bin ein Berliner."*

Sorensen, the man other than Kennedy who was most closely involved in drafting the president's speeches, emphasizes in his account of the day in Berlin that the words about not being able to work with the Communists were the president's own, not the product of the usual elaborate clearance process involving the State Department and the rest of the foreign policy and national security bureaucracy. "Departing from his text" is what the president did, according to Sorensen, who describes the passage as an "ad lib."[88] Powers and O'Donnell, in their book, call the passage "what his heart wanted him to say . . . spontaneous and unprepared."[89]

At a luncheon after the Berlin speech, Kennedy gave a toast "to the cause of freedom on both sides of the wall." Then, in an address at the Free University of Berlin, he declared:

> Reunification, I believe, will someday be a reality . . . We all know that a police state regime has been imposed on the Eastern sector of this city and country. The peaceful reunification of Berlin and Germany will, therefore, not be either quick or easy. We must first bring others to see their own true interests better than they do today. What will count in the long run are the realities of Western strength, the realities of Western commitment, the realities of Germany as a nation and a people, without regard to artificial boundaries of barbed wire. Those are the realities upon which we rely and on which history will move, and others, too, would do well to recognize them . . . What does liberty require? The answer is clear. A united Berlin in a United Germany, united by self-determination and living in peace.

Kennedy's themes at the time were somewhat at odds with each other. On the one hand, he was telling audiences that Soviet communism was an evil, aggressive system that needed to be rolled back and replaced with freedom. On the other hand, he was telling them that the United States should redouble its efforts to keep peaceful relations with the Soviet Union. Sometimes he included both messages in the same speech. Returning from Germany, Kennedy stopped in Ireland, from which his forebears departed on their journey to America. "Across the gulfs and barriers that now divide us, we must remember that there are no permanent enemies," Kennedy told the Irish parliament in Dublin. "Hostility today is a fact, but it is not a ruling law. The supreme reality of our time is our indivisibility as children of God and our common vulnerability on this planet." A few minutes later, in the same speech, Kennedy said, "The central issue of freedom, however, is between those who believe in self-determination and those in the East who would impose on others the harsh and oppressive Communist system."

Perhaps aware of the possible confusion caused by these two strands of thinking, the president tried to clarify matters with two more speeches. The first came at the Mormon Tabernacle in Salt Lake City, where, three years earlier, during the 1960 campaign, Kennedy had spoken about what he called the "struggle for supremacy between two conflicting ideologies; freedom under God versus ruthless, Godless tyranny."

On September 26, 1963, Kennedy returned to Salt Lake City and urged Americans weary of commitments in faraway places like Berlin and Vietnam to soldier on in the struggle for freedom and against communism:

> I realize that the burdens are heavy and I realize that there is a great temptation to urge that we relinquish them, that we have enough to do here in the United States, and we should not be so busy around the globe . . . To turn away now is to abandon the world to those whose ambition is to destroy a free society. To yield these burdens up after having carried them for more than 20 years is to surrender the freedom of our country inevitably, for without the United States, the chances of freedom surviving, let alone prevailing around the globe, are nonexistent . . . The burdens of maintaining an immense military establishment with one million Americans serving outside our frontiers, of financing a far-flung program of development assistance, of conducting a complex and baffling diplomacy, all weigh heavily upon us and cause some to counsel retreat . . . To renounce the world of freedom now, to abandon those who share our commitment, and retire into lonely and not so splendid isolation, would be to give communism the one hope which, in this twilight of disappointment for them, might repair their divisions and rekindle their hope.
>
> . . . Therefore, I think this country will continue its commitments to

support the world of freedom, for as we discharge that commitment we are heeding the command which Brigham Young heard from the Lord more than a century ago, the command he conveyed to his followers, "Go as pioneers . . . to a land of peace."

The second speech explaining Kennedy's view of relations with the Soviet Union and both the Cold War thaw and its limits came on October 19, in a speech at the University of Maine:

A pause in the cold war is not a lasting peace — and a detente does not equal disarmament. The United States must continue to seek a relaxation of tensions, but we have no cause to relax our vigilance . . .

A change in atmosphere and in emphasis is not a reversal of purpose. Mr. Khrushchev himself has said that there can be no coexistence in the field of ideology. In addition, there are still major areas of tension and conflict, from Berlin to Cuba to Southeast Asia. The United States and the Soviet Union still have wholly different concepts of the world, its freedom, its future. We still have wholly different views on the so-called wars of liberation and the use of subversion. And so long as these basic differences continue, they cannot and should not be concealed. They set limits to the possibilities of agreements, and they will give rise to further crises . . .

In times such as these, therefore, there is nothing inconsistent with signing an atmospheric nuclear test ban, on the one hand, and testing underground on the other; about being willing to sell to the Soviets our surplus wheat while refusing to sell strategic items; about probing their interest in a joint lunar landing while making a major effort to master this new environment; or about exploring the possibilities of disarmament while maintaining our stockpile of arms. For all of these moves, and all of these elements of American policy and allied policy towards the Soviet Union, are directed at a single, comprehensive goal — namely, convincing the Soviet leaders that it is dangerous for them to engage in direct or indirect aggression, futile for them to attempt to impose their will and their system on other unwilling people, and beneficial to them, as well as to the world, to join in the achievement of a genuine and enforceable peace . . . Let us always make clear our willingness to talk, if talk will help, and our readiness to fight, if fight we must . . . Let us distinguish between our hopes and our illusions, always hoping for steady progress toward less critically dangerous relations with the Soviets, but never laboring under any illusions about Communist methods or Communist goals.

. . . Let us recognize that we have made these gains and achieved this pause by the firmness we displayed a year ago as well as our restraint — by our efforts for defense as well as our efforts for peace.

This was the Kennedy foreign policy agenda, and its philosophy, in a nutshell: peace through strength, and "never laboring under any illusions about Communist methods or Communist goals."

A story illustrates how Kennedy, even in the fall of 1963, remained willing to challenge what he had called the "ruthless, Godless tyranny" of Soviet communism. The story is told by Lewis Weinstein. Weinstein was a Jew who had been born in Lithuania in 1905. He had come to America when he was fifteen months old, graduated from Harvard and Harvard Law School, served in the Army on Eisenhower's staff during World War II, and had returned to become a partner at the Boston law firm of Foley, Hoag & Eliot. There, one day in the summer of 1946, Weinstein's partner Thomas Eliot, whose grandfather had been Harvard president Charles W. Eliot, walked into Weinstein's office and said, "Lou, meet Jack Kennedy." From this classic Boston political moment — the Brahmin lawyer introducing the Irish-Catholic politician to a Jewish partner who could help him raise campaign contributions — an enduring relationship began.

By the fall of 1963, the deteriorating situation of the approximately three million Jews in Russia was beginning to attract broader international attention, particularly in the United States. Kennedy's White House files contain a copy of a resolution adopted unanimously by the Philadelphia City Council on October 24, urging the president to speak out about the matter. The Soviet Communists were denying Jews access to prayer books and Passover matzo, the resolution said.[90]

When American Jewish organizations tried the usual route of having friendly members of Congress contact the State Department, they were rebuffed. The assistant secretary of state for congressional relations, Frederick Dutton, sent Senator Kenneth Keating of New York a long letter acknowledging that Russian synagogues had been closed and Jewish cemeteries desecrated as part of "the long-term Soviet campaign against religion generally," but fretting that the American government could not do much about it. "It is doubtful if further protestations would be helpful to the Jews in the Soviet Union," the letter concluded.[91]

Weinstein went to Robert Kennedy and succeeded in having a mention of the Soviet closing of synagogues included in President Kennedy's September 1963 speech to the United Nations General Assembly. Weinstein persuaded the president to have Averell Harriman, the former governor of New York who was undersecretary of state, raise the matter with Khrushchev during a negotiating mission to Moscow on arms control. In a White House meeting with President Kennedy in November, Weinstein, who was soon to take over as chairman of the Conference of Presidents of Major American Jewish Organizations, launched into a plea on the issue. "You know, it's getting pretty bad," Weinstein said. "There are murder trials going on. They call them economic trials, but the defendant is always a Jew. He's charged with black market [trading] or something else like that, he's always convicted and executed. They're murder trials, in which the defendant is murdered and not the murderer."

Weinstein told Kennedy that Soviet authorities had slowed the flow of Jewish refugees out of Russia to a trickle. And he said no American president had intervened with the Russian authorities on behalf of the Jews since President Theodore Roosevelt protested to Tsar Nicholas II after the Kishinev massacre in 1903.

Kennedy replied, "Well, here's one president who's ready to do something."

He told Weinstein to organize a conference in Washington on the Soviet Jewry problem. The president told Weinstein to schedule the conference for a time soon after Kennedy returned from an upcoming political trip to Dallas.[92]

CHAPTER 9

The Death of a President

November 22, 1963–1968

Strengthening our security as well as our economy . . . by maintaining a more stable level of prices than almost any of our overseas competitors, and by cutting personal and corporate income taxes by some $11 billion, as I have proposed, [will] assure this Nation of the longest and strongest expansion in our peacetime economic history.

— JOHN F. KENNEDY, remarks prepared for delivery at the
  Dallas Trade Mart, November 22, 1963

Dallas

PRESIDENT KENNEDY SPENT — and planned to spend — Friday, November 22, 1963, in Texas doing just what he had done for his entire presidency and for much of his political career: quoting the Bible, making the case for a strong military that would defend freedom against the Communists, and promoting economic growth through a tax cut.

At a rally in front of his Fort Worth hotel that morning, Kennedy spoke of how "we have placed so much emphasis in the last 3 years in building a defense system second to none, until now the United States is stronger than it has ever been in its history."

To a breakfast of the Fort Worth Chamber of Commerce, Kennedy elaborated: "We have increased the defense budget of the United States by over 20 percent; increased the program of acquisition for Polaris submarines from 24 to 41; increased our Minuteman missile purchase program by more than 75 percent; doubled the number of strategic bombers and missiles on alert; doubled the number of nuclear weapons available in the strategic alert forces; increased the tactical nuclear forces deployed in Western Europe by over 60 percent; added five combat ready divisions to the Army of the United States, and five tactical fighter wings to the Air Force of the United States; increased our strategic airlift capability by 75 percent; and increased our special counter-insurgency forces which are engaged now in South Viet-Nam by 600 percent."

After Fort Worth, Kennedy flew the short distance to Dallas, then began a motorcade on the way to a speech at the Trade Mart. There he was scheduled to deliver remarks going into even greater detail on his military buildup. The prepared remarks for the speech show that he was to tie the nation's military strength to economic growth and to a stable dollar, and that he was to link economic growth to the tax cut. He would have spoken of "strengthening our security as well as our economy . . . by maintaining a more stable level of prices than almost any of our overseas competitors, and by cutting personal and corporate income taxes by some $11 billion, as I have proposed, to assure this Nation of the longest and strongest expansion in our peacetime economic history." He was fighting for a tax cut to the end.

The Trade Mart speech's text concluded with a quote from Psalm 127: "Except the Lord keep the city, the watchman waketh but in vain."

Kennedy's own watchmen failed him. Nine agents of his Secret Service detail had been out drinking past midnight; one was out until 5 a.m. that morning. The FBI's Dallas office had a file on Lee Harvey Oswald. The FBI knew Oswald had a job in the Texas School Book Depository, which the motorcade was to pass, according to the route published ahead of time in Dallas newspapers.[1]

The final blame for Kennedy's assassination, though, must lie not with the shortcomings of the Secret Service or the FBI, but with Oswald himself. The assassin's father had died of a heart attack two months before Oswald was born. Oswald had dropped out of school after ninth grade and spent three years in the Marine Corps, where he qualified as a sharpshooter but ultimately was released with an "undesirable discharge" after reportedly trying to renounce his American citizenship and become a citizen of the Soviet Union, where he spent thirty-two months.[2] When he defected in 1959 in Moscow, he was quoted in the press as saying he "could not be happy living under capitalism." On his way back to the United States, he wrote out two possible versions of an interview with American reporters: "Are you a communist? Yes, basically," and "Are you a communist? No of course not." He was estranged from his wife. In April 1963, after he had returned, he had fired a shot at former general Edwin Walker, a leader of the far-right, anti-Communist, and anti-Kennedy John Birch Society of Dallas.[3] In September Oswald tried to go to Cuba, but could not get a visa.[4]

This was the man who, at 12:30 p.m. Dallas time on November 22, perched in the sixth-floor window of the School Book Depository, fired shots from a 6.5-millimeter Mannlicher-Carcano rifle equipped with a telescopic sight, and killed the president of the United States.

Under interrogation after being captured by the Dallas police, the twenty-four-year-old Oswald asserted, "I'm not a Communist, I'm not a Leninist-Marxist, I'm a Marxist." Any further exploration of his motives was limited by the fact that Oswald was fatally shot two days later by a fifty-two-year-old Dallas strip-club operator named Jack Ruby. Ruby himself died of cancer in 1967.[5]

Kennedy died and was buried as he lived — as a Catholic. Father Oscar Huber administered the last rites at Parkland Hospital in Dallas, then led Jacqueline Kennedy and the president's personal physician, Admiral George Burkley, in the Lord's Prayer. "I am convinced that his soul had not left his body. This was a valid last sacrament," he told her.[6] After Kennedy's body and his widow had returned to Washington, there were Masses for the president's family on both Saturday and Sunday in the White House East Room, where the dead president lay on a bier. When the White House chief of protocol, Angier Biddle Duke, suggested a nondenominational or secular funeral on the grounds that "the President believed in the separation of church and state," the Kennedy family flatly rejected the idea, William Manchester reports in his book *The Death of a President*. Cardinal Cushing presided at the funeral Mass on Monday, at St. Matthew's, where Jacqueline Kennedy took communion. Afterward, Cushing also officiated at

Kennedy's burial at Arlington National Cemetery. Later, the tiny bodies of Patrick Bouvier Kennedy and of Kennedy's stillborn daughter from August 1956 were eventually buried alongside the president's.[7]

No sooner had Kennedy been laid to rest than the struggle began to define his legacy. On one side were a group of largely liberal journalists, historians, and former Kennedy administration officials; on the other side was the president's widow, Jacqueline Kennedy. She had a more accurate view of her husband's ideas than they did, but they were the ones who wrote history.

The most famous interview Jacqueline Kennedy gave after the assassination was the one at Hyannis Port with Theodore White for *Life* magazine on November 29, 1963, one week after her husband was killed, in which she quoted from a song: "Don't let it be forgot, that once there was a spot, for one brief shining moment that was known as Camelot."

White dictated his account of the interview by phone while *Life* was being held open after its deadline, at a cost of $30,000 an hour in printing plant overtime. The resulting article, he conceded in his 1978 memoir, "heavily edited her."[8]

White's 1978 memoir contained more material from the November 29 interview, but that, it turns out, was edited, too. Only in 1995, a year after Jacqueline Kennedy Onassis's death, did the JFK Library release White's full notes of the interview, following the terms of White's gift of the notes to the library. The president's widow had said she cared deeply about the eternal flame marking Kennedy's grave at Arlington: "I care about the flame . . . I wanted that flame." Among the lines that White cut in his heavy editing was this one from Jacqueline Kennedy: "All I wanted was his name on just that one booster, the one that would put us ahead of the Russians."[9] The line suggests that even right after Kennedy's death, his widow wanted JFK's legacy to be not some kind of peaceful cooperation with the Russians on the space program, but *beating them.*

A similar kind of editing of history took place in Ted Sorensen's draft of his 1965 book *Kennedy.* Sorensen's manuscript had declared that JFK "thought the *New York Times* the greatest newspaper in the world." Jacqueline Kennedy, who had agreed to read Sorensen's draft before publication, objected: "Are you sure? He had a great deal of disillusionment about them — nepotism — their columnists who never left DC — etc — just don't give them that much of a plug . . . because he really had a lot of contempt for the *Times*."[10] Notwithstanding her words and the president's own private remarks about David Halberstam's reporting, Sorensen's book as published said Kennedy thought the *Times* "less guilty of bias and sensationalism in its news stories than any other publication." The book quoted Kennedy as crediting the *Times*'s 1960 endorsement for his election, echoing a *Times* pitch for its help-wanted ads: "I got my job through the *New York Times*."[11]

Sorensen's handling of President Kennedy's view of the *New York Times,* while telling, is hardly the only example of how the aide's 1965 book rewrote the president's story in a way consonant with Sorensen's own dovish views and with the views of his peace-activist father, to whom the book was dedicated. The penultimate chapter of *Kennedy* was titled "The Strategy of Peace." On pages 730 to 733, it dealt with Kennedy's American University speech, about which Sorensen later told a biographer, "I really don't want to be quoted on the record of what I'm the author of, but I'm sure that I was the principal draftsman."[12] Kennedy's Berlin speech — "there are some who say in Europe and elsewhere we can work with the Communists. Let them come to Berlin" — as we have seen, was delivered *after* the American University speech. Yet in Sorensen's telling of the Kennedy administration, the story was reordered: the Berlin speech was mentioned on pages 331 and 601 of the Sorensen book.

The nonchronological telling fits the narrative that, as Sorensen put it later, Kennedy "started from his father's house as a conservative" and "gradually revised his priorities and principles, accommodating the more liberal positions I was urging upon him."[13] That describes Sorensen as the one with consistent principles and Kennedy as the malleable one, and it describes Sorensen as, in at least one important way, the more powerful partner in the relationship. Such a portrayal may have been flattering to the former aide, or somehow psychologically soothing to him. Whether the portrayal is an accurate one is a different matter. With the perspective of history, the principles of the president who gave the Berlin speech in 1963 and of the young congressman who in 1947 said on a Polish radio broadcast, "There can be no compromise with communism or any other 'ism' which is contrary to the rights of freedom-loving peoples," may seem more consistent than "revised."

Sorensen supported his contention that Kennedy became more liberal over time by writing that JFK "pardoned Communist leader Junius Scales, halted the postal interception of Communist propaganda, welcomed the controversial Linus Pauling into the White House."[14] All three of these points are misleading, however. Scales was not a "Communist leader" but a *former* Communist leader. Kennedy pardoned Scales only after receiving a letter favoring the pardon from the president of the International Ladies' Garment Workers' Union, David Dubinsky. Dubinsky, a friend of Kennedy's, had fought what Dubinsky described in the letter as an eleven-year-long "bitter struggle" against Communists in his union, and he wrote in his letter to Kennedy of "the vital battle against the Communist enemy." Dubinsky, citing the same former editor of the Communist *Daily Worker,* Louis Budenz, who had been the star witness years earlier against Harold Christoffel, said Scales had broken with the Communist Party. Dubinsky wrote to Kennedy that "many former Communists who have renounced the Party are among the most effective fighters against Communism."[15] That, not any conversion by Kennedy to leftism, is the most likely explanation of the Scales pardon.

On the postal interception issue, it is true that Kennedy, following an Eisenhower-Nixon recommendation, announced in March 1961 that he would end the interception program. But it is also true — and unmentioned by Sorensen — that on October 11, 1962, Kennedy, pronouncing himself "delighted," signed into law the Postal Service and Federal Employees Salary Act. That act included the Cunningham Amendment, named for its sponsor, Congressman Glenn Cunningham, Republican of Nebraska. The amendment stated, "Mail matter, except sealed letters, which originates or which is printed or otherwise prepared in a foreign country and which is determined by the Secretary of the Treasury pursuant to rules and regulations to be promulgated by him to be 'communist political propaganda,' shall be detained by the Postmaster General upon its arrival for delivery in the United

States, or upon its subsequent deposit in the United States domestic mails." It was the Kennedy administration's post office that in 1963 intercepted a copy of the *Peking Review* mailed to Corliss Lamont, and it was the Kennedy administration's lawyers who defended the law in court when Lamont challenged it in the litigation that ultimately gave rise to the Supreme Court case *Lamont v. Postmaster General.*[16]

As for Linus Pauling, he was invited to the White House not in connection with some reconciliation or conversion by President Kennedy to Pauling's left-wing political views, but rather as part of an April 1962 dinner that included Pauling as one of forty-six American Nobel laureates in attendance. Excluding Pauling would only have played into his hands by giving him more publicity. Sorensen's book mentioned Pauling's visit to the White House, but it did not mention that, as we have seen, even after the visit Pauling continued to agitate publicly against Kennedy's policies, including what he described as the president's "dirty cruel war" in Vietnam.

Nor did Sorensen's accuracy improve with time. In his 2008 book *Counselor,* Sorensen claimed, "In his foreign policy speeches, JFK stayed out of the terminology trap, the common tendency to label groups with names that put them beyond the pale of negotiation, such as 'Communist,' or 'enemy,' or 'evil.'"[17] Yet, as we have seen, at Assumption College in 1955, Kennedy spoke of the Cold War in terms of "Good versus Evil, right versus wrong." At the Mormon Tabernacle in 1960, Kennedy said, "The enemy is the communist system itself — implacable, insatiable, unceasing in its drive for world domination." And at Berlin in 1963, Kennedy said, "There are some who say in Europe and elsewhere we can work with the Communists. Let them come to Berlin."

Jacqueline Kennedy tried again with Arthur Schlesinger, as she had with White and Sorensen. In seven conversations between March and June 1964, which yielded eight and a half hours of tape-recorded interviews, the president's widow made clear how she felt about liberals. She described one Wisconsin newspaper reporter as "a terrible man. Again, a wild-eyed liberal creature." She said, "You can name so many violently liberal women in politics who were always suspicious of Jack." As for the warming of relations with the Soviet Union in 1963,

188 · JFK, CONSERVATIVE

Jacqueline Kennedy said the president never had any illusions. "When things got nicer about Khrushchev, you know, after the détente and everything, he always used to say — well, remember what he said after Vienna, that he really is a gangster, and so everybody mustn't get deluded. But if you deal with him out of firmness — it's different. But he never wanted people to think that now Khrushchev is the sweet, benign, undangerous person." Listing "the great things Jack did," she omitted the nuclear test ban treaty and the American University speech, but did include "the tax bill."[18]

When Schlesinger's book on the Kennedy administration, *A Thousand Days*, came out in 1965, it took the same approach Sorensen did, reversing the chronology of the Berlin and American University speeches. The Berlin speech appears on pages 884 and 885 of *A Thousand Days*; the American University speech and the reaction to it appear on pages 900 to 905, in a chapter titled "The Pursuit of Peace." In fairness, not all narratives must follow a strictly chronological sequence. This account has departed from such a structure at times. But with Schlesinger as with Sorensen, reversing the order of the two speeches is a specious way of advancing the liberal interpretive line being put forth by the presidential-aides-turned-authors. Schlesinger wrote that the American University speech, "in its modesty, clarity, and perception, repudiated the self-righteous cold war rhetoric of a succession of secretaries of state." He wrote further of Kennedy, "For two and a half years he had quietly striven to free his countrymen from the clichés of the cold war . . . The American University speech was the climax of a long campaign."[19]

Both Sorensen and Schlesinger, while quoting extensively from the American University speech in their books, entirely excised its two most hawkish lines: "As Americans, we find communism profoundly repugnant as a negation of personal freedom and dignity," and "The Communist drive to impose their political and economic system on others is the primary cause of world tension today."

Neither Sorensen nor Schlesinger deserve blanket condemnations. Their books are both valuable sources on many Kennedy-related topics. Schlesinger's in particular is beautifully written, particularly the opening and closing passages. Schlesinger, too, is humble enough to acknowledge that his effort was only a "personal memoir" that, "at best, can offer only a partial view." He acknowledged that recovering the president's own perspective would be the work of some future historian, "today perhaps a very young man," who would "read the volumes of reminiscence and analysis" and "immerse himself in the flood of papers in the Kennedy Library" and "do the best he can."[20] One can nonetheless understand at least one possible reason that Jacqueline Kennedy, in September 1966, was reportedly "deeply critical of all books about her husband, even Schlesinger's *A Thousand Days.*"[21]

If neither Sorensen nor Schlesinger would transmit Kennedy's legacy with full fidelity, perhaps Lyndon Johnson, the man Kennedy had chosen as his vice president, would do better. Johnson kept the Kennedy cabinet intact, at least initially. And when Johnson spoke to a joint session of Congress on November 27, 1963, he pressed for action on two of Kennedy's pieces of domestic legislation, the tax bill and the civil rights bill. "First, no memorial oration or eulogy could more eloquently honor President Kennedy's memory than the earliest possible passage of the civil rights bill for which he fought so long," Johnson said. "And second, no act of ours could more fittingly continue the work of President Kennedy than the early passage of the tax bill for which he fought all this long year."

The civil rights bill did pass, as did the tax cut, known as the Revenue Act of 1964. Johnson's strong relationships with key Senate conservatives, especially Harry Byrd of Virginia, who chaired the Finance Committee, helped. Congress did, however, tinker with the original tax proposal. Where Kennedy had wanted the top individual income tax rate lowered to 65 percent from 91 percent, the final law set it at 70 percent. Where Kennedy wanted to cut the top long-term capital gains rate to 19.5 percent (or the 65 percent rate applied to 30 percent of the gains) in exchange for getting rid of the automatic step-up in basis at death, the final law left the rate unchanged at 25 percent (or a 50 percent rate applied to 50 percent of the gains).[22]

Even the changed proposal, though, was enough of a rate reduction that the economy reacted precisely as Kennedy had predicted, with robust economic growth that in turn yielded increased federal revenues. Commerce Department statistics show that the American economy grew at a 7.4 percent annual rate in 1964, 8.4 percent in 1965, and 9.5 percent in 1966, far exceeding Kennedy's 5 percent target of the 1960 campaign, even after inflation is taken into account (the inflation-adjusted numbers, says the Commerce Department, are 5.8 percent in 1964, 6.4 percent in 1965, and 6.5 percent in 1966). As for federal revenues, they grew, in current dollars, to $112.6 billion in 1964, $116.8 billion in 1965, and $130.8 billion in 1966, from their level before the tax rate reductions of $106.6 billion in 1963, according to the historical tables of the White House Office of Management and Budget. Senator Barry Goldwater, who had opposed the cut, conceded, "Kennedy was right on this. His tax cut did stimulate the economy. Federal tax collection increased even at the lower rate."[23]

In a series of interviews conducted for the JFK Library's oral history program in 1964, Treasury Secretary Douglas Dillon made clear he hoped that Kennedy's tax cut would be the beginning of a pattern. "We felt that 70 [percent] was a little higher than desirable," he said. "Tax reduction will have to be a continuing part of any program to keep our economy in proper fiscal balance."

The interviewer followed up: "You see the '64 cut then as very likely being one of a series of additional cuts to come in future years?" Dillon replied, "Yes."

Dillon then speculated about at least two possible scenarios for such tax cuts. One was an end to the Cold War, in which, he said, "there would have to be quite a readjustment — a large reduction of expenditures accompanied by tax reduction." Another would be "a voluntary approach" under which a taxpayer "could forego voluntarily all loopholes, and as a counterpart obtain the benefit of a much lower rate schedule."[24]

Alas, President Johnson, rather than pressing for additional tax cuts, called in his January 1967 State of the Union address for "a surcharge of 6 percent on both corporate and individual income taxes." Johnson also abandoned Kennedy's restraint when it came to government spending; expenditures soared to $178 billion in 1968, from $111 billion in 1963, according to the historical tables of the Office of Management and Budget. These outlays were not only for military spending on the sharply escalated war in Vietnam, but also for the Great Society programs that went far beyond Kennedy's domestic agenda.

Apportioning credit, or blame, to Kennedy for legislation passed during the Johnson administration must be done with considerable care. The tax cut and the Civil Rights Act of 1964 were widely credited to Kennedy. Some historians go further and, in making the case that Kennedy was a liberal, credit him for Johnson-era programs such as Medicare and for the creation of the Department of Housing and Urban Development and the Office of Economic Opportunity, headed by Kennedy's brother-in-law R. Sargent Shriver, which included legal services for the poor and the Head Start program for early-childhood education.[25] Yet it was Johnson, not Kennedy, who gave priority to what he called the War on Poverty. Johnson himself, at least in one conversation the day after the assassination, made it clear that in so doing, he was shifting his approach from that of his predecessor. "I'm no budget slasher," Johnson told Walter Heller. "As a matter of fact, to tell the truth, John F. Kennedy was a little too conservative to suit my taste."[26]

Some of that may have been Johnson playing to his audience and trying to please Heller, a liberal economist and adviser to Kennedy. At about the same time, in different conversations, Johnson was telling conservatives and business leaders he would be more of a budget cutter than Kennedy was. But to the extent the comment to Heller signaled a shift rather than continuity, it was telling.

Any effort by Johnson to assume the Kennedy legacy fully, moreover, was complicated by the survival of Robert Kennedy, who, as attorney general and the close adviser and brother of the slain president, and with a speaking voice eerily similar to his brother's, was immediately the subject of national political attention and interest.

Robert Kennedy and his family made a presidential-style visit to Poland, where they were mobbed by adoring crowds despite a Communist news blackout on his visit.[27] When he returned, he was disappointed not to be called to the White House by Johnson.[28] Richard

Goodwin, who now served as President Johnson's chief speechwriter, wrote later of "the depth of Johnson's hostility toward Bobby Kennedy, the intensity of his desire to establish himself not as an heir to Kennedy, but as master and architect of a new Johnson administration." So, Goodwin accurately predicted in his diary, Johnson would not choose Robert Kennedy as his running mate in 1964: "LBJ probably hates Bobby so much that he won't take him under any circumstances."[29]

One staffer who worked for both Robert and John Kennedy, Milton Gwirtzman, recalled, "Three or four months after the assassination Johnson saw one of the Secret Service men wearing a PT-boat tie clip, and he took it off him and threw it away. And as I heard the story this particular Secret Service man walked over, retrieved it, and put it back on, and he was reassigned. Now, you know, there may be nothing at all in that story but Robert Kennedy heard that story. He believed it, and he didn't like it because it was disrespectful toward his brother."[30]

If President Johnson would not be John Kennedy's political heir, perhaps Robert Kennedy would. RFK detailed the history of his brother's administration in eleven oral history interview sessions, conducted by the Kennedy Library from February 1964 to August 1967. In addition, he wrote a memoir of the Cuban Missile Crisis, *Thirteen Days*. In one of the oral history sessions, on April 30, 1964, the interviewer, John B. Martin, pressed Robert Kennedy about Vietnam:

> KENNEDY: The president . . . had a strong, overwhelming reason for being in Vietnam and that we should win the war in Vietnam.
>
> MARTIN: What was the overwhelming reason?
>
> KENNEDY: Just the loss of all of Southeast Asia if you lost Vietnam. I think everybody was quite clear that the rest of Southeast Asia would fall.
>
> MARTIN: What if it did?
>
> KENNEDY: Just have profound effects as far as our position throughout the world, and our position in a rather vital part of the world. Also, it would affect what happened in India, of course, which in turn has an effect on the Middle East. Just as

it would have, everybody felt, a very adverse effect. It would have an effect on Indonesia, hundred million population. All of these countries would be affected by the fall of Vietnam to the Communists . . .

MARTIN: There was never any consideration given to pulling out?

KENNEDY: No.

MARTIN: . . . The president was convinced that we had to keep, had to stay in there . . .

KENNEDY: Yes.

MARTIN: . . . And couldn't lose it.

KENNEDY: Yes.

Others close to John F. Kennedy have since offered other assessments. Kenneth O'Donnell's 1970 book *"Johnny, We Hardly Knew Ye"* claimed Kennedy "told me privately" that "he had made up his mind that after his reelection he would take the risk of unpopularity and make a complete withdrawal of American military forces from Vietnam." The same book also quotes Kennedy telling O'Donnell and Dave Powers, "I'll never send draftees over there to fight."[31] Robert McNamara's 1995 book *In Retrospect* observes that in 1965 even David Halberstam wrote that choosing the option of an American withdrawal "means a drab, lifeless, and controlled society for people who deserve better . . . means that the United States' prestige will be lowered throughout the world . . . means that the pressure of Communism on the rest of Southeast Asia will intensify . . . means that throughout the world the enemies of the West will be encouraged to try insurgencies like the one in Vietnam." McNamara writes that President Kennedy never disclosed his intentions, but the former defense secretary also concludes, "John Kennedy would have eventually gotten out of Vietnam rather than move more deeply in."[32] In his 2009 memoir *True Compass*, Edward Kennedy writes, "Toward midsummer 1963, I was aware that my brother had qualms about Vietnam. He felt that we needed a new and different direction. He had a growing understanding that the conflict could not be resolved militarily, and I feel very strongly that he certainly would not have escalated it. I witnessed elements of this process unfolding, and Jack affirmed it to me himself in private conversations."[33]

President Kennedy and the national security team he brought into office have been faulted for leading the country into the Vietnam War without clear objectives, without a formal declaration of war, and without an exit strategy. The United States lost the war and along with it the lives of fifty-eight thousand American soldiers, sustaining significant damage to its international prestige. That criticism, however merited, should be discounted for the fact that South Vietnam fell to Communist North Vietnam only in April of 1975, more than eleven years after Kennedy's death, and only after Congress cut off the aid South Vietnam needed to defend itself under the peace agreement that had been reached in 1973. To this day, the leadership of Communist Vietnam imprisons political opponents and religious leaders and denies its citizens a free press or the right to organize free or independent labor unions.[34]

One of the many consequences of John F. Kennedy's assassination is that how he would have handled Vietnam is a matter of speculation rather than historical fact. Robert Kennedy's stance is one guide that may be useful, although not definitive. Even after leaving the Johnson administration and winning election in 1964 as a U.S. senator from New York, Robert Kennedy defended the Vietnam War. On May 15, 1967, in a joint television appearance on CBS with the governor of California, a Republican named Ronald Reagan, Robert Kennedy was confronted by a student who asserted, "I believe the war in Vietnam is illegal, immoral, politically unjustifiable and economically motivated." Senator Kennedy replied, "I don't agree with that. I have some reservations as I've stated them before about some aspects of the war, but I think that the United States is making every effort to try to make it possible for the people of South Vietnam to determine their own destiny . . . The fact is that the insurgency against — that's taking place in South Vietnam is being supported by North Vietnam. If both of us withdraw and let the people of South Vietnam determine and decide what they want . . . that's all we're interested in, that's all we're interested in accomplishing."

Reagan replied that he and Kennedy were "very much in agreement" on the point.[35] As late as March 1968, Kennedy, while favoring a halt to American bombing in Vietnam, said of the option to "pull out of South Vietnam unilaterally and raise the white flag": "I think that's unacceptable."[36]

For such statements, and for actions earlier in his career, he was protested and attacked by antiwar radicals. On April 19, 1968, at an appearance at the University of San Francisco, he was shouted down by demonstrators calling him a "fascist pig" and yelling "Victory for the Viet Cong."[37]

When Robert Kennedy finally veered against the war and also began to speak in passionate detail about race and poverty in America, it troubled some of John F. Kennedy's old allies, including Kennedy's assistant secretary of labor, Daniel Patrick Moynihan. "More and more, or so it seemed to me, he was being used by an all too familiar upper middle class radical," Moynihan wrote in July 1968. "The people who surrounded Bob when he later went to New York were precisely the ones who were against us — who held him and his brother and the whole tradition in the party that they represented in contempt . . . I would hate to see a memorial to Bob fashioned in the image of whatever is the current vogue in upper middle class models of social change on behalf of whatever segment of the lower orders that are currently most in favor in the salons of Central Park West. Community action, neighborhood corporations, black, green, yellow power, peril, or whatever. Bob Kennedy as a political man descended from a tradition of stable, working class urban politics. It is the only element, so far as I can see, in the political system that ever did anything for him or for his family. That tradition is very much isolated now, and very much in trouble."[38]

No matter Moynihan's concerns about "the people who surrounded Bob," as both a senator and a presidential candidate, Robert Kennedy nonetheless managed to convey some of his brother's conservative ideas and ideals. In a series of speeches in January 1966, Kennedy criticized the welfare programs that were expanding under President Johnson. "Recent studies have shown, for example, that higher welfare payments often encourage students to drop out of school, that they often encourage families to disintegrate, and that they often lead to lifelong dependency," he said, asserting that "there is factual support" for the position "that welfare was the worst thing that could have happened to the Negro."[39] On April 28, 1968, just under a month after President Johnson announced he would not seek reelection, the *New York Times* headlined an article on RFK's presidential campaign, "Kennedy: Meet the Conservative":

> First and foremost, Mr. Kennedy is emphasizing criticism of the Federal Government as a bureaucracy, he is championing local autonomy, and endorsing the old Republican slogan: "The best government is a government closest to the people."
>
> "We can't have the Federal Government in here telling people what's good for them," he told a college audience in Fort Wayne. "I want to bring that control back to the localities so that people can decide for themselves what they think is best for themselves."
>
> The senator is harshly critical of the concept of execution of welfare, that hallowed cornerstone of Democratic liberalism. "We've got to get away from the welfare system, the handout system and the idea of the dole," he said in Kokomo. "We've got to have jobs instead of welfare."

Robert Kennedy was assassinated on June 5, 1968, as he walked through the kitchen of the Ambassador Hotel in Los Angeles after winning the California Democratic presidential primary. A Jerusalem-born Jordanian citizen, Sirhan Sirhan, who was twenty-four at the time of the shooting, was convicted of the crime.

The death of Robert Kennedy was a tragedy in many ways small and large. Among other consequences, it meant that it would be more than a decade before John F. Kennedy's policies of tax cuts and a military buildup would be tried again.

CHAPTER 10

Passing the Torch

1968 to the Future

What he was, he was:
What he is fated to become
Depends on us.

— W. H. AUDEN, *Elegy for J.F.K.,* 1964[1]

R ICHARD NIXON WOULD DRIVE the nation in a direction far from where John Kennedy was steering it at the time of his death. On the surface, there were similarities between the men. Both had served in the Navy as officers; they entered Congress in the same year and served together on the Education and Labor Committee; and, until the 1960 campaign, they were on friendly terms. But the policies of their administrations contrasted starkly. The irony is that Nixon pursued a more liberal path than the conservative one Kennedy followed.

Under President Nixon, federal spending soared to $269 billion in 1974, from $184 billion in 1969, an increase of about 46 percent over five years. Nixon created the Occupational Safety and Health Administration, the National Transportation Safety Board, the Environmental Protection Agency, and the Consumer Product Safety Commission. He quadrupled the staff of the Equal Employment Opportunity Commission and increased the budget of the National Endowment for the Arts by 637 percent. He convened a White House nutrition summit, declared a federal War on Hunger and a War on Cancer, and campaigned for national health insurance and a government-run daycare program. He instituted the first federal Earth Week and signed the Clean Air Act of 1970. He imposed nationwide controls on wages and prices, created the Alternative Minimum Tax on personal income that stalks upper-middle-class taxpayers to this day, and closed the "gold window" that had allowed the dollar to be converted to a solid standard. He ended the war in Vietnam, warmed relations with the Soviet Union, and opened American ties with Communist China.[2]

Nixon had campaigned in 1968 on a pledge to "end the war" in Vietnam and replace the "era of confrontation" with the Soviet Union with an "era of negotiation." In his inaugural address, he spoke of peace as emphatically as Kennedy had stressed liberty and freedom. "For the first time, because the people of the world want peace, and the leaders of the world are afraid of war, the times are on the side of peace," Nixon said. "The greatest honor history can bestow is the title of peacemaker. This honor now beckons America — the chance to help lead the world at last out of the valley of turmoil and onto that high ground of peace that man has dreamed of since the dawn of civilization."

Nixon used the word "peace" or a variation of it fifteen times. "We shall plan now for the day when our wealth can be transferred from the destruction of war abroad to the urgent needs of our people at home . . . Let us take as our goal: Where peace is unknown, make it welcome; where peace is fragile, make it strong; where peace is temporary, make it permanent . . . I have taken an oath today in the presence of God and my countrymen to uphold and defend the Constitution of the United States. To that oath I now add this sacred commitment: I shall consecrate my office, my energies, and all the wisdom I can summon to the cause of peace among nations."

Nixon backed up his words with deeds. He negotiated and entered into an antiballistic missile treaty with the Soviet Union whose provisions restricted future presidents who hoped to deploy a system to defend America against incoming missiles. He negotiated and entered into a nuclear arms control agreement with the Soviet Union known as SALT I — the "SALT" stands for Strategic Arms Limitation Talks — that limited both land-based and submarine-based missiles.[3] He unilaterally renounced the use of biological weapons, and negotiated a

Biological Weapons Convention by which the USSR and other nations agreed to do the same (a treaty the Soviets promptly ignored, continuing research and development while the United States stopped work in the field). He negotiated an end to the Vietnam War, but after North Vietnam breached the peace and Congress cut off funds to enforce it, more than a million Vietnamese fled their country in small boats. And he negotiated new relations between America and China, meeting Mao Tse-tung, holding hands with him "for about a minute" and telling him, fawningly, "The chairman's writings moved a nation and changed the world."[4]

The opening to China has been hailed as a brilliant geostrategic stroke for exploiting a rift between China and the Soviet Union, but there has been little attention given to alternative scenarios or to exploring whether, if America had withheld recognition, the Chinese Communist government would have expired when the one in Moscow did. Just how far Nixon was willing to go in pursuit of improved relations with the Soviet Union was clear in his reaction to an attempt by American Jewish activists and members of Congress to link freedom of emigration for Soviet Jewry to Soviet trade privileges with the United States. Nixon fought vigorously against it, to the point of summoning fourteen Jewish leaders to a White House meeting at which Henry Kissinger asked them to get Congress to back down.[5] The president laid out his reasoning in a June 5, 1974, commencement address at the U.S. Naval Academy at Annapolis, in which he described American anticommunism as "simplistic and occasionally misguided," and warned that "unrealistic idealism could be impractical and potentially dangerous." Nixon went on: "We would not welcome the intervention of other countries in our domestic affairs, and we cannot expect them to be cooperative when we seek to intervene directly in theirs. We cannot gear our foreign policy to transformation of other societies."

The Soviet Jewry legislation, known as the Jackson-Vanik Amendment after its sponsors, Senator Henry Jackson and Representative Charles Vanik, was eventually passed after Nixon left office, and the continued differences over it illuminate better than nearly anything the differences between Nixon and the anti-Communist hawks. A hardliner against the Soviet Union who served in the Defense Department in the Reagan administration, Richard Perle, has called Jackson-Vanik "arguably the most important piece of legislation in the century." Perle, who as a member of Jackson's Senate staff helped to draft the amendment, argued, "It had a galvanizing effect on millions of Soviet citizens — Jews and non-Jews — who understood that people in the West . . . were willing to stand with people seeking freedom."[6] That, in turn, helped to topple the Soviet Union. Nixon, as late as a 1983 interview, called Jackson-Vanik "a great mistake."[7]

If Nixon was moving abroad to improve relations with the Communists in Russia, China, and Vietnam, he was also acting at home to bring a more socialist-style bureaucracy, central planning, and redistribution of wealth to America.

In a speech on August 15, 1971, Nixon imposed wage and price controls. "I am today ordering a freeze on all prices and wages throughout the United States for a period of 90 days," Nixon said, emphasizing that the action would be "temporary." The ninety-day freeze wound up lasting until April 1974, nearly three years. In the same speech, Nixon announced "an additional tax of 10 percent on goods imported into the United States," a reversal of Kennedy's free-trade policies.

On health care, Nixon asked Congress to enact what he called "comprehensive health insurance," which would offer benefits "identical for all Americans, regardless of age or income." The plan was to cover everyone, regardless of preexisting health conditions, and to cover services including not only hospitalization and doctors' visits, but also prescription drugs, medical devices, laboratory tests, and "treatment for mental illness, alcoholism and drug addiction." Nixon declared, in February 1974, "Comprehensive health insurance is an idea whose time has come in America. There has long been a need to assure every American financial access to high quality health care."[8]

On welfare, Nixon, advised by Daniel Patrick Moynihan, proposed a Family Assistance Plan that would guarantee a minimum income to every family. Ronald Reagan, then the governor of California, opposed it, warning of "the potential for evil in adding millions of new people to the relief rolls."[9]

Nixon signed into law a 20 percent increase in Social Security benefits that went into effect a month before the 1972 elections, setting Social Security on a course of expensive cost-of-living adjustments that policymakers ever since have struggled to find funds to maintain.[10]

After his Supreme Court nominees Clement Haynsworth and G. Harrold Carswell failed to win confirmation, Nixon elevated Harry Blackmun, who would become the author of the majority opinion in the landmark *Roe v. Wade* abortion rights decision. Two other justices who were part of the *Roe* majority, Lewis Powell Jr. and Chief Justice Warren Burger, were also Nixon nominees. Powell was the author of the majority opinion in *Regents of the University of California v. Bakke,* which found that some race-based affirmative action programs were constitutionally permissible. Nixon did, however, also appoint William Rehnquist, who dissented in both *Roe* and *Bakke.*

Unlike John F. Kennedy, who had to rely on aides, on family members, and, at least initially, on sympathetic journalists and historians to shape his legacy and his posthumous reputation, Nixon left the presidency scandal-tarred but with the ability to participate in debates over the issues of the day. Writing books, giving speeches, and granting the occasional interview, Nixon tried to dwell not on the Watergate scandal that brought him down but on foreign and domestic policy. He found President Reagan lacking in diplomatic outreach to Moscow, and he criticized Congress, after the Tiananmen Square massacre, for passing a law assuring that none of the forty thousand Chinese students in the United States would be returned to China against their will.

In one book, *In the Arena,* published in 1990, he wrote, "A day did not pass that I did not hate the Vietnam War." In the same volume, he claimed America was "fundamentally isolationist," deriding Kennedy's promise "to support any friend and oppose any foe to assure the success of liberty" as "bad policy." Anticipating, more than a decade in advance, the debates over the wars in Iraq and Afghanistan, he wrote, "We should not make the mistake of trying to impose our system on nations that have neither the traditions nor the institutions to make democracy work." In the same book, he encouraged the president to raise taxes.

And Nixon's influence, perhaps more than Kennedy's, was felt after his presidency by the continued public service of those who had worked in his administration. His United Nations ambassador, George H. W. Bush, became president of the United States. Leon Panetta, who served as chief of civil rights enforcement in Nixon's Department of Health, Education, and Welfare, became President Clinton's White House chief of staff and secretary of defense under President Obama. A deputy director of the Office of Management and Budget in the Nixon administration, Paul O'Neill, was President George W. Bush's Treasury secretary before resigning, complaining that Bush was cutting taxes too much and that the Iraq War was a mistake. Eventually following O'Neill into the office at Treasury was Henry Paulson, who had served on Nixon's Domestic Policy Council from April 1972 to December 1973, the period of wage and price controls. At the end of the George W. Bush administration, Paulson took a similarly aggressive approach during the financial crisis of 2008, using government money to shore up some privately owned businesses and to take over control of others.

Historians, journalists, and public figures, aided by the perspective of time, have been able to begin to see Nixon beyond Watergate, so much so that David Greenberg, now a history professor at Rutgers University, was able to write, in the March 2002 issue of the journal *Reviews in American History,* "The portrait of Nixon as a liberal has more recently been repeated so often by columnists and pundits that it now represents not a challenge to the conventional wisdom but the conventional wisdom itself." Greenberg's characterization may be correct about the circle of professional Nixon scholars, but, as he went on to emphasize, it is less so when it comes to Nixon in the popular imagination.

Nixon may have gone along with some liberal policies to reach accommodation with a Democratic Congress, but in private conversations he expressed more conservative views and impulses. For example, he widened the war in Vietnam before finally ending it. Yet the differences between Nixon and Kennedy remained stark. And as it happened, as Chris Matthews records in his book *Kennedy and Nixon,* Kennedy men helped bring down Nixon. JFK's solicitor general, Archibald Cox, was the Watergate special prosecutor. Kennedy's friend Ben Bradlee was the *Washington Post* editor who published the groundbreaking investigative journalism about the scandal.

Ultimately, what matters is not the particulars of any given year, or scandal, or individual appointee. Nor is it useful to get tangled in competing definitions of "conservative" and "liberal." What matters is the larger pattern and tradition that Kennedy represents — and Nixon opposed. Economic growth, limited government, peace through strength. Since the time of Kennedy and Nixon, the two parties flip-flopped on that tradition. Reagan seized it, while the Democrats mostly rejected it.

Nixon's handpicked successor, Gerald Ford, lost in 1976 to a Democratic peanut farmer who was governor of Georgia, Jimmy Carter. Carter's reputation, shaped in part by his post-presidential self-appointed diplomacy, nowadays is more Nixonian — a big-spending peacenik — than Kennedyesque. Carter twice ran for the Democratic nomination for president against a family member of John Kennedy — first, in 1976, against Sargent Shriver, who had been JFK's Peace Corps director and who was married to JFK's sister Eunice; then, in 1980, against Senator Edward Kennedy. So it would be natural that the relationship between Carter and the legacy of John Kennedy would be somewhat strained.

On the other hand, Carter, like JFK, was a former Navy officer and a religious Christian, so perhaps there would be some surprising affinities. During the 1976 campaign, the artist Jamie Wyeth gave a watercolor sketch of President Kennedy to Carter, who hung it first in his house in Plains, and later in the family quarters of the White House.[11] There were flashes of John F. Kennedy in Carter on both domestic and foreign policy fronts. President Carter appointed as chairman of the Federal Reserve a Kennedy administration Treasury Department official, Paul Volcker, who eventually (though too late for Carter's reelection) succeeded in reining in the runaway inflation of the time. Carter also signed into law the Steiger Amendment, named for William Steiger, a Republican congressman from Wisconsin. The amendment cut the capital gains tax to 28 percent from the effective 49.875 percent maximum level to which it had been increased by Nixon and Ford in

1969 and 1976.[12] Carter did this only after first denouncing the Steiger Amendment as "a step backward," claiming, "This proposal would add more than $2 billion to the Federal budget deficit. Eighty percent of its tax benefits would go to one-half of 1 percent of the American taxpayers, who make more than $100,000 a year. Three thousand millionaires would get tax reductions averaging $214,000. The other 99½ percent of our taxpayers would not do quite so well."[13] Nevertheless, Carter later decided to sign the tax cut into law.

Carter also followed the path President Kennedy had begun in rolling back federal regulations in the energy and transportation sectors. In doing so, he worked with Senator Edward Kennedy to pass the Airline Deregulation Act, or the Kennedy-Cannon bill, which led to the abolition of the Civil Aeronautics Board, to lower fares, and to the rise of discount carriers like People Express and Southwest.[14] The Motor Carrier Act of 1980, deregulating trucking, was another Kennedy-Carter joint effort. At a Miami Beach Democratic Party rally in late October before the 1978 midterm elections, Carter said: "Do you want a government that will get the regulatory agencies' and government agencies' nose out of the private sector's business and let our free enterprise system work in the United States? Well, that's the kind of government we're trying to bring you in Washington . . . When I came in as President, I promised that we were going to deregulate the airline industry . . . I'm committed in the future to bringing deregulation to other industries."[15]

On foreign policy, while Carter is best remembered for the weakness epitomized by the failed helicopter attempt to rescue the American hostages in Iran, he also took several symbolic steps to challenge the Soviet Union that broke with Nixonian détente, imposing an embargo on American grain exports to the Russians and boycotting the 1980 Moscow Olympics.

On October 20, 1979, visiting Boston for the dedication of the new John F. Kennedy Library, Carter tried to claim that in certain respects he reflected President Kennedy's legacy better than Senator Edward Kennedy, who was challenging Carter for the Democratic Party's nomination in 1980. "I feel a political kinship with President Kennedy that's very intense and also very personal," Carter said. He drew a contrast between his own — and, by implication, John F. Kennedy's — positions on spending restraint and on the military and those of Edward Kennedy:

> I think as far as fiscal prudence is concerned, balancing the budget, holding down unnecessary spending, being cautious about what kind of new programs we've put forth that are very expensive, we are in sharp disagreement. Senator Kennedy is much more inclined toward the old philosophy of pouring out new programs and new money to meet a social need. He may be right. I disagree with him. I'm much more inclined to try to make existing programs work efficiently and start up new programs only when it's absolutely necessary.
>
> I think in the matter of a commitment to our Nation's defense strength, I would be in favor of much stronger defense commitments than his record shows.

In the 1980 campaign against Ronald Reagan, Carter tried to liken his plan for a tax cut to President Kennedy's. "In 1963 John Kennedy made a proposal for a similar tax cut," Carter told the Associated Press on October 17, 1980.

But it was Reagan, an Irish American who had fought against Communists in his own labor union, the Screen Actors Guild, who would, in the judgment of many voters, more convincingly lay claim to Kennedy's legacy. As a home base for the 1980 campaign, Reagan rented a house near Middleburg, Virginia, known as Wexford. The name came from the county the Kennedy family had come from in Ireland. In fact, Jacqueline Kennedy had designed the house as a presidential retreat. It was on this estate, once owned by the Kennedys, that Reagan prepared for his presidential debate, with a Republican congressman from Michigan named David Stockman playing Carter, and with the columnist George Will and a Georgetown University professor named Jeane Kirkpatrick posing questions.[16] In his campaign, Reagan faulted Carter's defense policies for having "broken sharply with the views and policies of Harry Truman, John Kennedy, and many contemporary Democratic leaders."[17]

Reagan had begun picking up Kennedy's themes at least as far back as January 25, 1974, when, in an address that became famous as the "city upon a hill" speech, Reagan first made the classic Kennedy point that rights come not from the state but from God: "The difference is so subtle that we often overlook it, but it is so great that it tells the whole story. Those other constitutions say, 'Government grants you these rights,' and ours says, 'You are born with these rights, they are yours by the grace of God, and no government on earth can take them from you.'"

In the same 1974 speech, Reagan went on to quote the same line from John Winthrop that Kennedy had used in his January 9, 1961, address to the Massachusetts General Court. Reagan said, "Standing on the tiny deck of the *Arbella* in 1630 off the Massachusetts coast, John Winthrop said, 'We will be as a city upon a hill. The eyes of all people are upon us, so that if we deal falsely with our God in this work we have undertaken and so cause Him to withdraw His present help from us, we shall be made a story and a byword throughout the world.'"

Reagan returned to the phrase, and really made it his own, in his January 11, 1989, farewell speech to the nation:

> The past few days when I've been at that window upstairs, I've thought a bit of the "shining city upon a hill." The phrase comes from John Winthrop, who wrote it to describe the America he imagined. What he imagined was important because he was an early Pilgrim, an early freedom man. He journeyed here on what today we'd call a little wooden boat; and like the other Pilgrims, he was looking for a home that would be free.
>
> I've spoken of the shining city all my political life, but I don't know if I ever quite communicated what I saw when I said it. But in my mind it was a tall, proud city built on rocks stronger than oceans, windswept, God-blessed, and teeming with people of all kinds living in harmony and peace; a city with free ports that hummed with commerce and creativity. And if there had to be city walls, the walls had doors and the doors were open to anyone with the will and the heart to get here. That's how I saw it, and see it still.

Reagan echoed and even embraced Kennedy's views, not merely in rhetoric but in policy. In 1981, shortly after signing legislation cutting the top income tax rate from 70 percent to 50 percent, Reagan said at a Republican fundraiser in Chicago:

Let me just read you something. "Our true choice is not between tax reduction on the one hand and avoidance of large Federal deficits on the other. An economy stifled by restrictive tax rates will never produce enough revenue to balance the budget, just as it will never produce enough jobs or enough profits." John F. Kennedy said that back in 1962, when he was asking for a tax decrease, a cut in tax rates across the board. And he was proven right, because that — the last tax cut, literally, that we've had — actually produced more revenue for government, because the economy was stimulated and more people were working and there was more industry and productivity in America.[18]

He made a similar point two months later, speaking at a Republican fundraiser in Ohio, portraying his own historic tax cut as following "the same principle" as President Kennedy's:

John Kennedy knew this 20 years ago when he proposed a tax cut based on the same principle. He knew an economy stifled by restrictive tax rates can never produce enough revenue to balance the budget, just as it can never produce enough jobs or enough profits. History proved him right. After enactment of the Kennedy tax cut, the rate of increase in employment almost doubled. The rate of growth in gross national product went from a little over 3 percent before the tax cut to 5 percent after the tax cut, and personal savings jumped from 2.3 percent to 8 percent of the American people's earnings.[19]

Later, in July 1982, Reagan called his own tax cut "the first decent tax program since John Kennedy's tax cut nearly 20 years ago."[20] By 1985, when the nation's economy had begun to grow vigorously, Reagan said, "In truth, we can't take complete credit for the ideas that reignited our current economic growth. After all, John Kennedy had done what we had done, and great growth followed."[21] In his State of the Union address on February 4, 1986, Reagan said, "I believe our tax rate cuts for the people have done more to spur a spirit of risk-taking and help America's economy break free than any program since John Kennedy's tax cut almost a quarter century ago."

Reagan praised Kennedy not only for his tax cuts, but for his restraint in spending. "Through the Kennedy years, we kept spending in check. During those Kennedy years there was a tax cut proposed similar to our cut. It was enacted in 1964, and the economy grew then as it has grown now," Reagan said in a televised prime-time address in 1985 on the federal budget.[22]

After the October 1987 stock market plunge, in which the Dow Jones Industrial Average declined 22 percent, Reagan again cited Kennedy's example:

> Two significant stock market declines in this century that had two different aftermaths can help us determine our best course of action. In 1929 the market crashed, and later the economy sank and stayed sunk. In another case, in 1962 the stock market, over a 4-month period, lost almost a third of its value. This market slide was followed by the most robust period of growth in United States history.
>
> What made the difference? Well, after the 1929 market drop, President Herbert Hoover signed into law protectionist trade legislation; and in 1932, at the depth of the market crash, the Congress, taking exactly the wrong action, passed tax increases that condemned the people of America to the Great Depression. In stark contrast, in 1962, with a market in a critical decline, the Trade Expansion Act was passed; and President Kennedy proposed dramatic tax rate cuts. Our economy took off, and the American people enjoyed an unprecedented period of high growth and low inflation.[23]

Reagan also looked to Kennedy for inspiration on foreign policy and defense issues. On June 11, 1982, Reagan went to Berlin and said, "We all remember John Kennedy's stirring words when he visited Berlin. I can only add that we in America and in the West are still Berliners, too, and always will be." When Reagan returned to Berlin on June 12, 1987, to demand, "Mr. Gorbachev, tear down this wall!" his speech began, "Twenty-four years ago, President John F. Kennedy visited Berlin."

In November 1982, in a televised address to the American people on arms control, Reagan cited Kennedy's military spending as a model. "You often hear that the United States and the Soviet Union are in an arms race," he said. "Well, the truth is that while the Soviet Union has raced, we have not . . . In 1962, when John Kennedy was President, 46 percent, almost half of the Federal budget, went to our national defense. In recent years, about one quarter of our budget has gone to defense, while the share for social programs has nearly doubled . . .

Unless we demonstrate the will to rebuild our strength, the Soviets have little incentive to negotiate."[24]

Reagan made a similar point in April 1984: "The 1970's were marked by neglect of our defenses . . . Too many forgot John Kennedy's warning that only when our arms are certain beyond doubt can we be certain beyond doubt they will never be used."[25] And again in March 1985: "All the great leaders of our time, from Winston Churchill to John Kennedy, have understood that to maintain the peace we must maintain our strength. If we don't, our adversaries will be inspired to wild action by our weakness."[26]

In May 1984, Reagan turned to Kennedy for support on another foreign policy point, aid to anti-Communists in Latin America. In a televised prime-time address from the Oval Office, Reagan said:

> We're in the midst of what President John F. Kennedy called "a long twilight struggle" to defend freedom in the world. He understood the problem of Central America. He understood Castro. And he understood the long-term goals of the Soviet Union in this region.
>
> Twenty-three years ago, President Kennedy warned against the threat of Communist penetration in our hemisphere. He said, "I want it clearly understood that this government will not hesitate in meeting its primary obligations which are to the security of our nation." And the House and Senate supported him overwhelmingly by passing a law calling on the United States to prevent Cuba from extending its aggressive or subversive activities to any part of this hemisphere. Were John Kennedy alive today, I think he would be appalled by the gullibility of some who invoke his name.[27]

In the heat of the 1984 presidential campaign, Reagan portrayed himself as the heir to Kennedy, and he faulted the modern Democratic Party for straying from JFK's policies. "For the first time since the administration of John Kennedy, we cut tax rates significantly for every working American," Reagan said in an August 18 radio address.

In Warren, Michigan, on October 10, while running for reelection, Reagan noted the flip-flop of the parties: "Whenever I talk about Franklin Delano Roosevelt or Harry Truman or John F. Kennedy, my opponents start tearing their hair out. They just can't stand it. Well, of course they can't, because it highlights how far they, the leadership today of the Democratic Party, have strayed from the strength of the democratic political tradition . . . When John Kennedy was President, he didn't push a program of dreary mediocrity with endless tax increases on those who dream of better days. He challenged Americans, just as we're challenging you today, to make America grow and to make America great by pushing for lower personal income tax rates for all the working people of America. And there was a great similarity between his tax cut program and the one that we implemented in 1981."

After winning reelection, Reagan, in May of 1985, went to Senator Edward Kennedy's house in Virginia for a fundraiser for the John F. Kennedy Library Foundation. Reagan said then that President Kennedy had "understood the tension between good and evil in the history of man; understood, indeed, that much of the history of man can be seen in the constant working out of that tension. He knew that the United States had adversaries, real adversaries, and they weren't about to be put off by soft reason and good intentions. He tried always to be strong with them and shrewd. He wanted our defense system to be unsurpassed. He cared that his country could be safe."[28]

One can spot Reagan's portrait of Kennedy in print from time to time. One of Vermont Royster's successors as editor of the *Wall Street Journal*, Robert Bartley, wrote an account of the 1980s economic boom, *The Seven Fat Years and How to Do It Again*. Bartley explained that Reagan's tax cuts were inspired in part by JFK's: "The Kennedy tax cuts, passed after the martyred president's death, cut the top rate . . . The 1960s expansion ensued . . . Yes, it was possible for a tax cut to recoup revenues. The Kennedy tax cuts had."[29] A colleague of Bartley's on the *Journal*'s editorial page, Jude Wanniski, wrote, "In a real sense, the Reagan Revolution did not begin with Reagan . . . but with President Kennedy's 1962 proposal to get the country moving again by slashing the top rate on personal income to 65% from 91%." As Wanniski, who voted for Kennedy in 1960, told it, the Reagan tax cuts began in March 1976, when Wanniski, visiting Washington, stopped by the office of "another 'JFK,'" Jack French Kemp, a former professional quarterback who was a Republican congressman representing Buffalo, New York. Wanniski wrote, "I suggested he think of the Kennedy tax cuts as a model." When Kemp and Senator William Roth of Delaware took up the idea, Wanniski hailed it in a *Wall Street Journal* editorial, "JFK Strikes Again."[30] The Kemp-Roth tax cut was signed into law by Reagan as the Economic Recovery Tax Act of 1981.

By the mid-1980s, with the Sorensen and Schlesinger books nearly two decades old, even some journalists on the left, perhaps prompted by the president's rhetoric, were beginning to recognize parallels between Reagan and JFK. Richard Walton, who had worked for Voice of America in the Kennedy administration, told *Newsweek,* "It's amusing how much Kennedy resembles Ronald Reagan, or vice versa. I mean his interventionism, his meddling in the Caribbean and Latin America, his wanting to increase our missile strength, his almost holy-crusade view of the Soviet Union."[31] The February/March 1984 number of the left-leaning San Francisco–based magazine *Mother Jones* carried a piece by Adam Hochschild titled "Would JFK Be a Hero Now?" In it, Hochschild recalls being a college student and picketing the Kennedy White House with a peace group. He writes of Kennedy, "He accepted all the clichés of the Cold War and slung them about as carelessly and as sweepingly as any other president before Ronald Reagan." The piece went on: "He raised a campaign alarm about the 'missile gap' between the U.S. and the Soviet Union and continued his huge armaments buildup even when shown that the gap was imaginary. He presided over a large increase in U.S. military involvement in Vietnam while keeping much of it secret from the American public . . . By sanctioning the Bay of Pigs invasion, Kennedy gave Fidel Castro an incentive to allow Soviet missiles in Cuba, thus setting the stage for the missile crisis, for the humiliation of the Soviet Union ('I cut his balls off,' Kennedy said of Khrushchev) and for the long Soviet military buildup that followed . . . Kennedy's rhetoric two decades ago rivaled Reagan's today and often implied the same assumptions about America's right to make the world as we see fit."

By the 1980s, it was the Robert Bartleys and Ronald Reagans of the world celebrating Kennedy, and the peace movement veterans of *Mother Jones* criticizing JFK. The Soviet Union, in the end, was not just humiliated but defeated, thanks in part to the Reagan military buildup, to Pope John Paul II, and to the Poles, whose Solidarity union led by Lech Wałęsa challenged the puppets the Kremlin had installed in Warsaw: "History shows that on many occasions, Poland saved the continent of Europe from being over-ridden by aggressors and saved Christianity and civilization," as Kennedy had put it prophetically back in that 1947 radio broadcast. With the Soviet threat gone, and with Reagan's successor, President George H. W. Bush, having departed from the Reagan-Kennedy tradition by agreeing to an increase in income tax rates, voters were finally ready to return the White House to the Democrats.

Actually, not to "the Democrats," but to one particular Democrat, the governor of Arkansas, Bill Clinton. Clinton's formal introduction to the nation came in a thirteen-minute biographical video at the 1992 Democratic National Convention in New York City, "The Man from Hope." Nearly a full minute of the video was devoted to an encounter in the White House Rose Garden between President Kennedy and the seventeen-year-old Clinton. "It was in July of 1963 that I went to Washington and met President Kennedy at the Boys Nation program," Clinton said in the voice-over. "And he came out and you know made a few little comments. We were all standing there in alphabetical order so Arkansas was near the front of the line and I was the biggest kid there, so I made sure that I got to shake hands with him. And I remember just thinking what an incredible country this was, that somebody like me who came from a little town in Arkansas, who you know had no money, no political position or anything, would be given the opportunity to meet the president." The convention video then cut to Clinton's mother, Virginia Kelley, who said: "When he came home from Boys Nation with this picture of John Kennedy and himself shaking hands, I've never seen such an expression on a man's face in my life. He just had such pride." The archival White House footage of Kennedy and Clinton shaking hands was shown again briefly at the very end of the video, as Clinton's voice said, "I still believe in the promise of America."

In case any voters missed the point, the video that had been shown at the convention was condensed into a sixty-second television commercial. The footage of the Kennedy-Clinton handshake was an important part of that, too.

At times it seemed that Bill Clinton was not so much living his own

presidency as reliving JFK's. The day before Clinton's presidential inauguration, he visited Kennedy's grave at Arlington, where he knelt,
bowed his head, bit his lip, and left a single white rose.[32] Invited to
speak at the centennial of American University, President Clinton
noted that it was where Kennedy gave what "many Americans still believe . . . was the finest speech he ever delivered."[33] He appointed Jean
Kennedy Smith, a sister of John Kennedy, as ambassador to Ireland.
Signing into law the bill to create the AmeriCorps national service
program, Clinton used a pen JFK had used to sign the Peace Corps
into law thirty-two years earlier.[34] When Clinton pushed for freer trade
through the North American Free Trade Agreement, he went to the
Kennedy Library in Boston, spoke of President Kennedy's record on
trade, and said that "here in Boston, Congressman Joseph P. Kennedy,
his predecessor Speaker O'Neill, from the congressional seat that John
Kennedy once occupied, have endorsed this new expansion of America's interest. And I believe if President Kennedy were still representing
that seat in Congress, he would endorse it as well."[35] Arriving in Caracas, Clinton announced, "Thirty-six years ago, John Kennedy became
the first American President to visit Venezuela."[36] Anticipating another
foreign trip, he said, "In 3 weeks, when I travel to Africa, my first stop
will be Ghana, the first place President Kennedy's Peace Corps volunteers went to serve."[37]

Clinton's linking of his own career to Kennedy's set him up for criticism when his failures were compared with those of his role model.
When, in April 1993, federal agents raided the Branch Davidian compound in Waco, Texas, and seventy-five people died, some commentators likened it to the failed Bay of Pigs invasion in April of Kennedy's
first year.[38] When Clinton was caught in an extramarital affair with a
White House intern, pundits pondered whether it was DNA testing or
the attitudes of the press that had changed since the days of President
Kennedy, whose womanizing never mired his presidency in scandal or
produced an impeachment vote, as Clinton's did.

Clinton's successes can be compared to Kennedy's. Like Kennedy,
he lowered tariffs. Clinton's mechanism was the North American Free
Trade Agreement and the negotiations of the General Agreement on
Tariffs and Trade and its successor the World Trade Organization.

Lawrence Summers, who was Treasury secretary at the end of the Clinton administration, called the tariff reductions "the largest tax cut in the history of the world."[39] Where President Kennedy had sought to reduce the capital gains tax rate to 19.5 percent from 25 percent, Clinton in 1997 signed into law a reduction in the rate to 20 percent from 28 percent. As both John and Robert Kennedy had sought to, he reformed welfare to emphasize work. An economic boom followed the tax cuts and the welfare reform. As Kennedy had been willing, with caution, to flex American military muscle in Berlin, Cuba, and Vietnam, Clinton launched missile attacks against Sudan, Afghanistan, and Iraq, and used American planes to bomb targets in the former Yugoslavia.

Yet Clinton's failings, too, can be seen in contrast to Kennedy's actions. While JFK wanted to lower income taxes for everyone, Clinton increased the topmost rate to 39.6 percent, up from the 28 percent at which it had been left at the end of the Reagan administration, and from the 31 percent to which it had been raised by George H. W. Bush. And, unlike Kennedy, who increased defense spending, Clinton, citing eased tensions at the end of the Cold War, cut billions of dollars in Pentagon spending. In this he seemed to ignore Kennedy's argument, in *Why England Slept,* that "we must always keep our armaments equal to our commitments."

Clinton's vice president, Albert Gore Jr., in his speech accepting the presidential nomination at the Democratic Convention in Los Angeles in 2000, paid tribute to his father, the man who had opposed Kennedy's tax cuts: "Never in the years to come — in Congress, and in the United States Senate — did he lose sight of the reason he entered public service: to fight for the people, not the powerful." In terms that echoed his father's opposition to Kennedy's cuts, Gore vowed his own opposition to the plans of the Republican candidate, George W. Bush, for a new round of tax reductions. Gore told the convention and the national television audience:

> I will not go along with a huge tax cut for the wealthy at the expense of everyone else and wreck our good economy in the process.
> Under the tax plan the other side has proposed, for every ten dollars

that goes to the wealthiest one percent, middle class families would get one dime. And lower-income families would get one penny.

In fact, if you add it up, the average family would get about enough money to buy one extra Diet Coke a day.

About 62 cents in change. Let me tell you: that's not the kind of change I'm working for.

I'll fight for tax cuts that go to the right people — to the working families who have the toughest time paying taxes and saving for the future.

The 2000 election was a close one, but in February 2001, in his first Rose Garden event as president, transmitting his tax relief plan to Congress, it was President George W. Bush who cited President Kennedy:

Our economy faces this challenge: Investors and consumers have too little money, and the U.S. Treasury is holding too much. The Federal Government is simply pulling too much money out of the private economy, and this is a drag on our growth.

Over the past 6 years, the Federal share of our GDP has risen from 18 percent to 21 percent, about as much as our Government took during World War II. President John Kennedy faced a similar situation in the 1960s. He warned then against storing up dollars in Washington by taking away more than the Government needed to pay its necessary expenses. "High tax rates," he said, and I quote, "are no longer necessary. They are, in fact, harmful. These high tax rates do not leave enough money in private hands to keep this country's economy growing and healthy."

Forty years later our Treasury is full, and our people are overcharged. Returning some of their money is right, and it is urgent.[40]

At a fundraising dinner for Senator Jeff Sessions of Alabama, in June 2001, Bush linked himself to Kennedy and Reagan in the line of tax-cutting presidents, saying, "I was proud to do something that President John Kennedy was able to do and President Ronald Reagan was able to do, and that's to listen to the American people and to sign broad, meaningful, real tax relief."[41] On the other side of the budget ledger, spending, George W. Bush, like JFK, increased defense spending. As part of a "no child left behind" deal with Senator Edward Kennedy on education policy, Bush also increased federal education spending to $69 billion in 2008, from $42 billion in 2001. Medicare spending also soared, and Bush added a prescription drug benefit. JFK had spoken in favor of Medicare and for increased federal education spending, so on some level these may be seen as extensions of his stated policies, but on another level, they were departures from his practice of restraint when it came to domestic spending.

George W. Bush's 2004 reelection campaign was in some sense a battle over the Kennedy legacy. The Democratic candidate was a Catholic senator from Massachusetts who had attended prep school (St. Paul's, where he represented Kennedy in a class debate[42]) and then an Ivy League college (Yale), and had been an officer in the Navy during wartime combat. John Forbes Kerry even had JFK's initials. In the first presidential debate, Kerry went out of his way, three separate times, to link himself to Kennedy, and to accuse Bush's Iraq performance of failing to meet Kennedy's Cuban Missile Crisis standard. "We can remember," Kerry said, "when President Kennedy, in the Cuban missile crisis, sent his Secretary of State to Paris to meet with de Gaulle, and in the middle of the discussion to tell them about the missiles in Cuba, he said, 'Here, let me show you the photos.' And de Gaulle waved them off and said, 'No, no, no, no. The word of the President of the United States is good enough for me.' How many leaders in the world today would respond to us, as a result of what we've done, in that way?"

And: "We're going to build the strongest international network to prevent nuclear proliferation. This is the scale of what President Kennedy set out to do with the Nuclear Test Ban Treaty. It's our generation's equivalent, and I intend to get it done."

And: "We need to rebuild our alliances. I believe that Ronald Reagan, John Kennedy, and others did that more effectively, and I'm going to try to follow in their footsteps."

In the third presidential debate as well, Kerry tried repeatedly to paint himself as Kennedy's heir. "I pledge this to you, America: I will do it in the way that Franklin Roosevelt and Ronald Reagan and John Kennedy and others did, where we build the strongest alliances, where the world joins together," Kerry said. A question about abortion, stem cell research, and archbishops was also answered by Kerry by referring to JFK: "And as President Kennedy said when he ran for President, he said, 'I'm not running to be a Catholic President. I'm running to be a President who happens to be Catholic.' . . . But I know this, that President Kennedy, in his Inaugural Address, told all of us that, 'Here on Earth, God's work must truly be our own.' And that's what we have to — so I think that's the test of public service."

But when Bush went back out on the campaign trail in battleground states during the closing weeks of the campaign, the incumbent president was the one quoting John F. Kennedy on national security policy and accusing Kerry of betraying Kennedy's legacy. On October 25, 2004, in Council Bluffs, Iowa, President Bush said, "The party of Franklin Roosevelt and Harry Truman and John Kennedy is rightly remembered for confidence and resolve in times of war and hours of crisis. Senator Kerry has turned his back on 'pay any price' and 'bear any burden.' He's replaced those commitments with 'wait and see' and 'cut and run.'" Bush repeated that line in speeches in the days that followed in Davenport, Iowa; Greeley, Colorado; Dubuque, Iowa; Onalaska, Wisconsin; Cuba City, Wisconsin; Pontiac, Michigan; Yardley, Pennsylvania; Toledo, Ohio; Columbus, Ohio; Portsmouth, New Hampshire; Ashwaubenon, Wisconsin; Minneapolis, Minnesota; Grand Rapids, Michigan; and Orlando, Florida. Kennedy had used the "pay any price, bear any burden" line just once, in his inaugural; George W. Bush used it fifteen times in the heat of a reelection campaign.

On October 27, in Vienna, Ohio, Bush introduced a new Kennedy quotation into his campaign stump speech, dropping the "pay any price" line and replacing it with one drawn from the same Kennedy text. Bush said, "The Democratic Party has a great tradition of leading this country with strength and conviction in times of war. I think of Franklin Roosevelt's commitment to total victory. I think of Harry Truman's clear vision at the beginning of the cold war. I think of John Kennedy's brave declaration of American ideals. President Kennedy said, 'The rights of man come not from the generosity of the state, but from the hand of God.' Many Democrats look at my opponent and wonder where that great tradition of their party has gone." Bush repeated that line again in Lititz, Pennsylvania, before reverting, in subsequent speeches, to the "pay any price, bear any burden" language.

Bush cited Kennedy as his inspiration not only on taxes and foreign policy but also on trade. In remarks to the Economic Club of Washington, D.C., on October 26, 2005, Bush said, "As Presidents from John Kennedy to Ronald Reagan to Bill Clinton have recognized, trade is the most certain path to lasting prosperity for people not only here but around the world."

A final postscript to the Bush administration's attitude toward Kennedy came in April 2012, when the George W. Bush Institute, a think tank affiliated with Bush's presidential library, hosted a major conference in New York City on "Tax Policies for 4% Growth." The director of the institute's 4% Growth Project, Amity Shlaes, had an opinion piece in the *Wall Street Journal* on the day of the conference praising Kennedy for his approach to tax cuts. At the conference, George W. Bush himself used the same line from Luke — "To whom much is given, much is required" — that Kennedy had used and that had so pleased Rose Kennedy in his January 9, 1961, address to the Massachusetts legislature. As Bush looked on from the audience, Lawrence Lindsey, who had been Bush's chief economic adviser in the 2000 presidential campaign and who served as Bush's director of the National Economic Council, praised Kennedy for being "very aggressive at pushing tax cuts for both supply-side and demand-side reasons." Lindsey called the Kennedy tax cuts "a very positive experiment" and "among the most successful we ever had." He explained that the Kennedy reduction in the top income tax rate to 70 percent from 91 percent meant that instead of keeping 9 cents of every dollar earned, a taxpayer would keep 30 cents, more than tripling his after-tax return. Finally, the Republican chairman of the House Budget Committee, Paul Ryan, looking as slender and young as had Kennedy at the start of his career, recounted how, when "potatoes stopped growing in Ireland," his ancestors left for Boston. "Your rights come from God and nature, not from government," Ryan told the audience, repeating one of Kennedy's favorite themes.

George W. Bush's successor, Barack Obama, came into office with members of the Kennedy family and Ted Sorensen expressing hope that he would follow in JFK's footsteps. Caroline Kennedy had endorsed Obama's candidacy in a January 27, 2008, *New York Times* op-ed piece. "I have never had a president who inspired me the way people tell me that my father inspired them. But for the first time, I believe I have found the man who could be that president," she wrote, mentioning too that Obama "has spoken eloquently about the role of faith in his life." Caroline Kennedy joined several other members of the Kennedy family who appeared with Obama at American University for a campaign event on January 28. After Obama took office, the publisher of Ted Sorensen's book *Kennedy* released a revised edition with a new preface by Sorensen explaining that "Barack Obama paradoxically is much like John F. Kennedy" and listing eleven ways in which that was so. Some of these were vague — "Kennedy, like Obama, was a strong leader," and "Kennedy, like Obama, had a sense of history" — but others were intriguing. Obama was the first president since Kennedy to have moved to the White House directly after serving as a senator. They both entered the office relatively young. Kennedy was the first Catholic president; Obama was the first black president.

Initially, at least, it looked as though Obama might follow some of Kennedy's precedents. Just as Kennedy had held over some key Eisenhower-Nixon personnel, Obama retained George W. Bush's defense secretary, Robert Gates, and his FBI director, Robert Mueller. Obama also reappointed Bush's chairman of the Federal Reserve, Ben Bernanke.

And a defender of the Obama administration could certainly draw some parallels. Just as Kennedy pursued tariff reductions to increase American exports, Obama signed free-trade agreements with Colombia, Panama, and South Korea. Just as Kennedy pursued tax cuts as a path to stronger economic growth, Obama agreed to extend George W. Bush's tax cuts for four years and put in place a payroll tax cut of his own. Just as Kennedy was originally seen as antibusiness after privately referring to steel executives as sons-of-bitches, so Obama was resented for demonizing the financial industry after publicly referring to them as "fat cat bankers on Wall Street." Just as Kennedy continued and even accelerated the Cold War, Obama has continued and in some cases intensified George W. Bush's war on Islamist militants, by increasing American troop levels in Afghanistan; maintaining the detention center at Guantánamo Bay for those designated as terrorist enemy combatants; defending America's right to kill overseas, without a trial, those who are suspected of terrorism, including American citizens; and increasing targeted killings by drone strikes.

On further examination, though, Obama looks more like a Nixonian anti-Kennedy than a Kennedy. JFK told the New York Economic Club, "In short, it is a paradoxical truth that tax rates are too high today and tax revenues are too low and the soundest way to raise the revenues in the long run is to cut the rates now . . . The purpose of cutting taxes now is not to incur a budget deficit, but to achieve the more prosperous, expanding economy which can bring a budget surplus." Obama, who inherited a far larger deficit than did JFK, sent his Treasury secretary, Timothy Geithner, to tell the same club, "We can't offer Americans the illusion of tax cuts that pay for themselves. No responsible politician can offer the nation fiscal sustainability through trillions in unpaid-for tax cuts."[43] Kennedy increased military spending; Obama proposed to cut it. While Obama did cut tariffs and some taxes, he did so under pressure from Republicans in Congress, conveying the impression that, left to his own devices, the president would have preferred spending to tax cuts. While Kennedy wanted to cut taxes on everyone, including the rich, Obama pressed for increased taxes on those earning $250,000 a year or more. While Kennedy exercised spending restraint, Obama increased federal spending overall, to $3.6 trillion in 2011, from $3 trillion in 2008.

The contrast was so sharp that, increasingly, Obama's critics and rivals who were independents or Republican politicians argued that they, not Obama or the Democrats, were the real upholders of John F. Kennedy's legacy.

In 2006, when Joseph Lieberman ran for reelection to the Senate as an independent, Barack Obama endorsed the Democratic candidate, Ned Lamont, a great-nephew of the same Corliss Lamont who had been a vocal critic of Kennedy on Vietnam and on nuclear testing. In 2008, Lieberman endorsed and campaigned for the Republican presidential candidate, John McCain, not Obama. In 2010, Lieberman resisted Obama's call to raise taxes on upper-income earners, saying, "The more money we leave in private hands, the quicker our economic recovery will be . . . I know that many people, including the President, have argued that the tax cuts should not be continued for people making more than $200,000 a year, but to me these are the people we need to be using their income to spend and invest to spur growth and job creation . . . I want the top income earners in our country to have the confidence and the money to spend and invest over the next year, rather than worrying about paying more in taxes to the federal government."[44]

In January 2011, when Lieberman announced his plan to retire from the Senate at the end of his fourth term, he spoke of his pride in his work "across party lines in support of the strong, bipartisan American foreign and defense policies carried out by the four Presidents under whom I've been privileged to serve — Presidents Bush, Clinton, Bush, and Obama — policies which ousted the invading Iraqi military from Kuwait, ended the genocide of Muslims in the Balkans, and liberated Iraq, Afghanistan, and the world from brutally repressive, anti-American dictatorships."

Lieberman went on:

> My interest in public service was inspired by President John F. Kennedy, who . . . asked us to ask ourselves what we could do for our country and challenged us to bear any burden to assure the survival and success of liberty. The politics of President Kennedy — service to country, support of civil rights and social justice, pro-growth economic and tax policies, and a strong national defense — are still my politics, and they don't fit neatly into today's partisan political boxes any more either.

In Kennedy's home state of Massachusetts, a Republican candidate for U.S. Senate, Scott Brown, launched his campaign with a thirty-second commercial that began with video of President Kennedy in his August 13, 1962, "Radio and Television Report to the American People on the State of the National Economy." The black-and-white footage of Kennedy then morphed into an image of Brown, as the candidate continued reading the language of the Kennedy speech, which was the entire script of the ad: "The billions of dollars this bill will place in the hands of the consumer and our businessmen will have both immediate and permanent benefits to our economy. Every dollar released from taxation that is spent or invested will help create a new job and a new salary. And these new jobs and new salaries can create other jobs and other salaries and more customers and more growth for an expanding American economy." Brown campaigned against President Obama's spending and health care plan, and he eventually was elected with Tea Party support. After being sworn into office on February 4, 2010, in his first press conference as a senator, Brown said, "I've called throughout the campaign, and I've felt this way forever, that you need an across-the-board tax cut, almost a JFK-style tax cut."

Mitt Romney, the Republican presidential candidate and former governor of Massachusetts, had a profile that was in some ways similar to President Kennedy's. Both had been elected statewide in Massachusetts, both were handsome, and both had fathers who were prominent in business and public service. Kennedy was the first Catholic president; Romney would be the first Mormon to gain the nomination.[45] Romney had run against Edward Kennedy for Senate and lost in 1994. When Romney ran for president the first time, in the 2008 political cycle, he addressed the religious issue head-on with a speech, "Faith in America." Romney chose to deliver the speech in Texas, where JFK had famously addressed the Houston ministers, and his text drew an explicit parallel. "Almost 50 years ago another candidate from Massachusetts explained that he was an American running for President, not a Catholic running for President. Like him, I am an American running for President. I do not define my candidacy by my religion," Romney said. In the 2012 campaign, Romney repeatedly used the "shining city on a hill" language in high-profile remarks, like his victory speech on the night of the New Hampshire primary. The press, if they noticed the phrase at all, traced the words back to Reagan, not Kennedy.

The most prominent Kennedy moment in the 2012 Republican presidential campaign, though, came from Rick Santorum, a former senator from Pennsylvania. Santorum, like Kennedy, was a young Catholic who had served in the House before winning election to the Senate. Kennedy had had a stillborn daughter and a son who lived only two days; Santorum's family had also suffered the death of a child, who lived for only two hours after birth. Yet, rather than embracing Kennedy as a fellow tax-cutting, strong-foreign-policy, Catholic politician, Santorum chose to attack him. Just as polls showed Santorum on the rise, the Pennsylvanian told a television interviewer that JFK's 1960 campaign speech on church-state separation made him want to "throw up." Santorum said that "people of faith, at least according to John Kennedy, have no role in the public square." This was such an absurd misinterpretation, not only of Kennedy's Houston speech and of the 1960 campaign but of Kennedy's entire career, that Santorum's campaign never recovered from it.

The historian William Leuchtenburg titled his oft-revised book on the ways Franklin Roosevelt left his mark on his successors *In the Shadow of FDR*. He quoted Theodore White to the effect that "all contemporary national politics descend from Franklin Roosevelt."[46] That is still true to an extent, but given what we have seen, it might be amended to say that the presidents since Kennedy have operated "in the light of JFK." All three of the presidents since Kennedy who served two full terms — Reagan, Clinton, and George W. Bush — campaigned and at least in some sense governed as successors to Kennedy. One might suggest that the fact that Kennedy has been claimed by both Republican and Democratic presidents, and denounced by Barry Goldwater and *National Review* on the right, as well as by Corliss Lamont, Linus Pauling, and Albert Gore Sr. on the left, shows he was a centrist rather than a conservative. Or one might make the point that the Cold War liberals of Kennedy's era seem by the standards of the 1970s and later to fall within a conservative consensus; they were liberals, not radicals. In any event, if Republicans Reagan and George W. Bush relied on Kennedy for his tax cuts, his anticommunism, and his military strength, even Democrat Clinton cited him as an advocate of tariff reductions, and Carter described him as a proponent of a strong military and of domestic spending restraint.

In the end, Kennedy himself was probably right when he said that labels are less important; what matter more are the policies and the principles, for which the labels can be a convenient shorthand. Despite the posturing by every president since Kennedy, the one who most clearly embraced both sides of Kennedy's peace-through-strength and growth-through-tax-cuts is Ronald Reagan. It is a fascinating irony of our political history that Democrat John F. Kennedy set the policy course that was the basis for the most successful Republican president who followed him. And since Reagan, whenever a president has strayed from that course, he has suffered.

Politicians are important keepers of the Kennedy legacy, but there are others, too. Americans' memories of JFK are shaped not only by presidents and senators and authors, but also by memorials and museums. There the story is sometimes told unreliably and at other times relayed with more care.

The Sixth Floor Museum in Dallas owns the website JFK.org, which reports that 325,000 visitors a year pay the admission fee to see an exhibit summarizing President Kennedy's career and to look out, as did Oswald, through the windows of the Texas School Book Depository down onto Elm Street and the president's motorcade route. On the weekend morning I visited, youth groups and Japanese tourists were lined up outside well before the doors opened. The panels of the museum exhibit declare, "Massive new social programs were central to Kennedy's New Frontier philosophy . . . The administration provided the foundation for Medicare, the Mass Transportation Act and the War on Poverty."

Another panel asserts, "Economist Walter Heller, chairman of the Council of Economic Advisors, favored induced federal deficits at a time of economic growth to overcome high unemployment, a radical departure from the balanced budget philosophy of the previous administration." There is no mention of Douglas Dillon, or of Kennedy's October 12, 1960, speech favoring "a balanced budget over the course of the business cycle with surpluses during good times more than offsetting the deficits which may be incurred during slumps." No mention, either, of Kennedy's February 2, 1961, message: "This Administration is pledged to a Federal revenue system that balances the budget over the years of the economic cycle."

In the section of the Sixth Floor Museum on Kennedy's legacy, the exhibit's text says, "Kennedy's philosophy of using induced deficits to encourage domestic fiscal growth became a mainstay of American government under later administrations, both Democratic and Republican." This, like other aspects of the exhibit, misses the point. Kennedy's recipe for growth was not a deficit; it was a tax cut that, both by changing incentives and by putting more money in the hands of the private sector, would yield growth that would ultimately narrow the deficit by increasing federal revenues.

Visitors leaving the museum are funneled into one of its two gift shops. The first prominently displayed souvenir for sale on the day I visited was a poster of JFK featuring the phrase from his American University speech about how "we all breathe the same air."

If the Sixth Floor Museum, with its sniper's nest overlooking Dealey Plaza, has a certain unavoidable grimness and somber tone, then John F. Kennedy Park in Cambridge, Massachusetts, on JFK Street, nestled between the Charles River and Harvard's John F. Kennedy School of Government, has a more cheerful mood in spring. Birds chirp, toddlers toddle, and dandelions bloom. Students picnic, sunbathe, strum guitars, or toss Frisbees on the grass. And if they pay enough attention to the Kennedy quotes etched into the pink granite gates to the park, they will find evidence there, too, of some heavy-handed editing. The park was dedicated in 1987 by the Democrat who was then governor of Massachusetts, Michael Dukakis, and the words chosen can be read as a kind of rebuke of President Reagan. One gate carries a phrase from a Kennedy speech about an America "which will protect the beauty of our natural environment," notwithstanding the view of Kennedy aide Ralph Dungan that with the possible exception of the Cape Cod National Seashore, conservation "basically bored Kennedy — he was no Theodore Roosevelt."[47] Another gate displays a passage from the American University speech: "We all breathe the same air," again, but, again too, not the line from the same speech declaring that "we find communism profoundly repugnant as a negation of personal freedom and dignity," and not the line about how "the Communist drive to impose their political and economic system on others is the primary cause of world tension today."

The words etched into the pink granite leading to Kennedy's grave at Arlington, with its eternal flame, give a more accurate picture. Those words are all from Kennedy's inaugural address. They include the lines "We shall pay any price, bear any burden, meet any hardship, support any friend, oppose any foe, to assure the survival and success of liberty," and "Only a few generations have been granted the role of defending freedom in its hour of maximum danger." Neither of *those* passages is quoted on the gates of the Dukakis-era Kennedy Park in Cambridge. Some quotes are more appropriate for a city park, others for a military graveyard; the challenge is to be sure that the real Kennedy is not distorted by the choice of what to include or omit in each place.

The site where visitors probably get the most accurate sense of Kennedy is the John F. Kennedy Presidential Library and Museum in Boston, which, alas, draws about 100,000 fewer visitors a year than the Sixth Floor Museum in Dallas. Here, too, one might quibble; there are entire areas of the Boston museum devoted to the space program and the Peace Corps, but not to the Kennedy tariff reductions, military buildup, or tax cuts. But one leaves, at least, with the sense that on some fundamental level, the people who created the exhibits understood the truth about Kennedy and were not afraid to share it. The final image a visitor to the JFK Library sees before exiting to a large American flag and a view of Boston Harbor is a 6,834-pound, graffiti-covered section of the Berlin Wall, brought to the museum with the help of Kennedy's sister Jean Kennedy Smith. The exhibit panel features one picture of JFK speaking in Berlin, and another of President Reagan speaking on June 12, 1987, in the same spot. It seemed to be a recognition that Reagan was Kennedy's heir, and that the defeat of the Soviet empire that built the wall was a victory that can be attributed in part to the military buildups and moral clarity of both men.

Another place where the Kennedy family's direct involvement has helped to provide a more accurate picture of Kennedy is at 83 Beals Street in Brookline, Massachusetts, the house where John F. Kennedy was born. After he was killed, the family repurchased the property and Rose Kennedy made a project of restoring it and recording an audio tour.

In a certain way, the Beals Street house is deceptive. While John Kennedy was born there in 1917, the family moved out in 1920. And this place, where six Kennedys and two servants shared a single bathroom and central staircase, is far more modest than the various mansions in Palm Beach, Bronxville, and Hyannis Port where Kennedy spent more time, but which, unlike the Brookline house, are not open to the public. Perhaps appropriately, the John Fitzgerald Kennedy National Historic Site at 83 Beals Street has been subjected to the same domestic spending restraint that characterized the Kennedy administration; it is open only from May to October, saving the National Park Service the expense of hiring permanent, year-round park rangers rather than the less expensive seasonal guides.

When the house is open, visitors can walk through and see the Madonna and child hanging in the room where Kennedy was born in the twin bed near the window, see a plan of St. Peter's Basilica hanging in the dining room, and hear Rose Kennedy's recorded voice talking about how her children recited grace before meals and prayers before bed. The audio tour is succinct, but even so, for Kennedy's mother, nearly every room seems to bring up a religious reference: "I wanted the children christened as soon as possible . . . I wanted my children to realize that church was for every day of the week and not just for Sundays."

There is a small gift shop in the basement. The day I visited, the store displayed, along with its usual merchandise, a shallow discard-bin of books that had been sent for review but that the shop had decided not to stock. Among those were a couple of books about John F. Kennedy geared toward young children.

I read one of these books to my daughters when I rejoined them later in the day. When I finished reading, one of my daughters said to me, "Daddy, that's a sad story, because at the end he dies."

In responding, I thought of an interview I had conducted a few weeks earlier with Robert Morgenthau. Morgenthau's arc and Kennedy's were in some ways similar. They had first met in Hyannis Port when they were teenagers sailing in the same races. Both had fathers who served in Franklin Roosevelt's administration: Kennedy's as chairman of the Securities and Exchange Commission and ambassador to Great Britain, Morgenthau's as Treasury secretary. Both had gone from New York to New England prep schools where they were religious minorities: Morgenthau a Jew at Deerfield, Kennedy a Catholic at Choate. Both saw combat service as officers in the grueling naval warfare of World War II in the Pacific. Morgenthau had been close friends at Yale Law School with Kennedy's friend Byron White. In the

1960 campaign, Morgenthau, who lived in Riverdale and was a partner in the law firm of Patterson, Belknap, became Bronx County chairman of Citizens for Kennedy. President Kennedy then appointed Morgenthau United States attorney for the Southern District of New York, the chief federal prosecutor for the area that includes Manhattan. When Morgenthau ran for governor of New York in 1962 against Nelson Rockefeller, Kennedy came to the state to campaign with Morgenthau, including a session at the Carlyle Hotel in which the men taped a commercial. Kennedy spoke of "economic growth," and Morgenthau responded, "We must not have a tax increase."[48] On the day Kennedy was shot in Dallas, Morgenthau was eating lunch with Robert Kennedy at the attorney general's home in Virginia.

Morgenthau was ninety-two when I interviewed him, in September 2011, on a back porch overlooking the apple trees of his farm in New York's Hudson Valley. I had carefully written out a list of questions in advance. To some of them, such as what Kennedy's politics would have been had he lived, Morgenthau readily answered that he did not know. When I got to the end of the session, I asked him a question that was not on my list. Had Kennedy's reputation been overly hyped, or was there really something there?

Morgenthau did not hesitate. "That's bona fide," he said. "He was an inspiration to a lot of people."

That is what I told my daughter after reading her the book. Yes, it is a sad story because John F. Kennedy dies at the end. But he inspired a lot of people. His ideas did not die.

For *this* new generation, Kennedy's ideas and policies can be a valuable guide — an imperfect one, because circumstances have changed so much in the half century since his presidency, but nonetheless valuable. Remembering that tax cuts, free trade, a sound dollar, and limiting domestic government spending lead to economic growth, and that firmness and strength are a path to peace and freedom — as important as all those concepts are, they are only part of his political legacy.

Some truths, after all, transcend the bounds of time or circumstance or of a single living individual. Kennedy himself spoke, both in his inaugural address and in his speech at Faneuil Hall on July 4, 1946, about the idea that, as he put it in the inaugural, "the rights of man come not from the generosity of the state, but from the hand of God." It was an idea that had inspired Americans since July 4, 1776, an idea more powerful than any weapon, an idea that burns even brighter than the eternal flame at Kennedy's grave.

It is an idea that lives on in us.

And so, as Kennedy said, the torch has been passed.

Acknowledgments

This book comes out five years after my *Samuel Adams: A Life*. John F. Kennedy lived two hundred years after Samuel Adams did, but astute readers may notice certain similarities in the lives and ideas of the two men. While there are discontinuities, there are also continuities. So, too, with the lists of people who deserve to be thanked.

Bruce Nichols bought this book, as he did the last one, and fortunately for me and for the readers, this time he remained at the publishing house to improve the book with his thoughtful editing. Also at Houghton Mifflin Harcourt, Larry Cooper made his own round of deft edits. For this book, as for the last, Noah Phillips and K. C. Johnson read drafts and made helpful suggestions; this time around, Anne Mandelbaum joined the team of readers, and the book benefited from her critical comments and careful eye. At the proposal stage, Noah Phillips and Jade Chang were readers, as was Jonathan Fluger, who also accompanied me on visits to the Kennedy Center in Washington, to a Kennedy residence and nearby church in Georgetown, and to Kennedy's grave (and Medgar Evers's) at Arlington. The Wylie Agency represented me for this book as it did for the last; this time around, Scott Moyers and Andrew Wylie deserve the thanks.

Even in the age of the Internet, human librarians and archivists are a historian's friends. At the Wisconsin Historical Society, reference archivist Harry Miller not only found the Christoffel Papers, which were not listed in the online catalog, but cheerfully and efficiently arranged for the photocopying and shipment of copies of about 1,800 pages of them to me in New York. The archivist of the Boston Symphony Orchestra, Bridget Carr, researched the Boston Pops schedule for the

July 4 long weekend of 1946. Barbara Eden and Patrizia Sione at Cornell helped me gain access to the David Dubinsky Papers without making the trip to Ithaca. At the Kennedy Library, Stephen Plotkin and his colleagues were courteous and helpful.

Nonlibrarians can also be friends. Mitchell Moss pointed me to Andrew Greeley's book *The Irish Americans;* Michael Mandelbaum pointed me to Daniel Patrick Moynihan's letter about Robert Kennedy; Tom Rice pointed me to both George Marlin's book *The American Catholic Voter* and Michael Knox Beran's book on Robert Kennedy. Richard Tofel shared his insights into Kennedy's inaugural address with me over an enjoyable lunch in lower Manhattan. Peter Kann talked with me about Vietnam during a dinner for sustaining subscribers of the *New York Sun,* which is still publishing online at NYSun.com. Tim Groseclose pointed me to the Americans for Democratic Action's voting records for Kennedy's time in Congress.

This work builds on that of other historians, and I am grateful to the many scholars whose work is cited in the notes, the bibliography, and in the text of the book itself. Even if I sometimes disagree with their conclusions or interpretations, their work made the work of writing this book much easier than it otherwise would have been.

Seth Lipsky wrote a letter to the editor of the *Chicago Tribune* that was published on June 8, 1994, to clarify that paper's description of him as a "Kennedy liberal." My appreciation of Kennedy, especially in comparison to Nixon, was shaped in part by conversations while walking over the Brooklyn Bridge with Seth and Amity Shlaes.

I am grateful to my partners in FutureOfCapitalism, LLC, for their friendship, encouragement, and support, and for giving me the freedom and flexibility to complete this project.

Finally, most important, is family. My paternal grandparents, Teddy and Millie Stoll, have helped me, through their stories, to understand some of what it was like to live during World War II. My parents, Alan and Nina Stoll, took me to the John F. Kennedy Presidential Library and Museum in Massachusetts soon after it opened, and my return visits there with school and Scout groups helped foster my interest in Kennedy. My parents and my father-in-law, David Phillips, provided welcoming home bases during research trips to Massachusetts. My daughters, newborns as I was finishing the previous book, are now old enough that they accompanied me and my parents to the John F. Kennedy Museum in Hyannis and asked their own questions. They also cheered me on as I swam two miles in a Massachusetts pond trying to get a feel for JFK's Blackett Strait adventure. The final and biggest thanks go, as always, to my wife, Aliza, for her fine editing and for putting up with and taking care of the author.

Notes

PREFACE

1. The speech is online at the JFKL, www.jfklibrary.org/Research/Ready-Reference/
    JFK-Speeches/Independence-Day-Speech-1946.aspx. It was also covered by the
    Boston newspapers, including the *Boston Herald,* in their July 5 editions. Photo-
    graphs of the event are in the James Michael Curley Papers at Holy Cross College.

INTRODUCTION

1. Pierre Salinger, *With Kennedy* (Garden City, N.Y.: Doubleday, 1966), 66.
2. Evelyn Lincoln, *My Twelve Years with John F. Kennedy* (New York: David McKay,
    1965), 96.
3. Mary Davis Oral History, April 21, 1976, JFKL.
4. David Powers recalled that "the primary was tantamount to the election." Ken-
    nedy prevailed in November 1946, winning 69,093 votes to the 26,007 votes of the
    Republican candidate. David Powers interviewed by Herbert Parmet, January 26,
    1976, Oral History Research Office, Columbia University.
5. Arthur M. Schlesinger Jr., *A Thousand Days: John F. Kennedy in the White House*
    (Boston: Houghton Mifflin, 1965), 739.
6. Thomas J. Whalen, *Kennedy Versus Lodge: The 1952 Massachusetts Senate Race*
    (Boston: Northeastern University Press, 2000), 157.
7. Michael O'Brien, *John F. Kennedy: A Biography* (New York: Thomas Dunne Books,
    2005), 400; William E. Leuchtenburg, *In the Shadow of FDR: From Harry Truman
    to Bill Clinton* (Ithaca, N.Y.: Cornell University Press, 1983; second edition, 1994),
    79.
8. October 12, 1960, speech: www.presidency.ucsb.edu, www.presidency.ucsb.edu/ws/
    index.php?pid=25779&st=percent&st1=growth#ixzz1HRtOpNNv.
9. Whalen, *Kennedy Versus Lodge,* 112.
10. James A. Reed Oral History, June 16, 1964, JFKL. Later in the oral history interview
    Reed does say that Kennedy became more liberal in the 1956–1958 period.
11. Joseph W. Alsop Oral History, June 18 and 26, 1964, JFKL, 47–50, 72.
12. White House Staff Reflections on the New Frontier, January 24, 1981, JFKL.

13. Theodore Sorensen, "A Legacy of Inspiration," *Newsweek,* November 28, 1963, 72. Mentioned in Herbert S. Parmet, "The Kennedy Myth and American Politics," *History Teacher,* Vol. 24, No. 1 (November 1990), 32.

14. Dillon speech to Century Club, New York, October 20, 1993; a copy is with Dillon's oral history at JFKL. Dillon does describe Kennedy as "liberal in social policy."

15. Cato, "From Washington Straight," *National Review,* January 30, 1962.

16. Peter S. Canellos, "Compound Fracture," *Boston Globe,* July 21, 2011.

17. Remarks by Ellen Fitzpatrick, Fiftieth Anniversary Conference and Reunion, February 21, 2011, JFKL.

18. Alan Brinkley, *John F. Kennedy* (New York: Times Books, 2012), 4.

19. Robert A. Caro, *The Years of Lyndon Johnson: The Passage of Power* (New York: Knopf, 2012), 144.

20. Kent Beck, "What Was Liberalism in the 1950s?" *Political Science Quarterly,* Vol. 102, No. 2 (Summer 1987), 233–258.

21. Robert Cramer quoted in Whalen, *Kennedy Versus Lodge,* 80.

22. Robert Dallek, *An Unfinished Life: John F. Kennedy, 1917–1963* (Boston: Little, Brown, 2003), 4–5.

23. Benjamin C. Bradlee, *Conversations with Kennedy* (New York: Pocket Books, 1976), 85, 210.

24. Garry Wills, *The Kennedy Imprisonment* (Boston: Atlantic–Little, Brown, 1981), 33–34.

25. Theodore Sorensen, *Kennedy* (New York: Harper & Row, 1965), 29.

26. Theodore Sorensen, *Counselor* (New York: Harper, 2008), 405.

27. Bradlee, *Conversations with Kennedy,* 10.

28. John F. Kennedy, *Profiles in Courage* (New York: HarperCollins, 2003), 217. My attention was drawn to this passage by Tom Putnam's quoting of it in his remarks at the Fiftieth Anniversary Conference and Reunion, February 21, 2011, JFKL.

1. PT 109

1. Rose Fitzgerald Kennedy, *Times to Remember* (Garden City, N.Y.: Doubleday, 1974), 177.

2. O'Brien, *John F. Kennedy,* 80.

3. Dallek, *An Unfinished Life,* 43.

4. Leuchtenburg, *In the Shadow of FDR,* 69.

5. "Kennedy Decries State Dominance / Former Ambassador Urges Boy Scout Leaders to Stress Dignity of the Individual," *New York Times,* October 7, 1945; Richard J. Whalen, *The Founding Father: The Story of Joseph P. Kennedy* (New York: New American Library, 1964), 403.

6. Rose Kennedy, *Times to Remember,* 172–173.

7. Doris Kearns Goodwin, *The Fitzgeralds and the Kennedys* (New York: Simon & Schuster, 1987), 275, 280–281, 565.

8. Goodwin, *The Fitzgeralds and the Kennedys,* 566.

9. Robert J. Donovan, *PT 109: John F. Kennedy in World War II* (New York: McGraw-Hill, 1961), 102.

10. Donovan, *PT 109*, 21, 105, 117.

11. Donovan, *PT 109*, 52, 113.

12. O'Brien, *John F. Kennedy*, 93.

13. O'Brien, *John F. Kennedy*, 95.

14. Goodwin, *The Fitzgeralds and the Kennedys*, 583.

15. www.thecrimson.com/article/1939/10/9/peace-in-our-time-pmilitant-democratic. See also O'Brien, *John F. Kennedy*, 98–99, who calls the editorial "dishonorable" and "exceptionally naïve."

16. James G. Hershberg, *James B. Conant: Harvard to Hiroshima and the Making of the Nuclear Age* (New York: Knopf, 1993), 120.

17. www.thecrimson.com/article/1940/6/9/the-mail-pto-the-editor-of.

18. John F. Kennedy, *Why England Slept* (New York: Wilfred Funk, 1940), xxvii–xxviii, 223–224.

19. John Kennedy had originally recounted the tale to Hersey in a Manhattan nightclub. Hersey asked him if he would mind if he, Hersey, tried to write it up for *Life*. *Life* rejected it, and it wound up in *The New Yorker*, where it was Hersey's debut article. Hersey's editor, Harold Ross, queried his account of the message on the coconut for the coast watchers with the note, "With what, for God's sake, blood?" Kennedy was shown a draft of the article before it was published. John Hersey interviewed by Herbert Parmet, December 8, 1976, Oral History Research Office, Columbia University.

20. Bruce Caldwell, Introduction, in F. A. Hayek, *The Road to Serfdom* (Chicago: University of Chicago Press, 2007), 19.

21. Kenneth P. O'Donnell and David F. Powers with Joe McCarthy, *"Johnny, We Hardly Knew Ye": Memories of John Fitzgerald Kennedy* (Boston: Little, Brown, 1970), 66–67.

2. CONGRESSMAN, 1946–1952

1. A copy is in JFKL. The "death to him was less a setting forth than a returning" quotation is from John Buchan's *Pilgrim's Way*, and is mentioned in Lawrence Leamer, *The Kennedy Men* (New York: William Morrow, 2001), 185.

2. O'Brien, *John F. Kennedy*, 205. Other sources put the amount at $600,000.

3. George Marlin, *The American Catholic Voter: 200 Years of Political Impact* (South Bend, Ind.: St. Augustine's Press, 2006), 198–220.

4. Richard Cardinal Cushing Oral History, 1966, JFKL.

5. O'Brien, *John F. Kennedy*, 216.

6. David M. Oshinsky, *A Conspiracy So Immense: The World of Joe McCarthy* (New York: Free Press, 1983), 108–114.

7. Robert H. Zieger, *John L. Lewis: Labor Leader* (Boston: Twayne, 1988), 101; Bert

Cochran, *Labor and Communism: The Conflict That Shaped American Unions* (Princeton, N.J.: Princeton University Press, 1977), 95–96.

8. Cochran, *Labor and Communism*, 267–270; Nelson Lichtenstein, *Labor's War at Home: The CIO in World War II* (New York: Cambridge University Press, 1982), 234–237.

9. Zieger, *John L. Lewis*, 165.

10. Cochran, *Labor and Communism*, 249–250.

11. A transcript of the hearings is in the Wisconsin Historical Society, Harold R. Christoffel Papers, MSS 1046, Box 7, Folder 2.

12. Christoffel Papers, Box 6, Folder 1.5.

13. Christoffel Papers, Box 3, Folder 5.

14. *Milwaukee Journal,* March 3, 1948, in Christoffel Papers, Box 5, Folder 5.

15. *Milwaukee Journal,* February 22, 1948, in Christoffel Papers, Box 5, Folder 5.

16. *Milwaukee Journal,* March 5, 1948, in Christoffel Papers, Box 5, Folder 5. The Supreme Court, in a 5-to-4 decision announced June 27, 1949, sent the case back for retrial, ruling that the government needed to prove that at least thirteen of the twenty-five committee members were present during the hearing. The court's opinion stated, "Evidence was adduced at the trial from which a jury might have concluded that, at the time of the allegedly perjurious answers, less than a quorum — as few as six — of the committee were in attendance." (*Christoffel v. United States,* 338 U.S. 84 ([1949].) Kennedy reacted by saying, "What a travesty on justice, that a Communist witness testifies untruthfully before a recognized committee of the House and then escapes the consequences of perjury by a technical claim that a specified number of Congressmen were not present at a particular moment." (O'Brien, *John F. Kennedy,* 215; Chris Matthews, *Kennedy and Nixon: The Rivalry That Shaped Postwar America* [New York: Simon & Schuster, 1996], 52–54.)

During the second trial, which lasted four weeks in early 1950, the government's star witness was Louis Budenz, a former editor of the Communist *Daily Worker,* who testified that an active Communist introduced Christoffel at a meeting as "a good Bolshevik" and that another active Communist greeted Christoffel as "comrade." Congressman Kennedy himself also had his diary subpoenaed and was called as a witness at the second trial on the key point of whether there had been a quorum. Kennedy's testimony was crucial because, though the government claimed fourteen congressmen were present at the hearing, one, Thomas Owens of Chicago, had since died. The defense claimed that Kennedy had spent the Saturday afternoon of Christoffel's testimony before Congress at the wedding of Lydia Langer, daughter of Senator William Langer, a Republican from North Dakota. One of Kennedy's sisters was a bridesmaid in the ceremony. Kennedy testified that he could not recall whether he went to the wedding or the reception. Christoffel's lawyer, John Rogge, said the testimony of Kennedy and several other congressmen who claimed they were present at the hearing was false; the printed record of the hearing indicated that only nine congressmen were present. "It is the final irony of the Christoffel affair," Rogge said, "that this charge of perjury against an innocent man rests ultimately upon the willingness of his accusers to perjure themselves." (This account is drawn from undated clips from the *Milwaukee Journal* in Christoffel Papers, Box 5, Folders 5 and 6, and Box 3, Folder 1.)

Rogge did his best to prove that Kennedy was lying. He called the secretary of St. John's Church, who produced records showing that the Langer wedding took place at 4:30 on the afternoon Christoffel testified. The pivotal testimony was at 5 p.m., so if Kennedy had attended the wedding ceremony, he would have missed Christoffel's false testimony. Rogge also called the secretary of the White House Correspondents' Association, who produced the seating list for the association's dinner for President Truman the evening of March 1; Kennedy was an invited guest. In the end, the testimony of Kennedy and the other congressmen who said there had been a quorum was apparently more believable to the jury than were the witnesses who said there had not been a quorum. On February 23, 1950, this second jury convicted Christoffel yet again. (*Milwaukee Journal,* February 24, 1950, in Christoffel Papers, Box 5, Folder 5.)

One hesitates to second-guess the jury's judgment from a distance of more than sixty years. Kennedy and the other congressmen certainly had a motive to lie — it would not look good to their constituents if a Communist sympathizer or perjurer escaped punishment because committee members had chosen to be absent or out socializing when they should have been in the hearing. There is no evidence in the transcript of Kennedy's presence in the Saturday afternoon portion of Christoffel's testimony. The House voted to withhold the records of the brief Saturday afternoon executive session, which might have indicated which congressmen were present. On the other hand, Christoffel did not produce any witnesses who could place Kennedy at the wedding ceremony, and Kennedy shows every indication of having been interested enough in the topic of the hearing to sit through it. If he lied about his presence at the hearing, so did Nixon and the other congressmen who testified that a quorum was present at the time of Christoffel's testimony. Christoffel himself did not take the stand in either trial.

In appealing this second conviction to the Supreme Court in 1952, Christoffel's lawyers again raised doubts about whether Kennedy was really at the hearing: "The testimony of Representative John Kennedy on the question of his presence during the crucial time is not particularly clear. At 4:30 that afternoon Senator Langer's daughter was being married. The wedding took place at St. John's Church on the corner of 16th and 8th Street [*sic*]. Representative Kennedy testified that he remembered going to 16th Street and then stated that he probably went to the reception and not the wedding." (The church is actually at 16th and H streets. Petition for Writ of Certiorari to the U.S. Court of Appeals for the District of Columbia Circuit, Christoffel Papers, Box 35, Folder 6.)

This time around, though, the Supreme Court declined to hear the appeal. Rogge ended up going to court to try to collect at least some of the $18,825.96 in legal fees and expenses he said he was owed for his work and that his client was unable to pay. (Christoffel Papers, Box 3, Folder 4.) Christoffel served three years in federal prison in Terre Haute, Indiana. (Christoffel Biography in finding aid for Christoffel Papers at Wisconsin Historical Society.) Kennedy issued a press release asserting, "The Communists, when I demanded that Christoffel be indicted, called 'Witch Hunter,' but I knew I was right. Now everybody should know." (Sean J. Savage, *JFK, LBJ, and the Democratic Party* [Albany: State University of New York Press, 2004], 8.)

17. Matthews, *Kennedy and Nixon*, 17, 52.
18. WNAC speech, "Justice for Poland," March 7, 1948, in David Powers Papers, Box 29, JFKL. It is not clear who wrote the original draft that Kennedy edited.
19. Hannah Pakula, *The Last Empress: Madame Chiang Kai-shek and the Birth of Modern China* (New York: Simon & Schuster, 2009), 564.
20. Schlesinger, *A Thousand Days*, 13.
21. Sorensen, *Counselor*, 99.
22. Whalen, *Kennedy Versus Lodge*, 34.
23. O'Brien, *John F. Kennedy*, 245.
24. Whalen, *Kennedy Versus Lodge*, 95.
25. Ralph Dungan Oral History, December 9, 1967, JFKL, 27–28.
26. The claim that Joseph Kennedy was a bootlegger whose fortune arose from smuggling liquor illegally in violation of Prohibition appears to be unsupported by any reliable evidence. Daniel Okrent treats the issue with care in *Last Call: The Rise and Fall of Prohibition* (New York: Scribner, 2010), 366–371.
27. Whalen, *Kennedy Versus Lodge*, 112.
28. O'Brien, *John F. Kennedy*, 247. Lodge was also, generally, a strong supporter of Truman's foreign policy; see Robert David Johnson, *Congress and the Cold War* (New York: Cambridge University Press, 2005).
29. Whalen, *Kennedy Versus Lodge*, 117–124.
30. Joseph Kennedy claimed the loan, $500,000, was repaid on time with full interest. (Whalen, *Kennedy Versus Lodge*, 131.)
31. Whalen, *Kennedy Versus Lodge*, 133–134.
32. O'Brien, *John F. Kennedy*, 218.
33. Whalen, *Kennedy Versus Lodge*, 103.
34. Whalen, *Kennedy Versus Lodge*, 154.

3. SENATOR KENNEDY, 1953–1959

1. Savage, *JFK, LBJ, and the Democratic Party*, 15.
2. Whalen, *Kennedy Versus Lodge*, 110–111; J. Anthony Lukas, *Common Ground* (New York: Vintage Books, 1986), 379.
3. Sorensen, *Kennedy*, 37.
4. J. Julius Fanta, *Sailing with President Kennedy: The White House Yachtsman* (New York: Sea Lore Publishing, 1968), 48; Clint Hill with Lisa McCubbin, *Mrs. Kennedy and Me* (New York: Gallery Books, 2012), 100. JFKL, www.jfklibrary.org/Research/

Ready-Reference/JBKO-Miscellaneous-Information/Wedding-Details.aspx, is the source for the 300-acre number; other sources put the size of the estate at 97 acres or at 48 acres.

5. 1,700 guests: Lincoln, *My Twelve Years with John F. Kennedy,* 41; 1,200 guests: www .jfklibrary.org/Research/Ready-Reference/JBKO-Miscellaneous-Information/ Wedding-Details.aspx. Rose Fitzgerald Kennedy, *Times to Remember,* 351, puts the number at "more than twelve hundred" and says that it took guests almost two hours to pass through the receiving line to meet the couple.

6. Paul B. Fay Jr., *The Pleasure of His Company* (New York: Harper & Row, 1966), 149. Lawrence F. O'Brien, *No Final Victories: A Life in Politics from John F. Kennedy to Watergate* (Garden City, N.Y.: Doubleday, 1974), 42, puts the number of guests at "about five hundred men."

7. Conrad Black, *Richard M. Nixon: A Life in Full* (New York: PublicAffairs, 2007), 277; Oshinsky, *A Conspiracy So Immense,* 33.

8. Oshinsky, *A Conspiracy So Immense,* 462–465.

9. Sorensen, *Counselor,* 154–155.

10. O'Brien, *John F. Kennedy,* 306–307.

11. Jacqueline Kennedy, *Historic Conversations on Life with John F. Kennedy* (New York: Hyperion, 2011), 9–10.

12. Schlesinger, *A Thousand Days,* 9.

13. www.jfklibrary.org/Research/Ready-Reference/JFK-Miscellaneous-Information/ Election-1958.aspx.

14. Sorensen, *Kennedy,* 75–76.

15. Sorensen, *Counselor,* 16, 24, 36–37, 39–45, 96, 98–99.

16. Chris Matthews, *Jack Kennedy: Elusive Hero* (New York: Simon & Schuster, 2011), 123.

17. Sorensen, *Counselor,* 238.

18. Richard W. Stevenson, "David Powers, 85, Aide to John Kennedy, Dies," *New York Times,* March 28, 1998. www.nytimes.com/1998/03/28/us/david-powers-85-aide -to-john-kennedy-dies.html.

19. Steven Lomazow and Eric Fettman, *FDR's Deadly Secret* (New York: PublicAffairs, 2010), 167–168.

20. Schlesinger, *A Thousand Days,* 310–311.

21. O'Brien, *John F. Kennedy,* 353.

22. O'Brien, *John F. Kennedy,* 234, 354–356.

23. O'Brien, *John F. Kennedy,* 357–358; Schlesinger, *A Thousand Days,* 553.

24. Schlesinger, *A Thousand Days,* 522.

25. Schlesinger, *A Thousand Days,* 622.

26. Kyle Longley, *Senator Albert Gore, Sr.: Tennessee Maverick* (Baton Rouge: Louisiana State University Press), 2004, 125–126; Richard F. Weingroff, "Kill the Bill: Why the U.S. House of Representatives Rejected the Interstate Highway System in 1955," www.fhwa.dot.gov/infrastructure/killbill.cfm.

27. Sorensen, *Kennedy,* 45.

28. Sorensen, *Kennedy*, 62.

29. Ralph Dungan Oral History, JFKL, 43–44.

30. www.nytimes.com/1993/12/28/obituaries/dave-beck-99-teamsters-chief-con victed-of-corruption-is-dead.html.

31. Sorensen, *Kennedy*, 54.

32. Barry Goldwater, *Conscience of a Conservative* (Blacksburg, Va.: Wilder Publications, 2009), 27.

33. Barry Goldwater, *With No Apologies* (New York: William Morrow, 1979), 74–75.

34. The Americans for Democratic Action's voting records are a useful yardstick of such votes. They are available at www.adaction.org/pages/publications/voting-records.php. The public housing votes were June 7, 1955, May 24, 1956, May 29, 1957, and August 12, 1959. The Social Security disability votes were July 17, 1956, May 28, 1958, and August 16, 1958. The unemployment benefits votes were May 27, 1958, and March 25, 1959. The school construction vote was August 13, 1958.

35. Dallek, *An Unfinished Life*, 31.

36. Lincoln, *My Twelve Years with John F. Kennedy*, 210.

37. O'Brien, *John F. Kennedy*, 294.

38. Sorensen, *Kennedy*, 16.

39. I used the federal government's inflation calculator at data.bls.gov/cgi-bin/cpicalc .pl.

40. O'Brien, *John. F. Kennedy*, 342.

41. Michael Knox Beran, *The Last Patrician: Bobby Kennedy and the End of American Aristocracy* (New York: St. Martin's Press, 1998), 5, writes that the *Fortune* estimate was "roughly double the actual figure."

42. Lincoln, *My Twelve Years with John F. Kennedy*, 26.

43. O'Brien, *John F. Kennedy*, 30–31; Goodwin, *The Fitzgeralds and the Kennedys*, 325.

44. Bradlee, *Conversations with Kennedy*, 41.

45. O'Brien, *John F. Kennedy*, 177.

46. Robert Morgenthau interview with the author, September 18, 2011.

47. O'Brien, *John F. Kennedy*, 173; Rose Kennedy, *Times to Remember*, 286.

4. PRESIDENTIAL CAMPAIGN, 1960

1. Matthews, *Jack Kennedy*, 293.

2. Richard Nixon, *RN: The Memoirs of Richard Nixon* (New York: Grosset & Dunlap, 1978), 219.

3. Nixon, *RN*, 221.

4. Theodore White, *The Making of the President 1960* (Cutchogue, N.Y.: Buccaneer Books, 1961), 291.

5. Ira Stoll, *Samuel Adams: A Life* (New York: Free Press, 2008), 14, 15, 99, 176.

6. John Fea, *Was America Founded as a Christian Nation?: A Historical Introduction* (Louisville: Westminster John Knox Press, 2011), 196.

7. John Higham, *Strangers in the Land: Patterns of American Nativism, 1860–1925*, second edition (New Brunswick, N.J.: Rutgers University Press, 1988), 7.

8. www.nps.gov/nr/travel/presidents/washington_monument.html; Kathleen Kennedy Townsend, "What Rick Santorum Doesn't Understand About JFK," *Washington Post*, March 2, 2012; Art Bromirski, "Monumental Bigotry: What Happened to the Pope's Gift," *Catholic Digest*, November 1948, 113–115.

9. Kenneth T. Jackson, *The Ku Klux Klan in the City, 1915–1930* (New York: Oxford University Press, 1967), 20.

10. Council of Economic Advisers Oral History, August 1, 1964, JFKL, 28, 92.

11. Taylor Branch, *Parting the Waters: America in the King Years, 1954–63* (New York: Simon & Schuster, 1988), 362–370. See also Schlesinger, *A Thousand Days*, 74.

12. Sorensen, *Kennedy*, 217.

13. Robert A. Slayton, "When a Catholic Terrified the Heartland," *New York Times*, December 10, 2011. campaignstops.blogs.nytimes.com/2011/12/10/when-a-catholic-terrified-the-heartland.

14. Andrew M. Greeley, *The Irish Americans: The Rise to Money and Power* (New York: Harper & Row, 1981), 11.

15. Carl Solberg, *Hubert Humphrey: A Biography* (New York: W. W. Norton, 1984), 99.

16. Winthrop Griffith, *Humphrey: A Candid Biography* (New York: William Morrow, 1965), 146–149.

17. Solberg, *Hubert Humphrey*, 157–159.

18. White, *The Making of the President 1960*, 89.

19. White, *The Making of the President 1960*, 95.

20. Houvouras was the son of a Greek immigrant father and an Italian-American mother who owned a metal-plating business in Huntington, West Virginia. For more details on his life, see www.huntingtonquarterly.com/articles/issue54/ajh.html.

21. Andrew J. Houvouras Oral History, July 10, 1964, JFKL.

22. White, *The Making of the President 1960*, 339–340. The speech is also online at www.presidency.ucsb.edu/ws/index.php?pid=25671#axzz1fZPd0N84. Kennedy's Lincoln history here is sloppy. The quotation appears in no Lincoln letter. If it was ever uttered by Lincoln, it was in a face-to-face conversation with Newton Bateman that Bateman is said to have recounted to Lincoln biographer Josiah Holland.

23. Marlin, in *The American Catholic Voter*, 257–259, suggests that inner-city Catholic votes in New York, Chicago, Newark, Detroit, St. Louis, and Philadelphia provided Kennedy's margin of victory in the 1960 election.

24. Peter Edson, "New Jersey Political Race Had Interesting Background; Both Candidates Ex-Catholics," *Florence* (Alabama) *Times*, November 15, 1957, 3. news.google.com/newspapers?nid=1842&dat=19571115&id=KhcsAAAAIBAJ&sjid=isgEAAAAIBAJ&pg=2950,5036306.

25. Theodore C. Sorensen Papers, JFKL, Box 6.

26. pewforum.org/Politics-and-Elections/Much-Hope-Modest-Change-for-Democrats-Religion-in-the-2008-Presidential-Election.aspx.

27. www.gallup.com/poll/124649/Religious-Intensity-Remains-Powerful-Predictor-Politics.aspx.

28. www.gallup.com/poll/128276/increasing-number-no-religious-identity.aspx.

29. www.presidency.ucsb.edu; www.presidency.ucsb.edu/ws/index.php?pid=25966&st=fail&st1=freedom#ixzz1Ic1YaOov.

30. www.presidency.ucsb.edu/ws/index.php?pid=74188.

31. Schlesinger, *A Thousand Days*, 72–73; Richard Goodwin, *Remembering America: A Voice from the Sixties* (New York: Harper & Row, 1988), 124–126.

32. www.presidency.ucsb.edu/ws/index.php?pid=25660.

33. Sorensen, *Kennedy*, 170.

34. Council of Economic Advisers Oral History, August 1, 1964, JFKL, 87–88.

35. Schlesinger, *A Thousand Days*, 568.

36. John F. Kennedy, *The Strategy of Peace* (New York: Popular Library, 1961), tactical nukes, 46; Eisenhower budget, 68, 223; missile defense, 70; more missiles, conventional forces, 225–226; test ban, 46.

37. O'Brien, *John F. Kennedy*, 404.

38. White, *The Making of the President 1960*, 200, 388–389.

39. Kennedy, *The Strategy of Peace*, Germany, xii (from June 14, 1960, Senate speech); 123, 43, 115.

40. Kennedy, *The Strategy of Peace*, 217–220.

41. Council of Economic Advisers Oral History, August 1, 1964, JFKL, 73.

42. www.jfklibrary.org/Research/Ready-Reference/JFK-Speeches/Remarks-of-Senator-John-F-Kennedy-at-Bethany-College-Bethany-West-Virginia-April-19-1960.aspx.

43. www.presidency.ucsb.edu/ws/index.php?pid=74188.

44. www.presidency.ucsb.edu/ws/index.php?pid=25655.

45. White, *The Making of the President 1960*, 389.

46. "Russian v. U.S. Growth: The Latest International Numbers Game," *Time*, December 14, 1959. www.time.com/time/magazine/article/0,9171,894385,00.html.

47. Robert M. Collins, *More: The Politics of Economic Growth in Postwar America* (New York: Oxford University Press, 2002), 45; Henry Hazlitt, "Wrong Aims and Means," *Newsweek*, March 9, 1959.

48. books.google.com/books?id=v0QEAAAAMBAJ&lpg=PA39&ots=VnHBk29ZUD&vq=Nixon%2520Growthmanship%2520parl&dq=Nixon%20Growthmanship%20parlor%20game&pg=PA39#v=onepage&q=Nixon%2520Growthmanship%2520parl&f=false.

49. www.presidency.ucsb.edu/ws/index.php?pid=25779.

50. Schlesinger, *A Thousand Days*, 11.

51. Schlesinger, *A Thousand Days*, 14.

52. Schlesinger, *A Thousand Days*, 91.

53. Chester Bowles Oral History, February 2, 1965, JFKL, 3.

54. Sorensen, *Kennedy*, 168.

55. O'Donnell and Powers, *"Johnny, We Hardly Knew Ye,"* 193–194.

56. Schlesinger, *A Thousand Days*, 66.
57. Hyman Bookbinder Oral History, July 22, 1964, JFKL.
58. Robert D. Parmet, *The Master of Seventh Avenue: David Dubinsky and the American Labor Movement* (New York: NYU Press, 2005), 199.
59. Address of John F. Kennedy upon Accepting the Liberal Party Nomination for President, New York, New York, September 14, 1960. www.jfklibrary.org/Research/Ready-Reference/JFK-Speeches/Address-of-John-F-Kennedy-upon-Accepting-the-Liberal-Party-Nomination-for-President-New-York-New-Yor.aspx.
60. Sorensen, *Kennedy*, 170.
61. Sorensen, *Kennedy*, 185.
62. Kennedy, *The Strategy of Peace*, 266.
63. White, *The Making of the President 1960*, 331. Kennedy's hand: O'Donnell and Powers, *"Johnny, We Hardly Knew Ye,"* 155; Fay, *The Pleasure of His Company*, 61.
64. www.american.edu/spa/cdem/upload/2008pdfoffinaledited.pdf. The American Presidency Project at the University of California, Santa Barbara, has different data that also says the 1960 election was marked by a high turnout. The UCSB figures put that turnout at 62.77 percent of the voting age population, second only to the 63.3 percent turnout in 1952, for a high in the presidential elections from 1912 to 2008. See www.presidency.ucsb.edu/data/turnout.php.
65. Sorensen, *Kennedy*, 219, 221.
66. O'Donnell and Powers, *"Johnny, We Hardly Knew Ye,"* 225. Rose Kennedy, *Times to Remember*, 376, puts the timing at "around four-thirty."

5. TRANSITION AND INAUGURATION, NOVEMBER 1960–JANUARY 20, 1961

1. O'Donnell and Powers, *"Johnny, We Hardly Knew Ye,"* 234.
2. Sorensen, *Kennedy*, 252.
3. Douglas Dillon Oral History, January 30, 1964, JFKL.
4. Schlesinger, *A Thousand Days*, 134–135.
5. Albert Gore Sr., *Let the Glory Out: My South and Its Politics* (New York: Viking, 1972), 146–147.
6. Schlesinger, *A Thousand Days*, 209.
7. Sorensen, *Kennedy*, 263.
8. Schlesinger, *A Thousand Days*, 143.
9. Royster to Kilgore, January 5, 1961, in Vermont Connecticut Royster Papers, University of North Carolina, Chapel Hill, Louis Round Wilson Special Collections Library, Southern Historical Collection.
10. Schlesinger, *A Thousand Days*, 148–149.
11. Schlesinger, *A Thousand Days*, 429.
12. Schlesinger, *A Thousand Days*, 572.
13. Sorensen, *Kennedy*, 595.
14. O'Brien, *John F. Kennedy*, 502.

15. Bradlee, *Conversations with Kennedy,* 71–72.
16. Schlesinger, *A Thousand Days,* 472.
17. Chester Bowles Oral History, JFKL, 87–89.
18. Schlesinger, *A Thousand Days,* 694–695.
19. Schlesinger, *A Thousand Days,* 170–171.
20. Schlesinger, *A Thousand Days,* 642.
21. Lincoln, *My Twelve Years with John F. Kennedy,* 249.
22. Schlesinger, *A Thousand Days,* 211–212.
23. www.jfklibrary.org/Research/Ready-Reference/JFK-Speeches/Address-of-Pres
    ident-Elect-John-F-Kennedy-Delivered-to-a-Joint-Convention-of-the-General
    -Court-of-th.aspx.
24. Rose Kennedy, *Times to Remember,* 387–388.
25. Richard J. Tofel, *Sounding the Trumpet: The Making of John F. Kennedy's Inaugural
    Address* (Chicago: Ivan R. Dee, 2005), 81.
26. Richard Reeves, *President Kennedy: Profile of Power* (New York: Simon & Schuster,
    1993), 29–30.
27. Rose Kennedy, *Times to Remember,* 384.
28. Tofel, *Sounding the Trumpet,* 17–19, 136. Kennedy may have been correct about the
    degree of fervor, but Eisenhower's 1957 inauguration had also featured four prayers,
    from Jewish, Catholic, Protestant, and Greek Orthodox clergymen.
29. The Bible is displayed at the Kennedy Library's museum. Tofel, *Sounding the Trum-
    pet,* 22–23.
30. Thurston Clarke, *Ask Not: The Inauguration of John F. Kennedy and the Speech That
    Changed America* (New York: Henry Holt, 2004), 33.
31. Sorensen, *Counselor,* 224.
32. Matthews, *Kennedy and Nixon,* 190.
33. Clarke, *Ask Not,* 13.

6. THE NEW FRONTIER: DOMESTIC POLICY, JANUARY 20, 1961–NOVEMBER 1963

1. An audio recording of the meeting is available at millercenter.org/scripps/archive/
   presidentialrecordings/kennedy/1962/11_1962.
2. G. Calvin Mackenzie and Robert Weisbrot, *The Liberal Hour: Washington and the
   Politics of Change in the 1960s* (New York: Penguin, 2008), 75, 90.
3. Lawrence F. O'Brien, *No Final Victories: A Life in Politics from John F. Kennedy to
   Watergate* (Garden City, N.Y.: Doubleday, 1974), 104, 135.
4. A transcript of the November 21, 1962, meeting is at history.nasa.gov/JFK-Webb
   conv/pages/transcript.pdf. For background on the meeting, see Barton C. Hacker
   and James M. Grimwood, *On the Shoulders of Titans: A History of Project Gemini*
   (Washington: NASA, 1977), 107–108.
5. Data from the Bureau of Labor Statistics and the Bureau of Economic Analysis,
   available from their websites, bls.gov and bea.gov.

6. Galbraith to Kennedy, March 25, 1961, in John Kenneth Galbraith, *Letters to Kennedy* (Cambridge, Mass.: Harvard University Press, 1998), 42.
7. Gore, *Let the Glory Out*, 142–146.
8. David L. Stebenne, *Arthur J. Goldberg: New Deal Liberal* (New York: Oxford University Press, 1996), 240–241.
9. Sorensen, *Kennedy*, 398.
10. David Bell Oral History, July 11, 1964, JFKL, 51.
11. David Bell Oral History, 60–62.
12. Schlesinger, *A Thousand Days*, 629.
13. Schlesinger, *A Thousand Days*, 1014.
14. Council of Economic Advisers Oral History, 385–386.
15. Salinger, *With Kennedy*, 74.
16. Sorensen, *Kennedy*, 413, 415.
17. White House Staff Reflections on the New Frontier, January 24, 1981, JFKL.
18. Royster to Barney Kilgore, December 14, 1961, in Vermont Connecticut Royster Papers.
19. Council of Economic Advisers Oral History, Appendix A, Note 7d, also 218–219.
20. Galbraith to Kennedy, December 30, 1960, in Galbraith, *Letters to Kennedy*, 38.
21. Savage, *JFK, LBJ, and the Democratic Party*, 92–94, 110–111.
22. Carl M. Brauer, "Kennedy, Johnson, and the War on Poverty," *Journal of American History*, Vol. 69, No. 1 (June 1982), 108, 113.
23. Schlesinger, *A Thousand Days*, 1012.
24. Nixon, *RN*, 235. Nixon's memoir is not necessarily the most credible source but, with that caution, is nonetheless worth a mention.
25. Schlesinger, *A Thousand Days*, 654.
26. Bradlee, *Conversations with Kennedy*, 95.
27. Council of Economic Advisers Oral History, Appendix A, Note 1.
28. Stebenne, *Arthur J. Goldberg*, 204, 214, 292–295.
29. Bradlee, *Conversations with Kennedy*, 78.
30. Bradlee, *Conversations with Kennedy*, 104.
31. Sorensen, *Kennedy*, 423–424.
32. Schlesinger, *A Thousand Days*, 638.
33. Schlesinger, *A Thousand Days*, 754.
34. Sorensen, *Kennedy*, 462.
35. Sorensen, *Kennedy*, 461.
36. Sorensen, *Kennedy*, 467.
37. Sorensen, *Kennedy*, 439.
38. See, for example, Amity Shlaes, "Real Men in Maine Have Wife Who's a Teacher," March 1, 2010, www.bloomberg.com/news/2010-03-01/real-men-in-maine-have -a-wife-who-s-a-teacher-amity-shlaes.html; Daniel Henninger, "The Fall of the House of Kennedy," *Wall Street Journal*, January 21, 2010, online.wsj.com/article/ SB10001424052748704320104575015010515688120.html. Henninger writes, "In 1962, President John F. Kennedy planted the seeds that grew the modern Democratic

Party. That year, JFK signed executive order 10988 allowing the unionization of the federal work force. This changed everything in the American political system. Kennedy's order swung open the door for the inexorable rise of a unionized public work force in many states and cities.

"This in turn led to the fantastic growth in membership of the public employee unions — the American Federation of State, County and Municipal Employees (AFSCME), the Service Employees International Union (SEIU) and the teachers' National Education Association.

"They broke the public's bank. More than that, they entrenched a system of taking money from members' dues and spending it on political campaigns. Over time, this transformed the Democratic Party into a public-sector dependency."

39. Presidential press conferences, October 9, 1963, and February 21, 1963. www.presidency.ucsb.edu/ws/index.php?pid=9460 and www.presidency.ucsb.edu/ws/index.php?pid=9573.
40. Schlesinger, *A Thousand Days*, 651.
41. Sorensen, *Kennedy*, 465.
42. Longley, *Senator Albert Gore, Sr.*, 179.
43. Schlesinger, *A Thousand Days*, 976.
44. Douglas Dillon Oral History, November 10, 1964.
45. White House Staff Reflections on the New Frontier, January 24, 1981.
46. Nick Bryant, *The Bystander: John F. Kennedy and the Struggle for Black Equality* (New York: Basic Books, 2006), 145.
47. Goodwin, *Remembering America*, 4–5.
48. www.uscg.mil/history/uscghist/African_American_Photo_Gallery.asp. See also Fanta, *Sailing with President Kennedy*, 40. Fanta puts Smith's graduation in 1965, but contemporary press accounts ("Baltimore Youth Coast Guard's 1st Negro Ensign," *Jet*, June 23, 1966, 4) make clear that it was in 1966.
49. "Hatcher's Son Integrates White House School," *Jet*, October 4, 1962, 14.
50. reason.com/archives/2011/11/14/a-fitting-tribute-to-medgar-evers. See also, generally, Adam Nossiter, *Of Long Memory: Mississippi and the Murder of Medgar Evers* (Reading, Mass.: Addison-Wesley, 1994), and Myrlie Evers-Williams and Manning Marable, eds., *The Autobiography of Medgar Evers* (New York: Basic Civitas Books, 2005).
51. Myrlie Evers, *For Us, the Living* (Jackson: University Press of Mississippi, 1996), 327–328. See also Branch, *Parting the Waters*, 833, and Reeves, *President Kennedy*, 528.
52. Savage, *JFK, LBJ, and the Democratic Party*, 19; Guy Paul Land, "John F. Kennedy's Southern Strategy, 1956–1960," *North Carolina Historical Review*, Vol. 56, No. 1 (January 1979), 41–63.
53. Harris Wofford, *Of Kennedys and Kings: Making Sense of the Sixties* (Pittsburgh: University of Pittsburgh Press, 1980), 153–156.
54. Irving Bernstein, *Promises Kept: John F. Kennedy's New Frontier* (New York: Oxford University Press, 1991), 110.

55. Schlesinger, *A Thousand Days,* 930, 939.
56. Schlesinger, *A Thousand Days,* 969.
57. Schlesinger, *A Thousand Days,* 972.
58. O'Brien, *John F. Kennedy,* 852–853.
59. Reeves, *President Kennedy,* 585.
60. Bernstein, *Promises Kept,* 108.
61. Bernstein, *Promises Kept,* 76–84.
62. Bernstein, *Promises Kept,* 97–101.
63. Schlesinger, *A Thousand Days,* 709.
64. Bernstein, *Promises Kept,* 70–71; Reeves, *President Kennedy,* 466 (Reeves, inaccurately, gives his name as William *Howard* Cox).
65. "Thurgood Marshall Courthouse," editorial, *New York Sun,* April 15, 2003. www.nysun.com/editorials/thurgood-marshall-courthouse/77602.
66. Bradlee, *Conversations with Kennedy,* 164–165.
67. White House Staff Reflections on the New Frontier, January 24, 1981, 131–132.
68. Richard Cardinal Cushing Oral History, 1966, JFKL; Reeves, *President Kennedy,* 552–553.
69. O'Donnell and Powers, *"Johnny, We Hardly Knew Ye,"* 316, 264, 183.
70. For an example of such an objection, see Alan Dershowitz, *Rights from Wrongs: A Secular Theory of the Origins of Rights* (New York: Basic Books, 2005), 18: "If rights come from God or nature, how can we ever know if a particular right exists? Neither God nor nature speaks directly to us."
71. William Manchester, *The Death of a President* (New York: Harper & Row, 1967), 55.
72. Sorensen, *Kennedy,* 19.
73. Sorensen, *Kennedy,* 249.
74. Sorensen, *Kennedy,* 377.
75. Fanta, *Sailing with President Kennedy,* 38.
76. Matthews, *Jack Kennedy,* 49.
77. Barbara Sinatra, *Lady Blue Eyes: My Life with Frank* (New York: Crown Archetype, 2011), 83.
78. Nassir Ghaemi, *A First-Rate Madness: Uncovering the Links Between Leadership and Mental Illness* (New York: Penguin, 2011), 173, 175.

7. TAX CUTTER, 1960–1963

1. George Ball, *The Past Has Another Pattern* (New York: W. W. Norton, 1982), 101, 103–104.
2. Ball, *The Past Has Another Pattern,* 160–161; Schlesinger, *A Thousand Days,* 156–157.
3. Royster to Barney Kilgore, December 14, 1961, in Vermont Connecticut Royster Papers.
4. Schlesinger, *A Thousand Days,* 724.
5. Ball, *The Past Has Another Pattern,* 190–191.
6. O'Brien, *John F. Kennedy,* 640.

7. Christopher J. Neely, "An Introduction to Capital Controls," Federal Reserve Bank of St. Louis *Review,* November/December 1999.

8. Sorensen, *Kennedy,* 401.

9. Bradlee, *Conversations with Kennedy,* 81.

10. Galbraith, *Letters to Kennedy,* 48.

11. These memos are in JFKL, Presidential Papers. President's Office Files. Departments and Agencies. Council of Economic Advisers, June 1962, 1–15. www.jfkli brary.org/Asset-Viewer/Archives/JFKPOF-074-008.aspx.

12. August 6, 1962, meeting with Wilbur Mills. Transcript at millercenter.org/scripps/ archive/presidentialrecordings/kennedy/1962/08_1962.

13. Theodore Sorensen Oral History, May 20, 1964, JFKL.

14. President's Office Files, Special Correspondence, "Graham, Philip L." JFKL. www .jfklibrary.org/Asset-Viewer/Archives/JFKPOF-030-003.aspx.

15. Gore, *Let the Glory Out,* 154–156. See also Albert Gore Oral History, August 13 and 21, 1964, JFKL.

16. Sorensen, *Kennedy,* 430.

17. Theodore Sorensen Oral History, May 20, 1964, 155. www.jfklibrary.org/Asset -Viewer/Archives/JFKOH-TCS-06.aspx.

18. Sorensen, *Kennedy,* 431.

19. "The Possible and the Perfect," *Wall Street Journal,* December 17, 1962.

20. "The Coming Tax Cut," *National Review,* December 31, 1962.

21. Walter Heller and Kermit Gordon Oral History, September 14, 1972, JFKL.

22. Herbert Stein, *The Fiscal Revolution in America* (Chicago: University of Chicago Press, 1969), 444, 446.

23. www.dirksencenter.org/emd_audio/9.18.63/press091863.pdf.

24. Goldwater, *With No Apologies,* 156.

25. Longley, *Senator Albert Gore, Sr.,* 170–171.

26. Douglas Dillon Oral History, 1964, JFKL.

27. "$11 Billion Tax-Cut Bill Voted by House; Senate Drive for Passage Opens," *Toledo Blade,* September 26, 1963, 1.

8. THE COLD WAR AND THE FREEDOM DOCTRINE, JANUARY 20, 1961–NOVEMBER 1963

1. Sorensen, *Kennedy,* 228.

2. Remarks by Harris Wofford, Fiftieth Anniversary Conference and Reunion, February 21, 2011, JFKL.

3. Nixon claimed in his memoirs that his own debate stance on the issue was a falsehood, taken "in order to protect the secrecy" of the government's plan to aid the Cuban exiles. (Nixon, *RN,* 220–221.)

4. Goodwin, *Remembering America,* 177.

5. Chester Bowles, *Promises to Keep: My Years in Public Life, 1941–1969* (New York: Harper & Row, 1971), 328.

6. Goodwin, *Remembering America*, 177.

7. Schlesinger, *A Thousand Days*, 252–253. Goldwater, in *With No Apologies*, 138, reports an April 15, 1961, meeting with Kennedy in which Kennedy told him, "Schlesinger thinks it's a mistake. Chester Bowles is opposed. Teddy Sorensen has been against it from the day we took office." Sorensen's own recollection is that "at the time, I was wholly preoccupied with the president's domestic agenda . . . I did not press him." (Sorensen, *Counselor*, 316.)

8. www.jfklibrary.org/JFK/JFK-in-History/The-Bay-of-Pigs.aspx; Reeves, *President Kennedy*, 89–95; Schlesinger, *A Thousand Days*, 270–278.

9. Schlesinger, *A Thousand Days*, 285–286.

10. Schlesinger, *A Thousand Days*, 783.

11. Copy in Arthur Schlesinger's May 1962 file, Presidential Papers, JFKL. www.jfklibrary.org/Asset-Viewer/Archives/JFKPOF-065-013.aspx.

12. Timothy Naftali and Philip Zelikow, eds., *The Presidential Recordings: John F. Kennedy*, Vol. 2 (New York: W. W. Norton, 2001), 457.

13. Robert Kennedy, *Thirteen Days: A Memoir of the Cuban Missile Crisis* (New York: W. W. Norton, 1969), 26–28.

14. Naftali and Zelikow, *The Presidential Recordings: John F. Kennedy*, Vol. 2, 442.

15. Robert Kennedy, *Thirteen Days*, 43; Ball, *The Past Has Another Pattern*, 292.

16. Tony Judt, *Reappraisals: Reflections on the Forgotten Twentieth Century* (New York: Penguin, 2008), 336; also partially quoted in O'Brien, *John F. Kennedy*, 673.

17. Naftali and Zelikow, *The Presidential Recordings: John F. Kennedy*, Vol. 2, 576.

18. Theodore C. Sorensen interview with Herbert S. Parmet, May 17, 1977, Oral History Research Office, Columbia University.

19. O'Donnell and Powers, *"Johnny, We Hardly Knew Ye,"* 322–323.

20. Robert Lovett Oral History, July 20 and August 17, 1964, JFKL.

21. Schlesinger, *A Thousand Days*, 817.

22. Ball, *The Past Has Another Pattern*, 300.

23. Robert Kennedy, *Thirteen Days*, 52.

24. Hill, *Mrs. Kennedy and Me*, 196.

25. Ball, *The Past Has Another Pattern*, 304–305.

26. Reeves, *President Kennedy*, 402.

27. O'Donnell and Powers, *"Johnny, We Hardly Knew Ye,"* 316, 326, 341.

28. Matthews, *Jack Kennedy*, 373.

29. For two examples of this argument, see J. E. Dyer, "Not So Fast with the '1962' Allusions," www.commentarymagazine.com/2010/12/29/not-so-fast-with-the-%E2%80%9C1962%E2%80%9D-allusions, and letter to the editor by John W. Bowling in the January 1983 issue of *Commentary*, www.commentarymagazine.com/article/the-cuban-missile-crisis.

30. Robert Kennedy, *Thirteen Days*, 108–109.

31. www.commentarymagazine.com/article/the-cuban-missile-crisis.

32. Cuban Prisoners Exchange Panel Oral History Interview, June 2, 1964, JFKL (John B. Jones, Louis B. Oberdorfer, and Mitchell Rogovin).

33. Cushing Oral History, 1966, JFKL.

34. Sorensen, *Kennedy,* 308.

35. Her remarks were on display in March 2012 at the JFKL museum.

36. David Talbot, *Brothers: The Hidden History of the Kennedy Years* (New York: Free Press, 2007), 176.

37. O'Brien, *John F. Kennedy,* 648–657; Reeves, *President Kennedy,* 335–337; Talbot, *Brothers,* 93–97.

38. Richard Helms, "Cuba and Consequences," *Newsweek,* November 28, 1983, 75.

39. "U.S Envoy, Not CIA Agent, Blamed in Mandela Arrest," *Los Angeles Times,* June 18, 1990, articles.latimes.com/1990-06-18/news/mn-268_1_cia-agent; David Johnston, "CIA Tie Reported in Mandela Arrest," *New York Times,* June 10, 1990, www.nytimes.com/1990/06/10/world/cia-tie-reported-in-mandela-arrest.html. Timothy Weiner, *Legacy of Ashes* (New York: Doubleday, 2007), 362, without giving a source, flatly states that the CIA was involved in Mandela's arrest.

40. Hill, *Mrs. Kennedy and Me,* 104.

41. See Schlesinger, *A Thousand Days,* 732.

42. Fanta, *Sailing with President Kennedy,* 69.

43. Jacqueline Kennedy, *Historic Conversations on Life with John F. Kennedy,* 293.

44. Frederick Kempe, *Berlin 1961: Kennedy, Khrushchev, and the Most Dangerous Place on Earth* (New York: G. P. Putnam's Sons, 2011), 240, 250; Sorensen, *Kennedy,* 545; www.state.gov/www/about_state/history/vol_v/86_89.html.

45. Lincoln, *My Twelve Years with John F. Kennedy,* 274.

46. Sorensen, *Kennedy,* 627, 417.

47. Reeves, *President Kennedy,* 438; Schlesinger, *A Thousand Days,* 856–865.

48. Warren Bass, *Support Any Friend: Kennedy's Middle East and the Making of the U.S.-Israel Alliance* (New York: Oxford University Press, 2003), 145.

49. Sorensen, *Kennedy,* 632–633.

50. Seth Gitell, *Broken Promise: The Story of U.S. Army Special Forces and the Dega People in the Central Highlands of South Vietnam, 1961–1965* (Houston: Radix Press, 1996), 20–21. Gitell is in part quoting David Halberstam, *The Best and the Brightest* (New York: Penguin, 1972), 154.

51. Sorensen, *Kennedy,* 632–633.

52. Sorensen, *Kennedy,* 647.

53. Schlesinger, *A Thousand Days,* 333, 336, 340.

54. Jacqueline Kennedy, *Historic Conversations on Life with John F. Kennedy,* 201.

55. Sorensen, *Kennedy,* 647.

56. Mark Moyar, *Triumph Forsaken: The Vietnam War, 1954–1965* (New York: Cambridge University Press, 2006), xv, 211.

57. Kempe, *Berlin 1961,* 384–386, 451–452, 468, 472, 481.

58. Kempe, *Berlin 1961,* xxiv, 400, 417.

59. Sorensen, *Kennedy,* 654.

60. O'Brien, *John F. Kennedy,* 616.

61. The letter is on display at the JFKL museum.

62. Moyar, *Triumph Forsaken*, 272–273.

63. *Foreign Relations of the United States, 1961–1963*, Vol. 4: Vietnam, August–December 1963, Document 274. history.state.gov/historicaldocuments/frus1961-63v04/d274.

64. Schlesinger, *A Thousand Days*, 998.

65. whitehousetapes.net/clip/john-kennedy-john-kennedy-jr-caroline-kennedy-jfks-memoir-dictation-assassination-diem.

66. Schlesinger, *A Thousand Days*, 413–414.

67. Chester Bowles Oral History, 17, 20.

68. Joseph Alsop Oral History, 15.

69. O'Brien, *John F. Kennedy*, 552.

70. Schlesinger, *A Thousand Days*, 423.

71. See Jamison A. Hill, "Veteran Reporter Dies in Crash," *Harvard Crimson*, April 24, 2007. www.thecrimson.com/article/2007/4/24/veteran-reporter-dies-in-crash-from.

72. Moyar, *Triumph Forsaken*, 252.

73. history.state.gov/historicaldocuments/frus1961-63v04/d143.

74. history.state.gov/historicaldocuments/frus1961-63v04/d141.

75. O'Brien, *John F. Kennedy*, 857.

76. O'Brien, *John F. Kennedy*, 861.

77. "The Choice of a Candidate," October 27, 1960, p. 36.

78. Susan E. Tifft and Alex S. Jones, *The Trust: The Private and Powerful Family Behind the* New York Times (Boston: Little, Brown, 1999), 388.

79. O'Brien, *John F. Kennedy*, 862.

80. Tifft and Jones, *The Trust*, 389.

81. Gladwin Hill, "U.S. Held Dodging Test of Mail Law," *New York Times*, October 24, 1963, 25.

82. Schlesinger, *A Thousand Days*, 498–499.

83. Rose Kennedy, *Times to Remember*, 242.

84. O'Donnell and Powers, *"Johnny, We Hardly Knew Ye,"* 374.

85. Schlesinger, *A Thousand Days*, 497, 482.

86. White House Staff Reflections on the New Frontier, January 24, 1981.

87. Kempe, *Berlin 1961*, 498–499.

88. Sorensen, *Kennedy*, 331–332.

89. O'Donnell and Powers, *"Johnny, We Hardly Knew Ye,"* 360.

90. Papers of John F. Kennedy. Presidential Papers. White House Central Subject Files: Human Rights, 4–3, Worship (Religion), General. www.jfklibrary.org/Asset-Viewer/Archives/JFKWHCSF-0375-008.aspx.

91. *Foreign Relations of the United States, 1961–1963*, Vol. 5: Soviet Union, Document 210, 456.

92. Biographical information on Weinstein is at findingaids.cjh.org/?pID=236266#ao. The account is drawn from Weinstein's June 3, 1982, oral history at JFKL and from

Lewis H. Weinstein, "John F. Kennedy: A Personal Memoir, 1946–1963," *American Jewish History*, Vol. 75, No. 1 (September 1985), 5–30.

9. THE DEATH OF A PRESIDENT, NOVEMBER 22, 1963–1968

1. Manchester, *The Death of a President*, 88, 32–33.
2. Manchester, *The Death of a President*, 89, 92, 286; Warren Commission exhibit 780.
3. James Pierson, *Camelot and the Cultural Revolution* (New York: Encounter Books, 2007), 144, 121, 150; Warren Commission exhibit 100; Manchester, *The Death of a President*, 97.
4. Manchester, *The Death of a President*, 93, 101.
5. Manchester, *The Death of a President*, 94, 456, 334, 634; Robert B. Semple Jr., ed., *Four Days in November: The Original Coverage of the John F. Kennedy Assassination by the Staff of the* New York Times (New York: St. Martin's Press, 2003), 567. Exploration of Oswald's motives was limited but not entirely foreclosed; the December 10, 1963, issue of *National Review* described him as "a Communist hoodlum" and "a psychopathic Communist."
6. Manchester, *The Death of a President*, 216–217.
7. Manchester, *The Death of a President*, 460–463, 515, 422, 587, 599.
8. Theodore H. White, *In Search of History* (New York: Harper & Row, 1978), 519–524.
9. Sorensen Papers, JFKL, Box 123, contains a full copy of the "Camelot" documents. The quote is from White's notes, typed later, on December 19, 1963. It also appears in a 1995 Associated Press dispatch by Glen Johnson on the release of the documents, "Camelot Revisited."
10. Sorensen, *Counselor*, 405–406.
11. Sorensen, *Kennedy*, 318, 169.
12. Sorensen interview with Herbert S. Parmet, May 17, 1977, Oral History Research Office, Columbia University. In framing the question, Parmet had described the speech to Sorensen as "one of the greatest speeches he ever gave."
13. Sorensen, *Counselor*, 521.
14. Sorensen, *Kennedy*, 26.
15. Dubinsky to Kennedy, December 5, 1962, Kheel Center for Labor-Management Documentation and Archives, Martin Catherwood Library, Cornell University Industrial and Labor Relations School. Victor Navasky, in *Kennedy Justice* (New York: Atheneum, 1971), 38, also makes the point that the Scales pardon "was not an outright repudiation of the cold-war assumptions" because Scales had "repudiated" communism. Navasky quotes a letter from a Washington lawyer, Joseph Rauh, to Arthur Schlesinger: "Far from clemency for Scales being a pro-Communist act, it is actually an anti-Communist act. The Communists do not really want Scales out of jail as he is not *their* cause."
16. The Kennedy administration did reportedly oppose the Cunningham Amendment

when it was under discussion in Congress. It was Kennedy's solicitor general, Archibald Cox, who defended the law before the Supreme Court.

17. Sorensen, *Counselor,* 138.
18. Jacqueline Kennedy, *Historic Conversations on Life with John F. Kennedy,* 77, 241, 347, 273.
19. Schlesinger, *A Thousand Days,* 909, 913.
20. Schlesinger, *A Thousand Days,* x.
21. Sam Kashner, "A Clash of Camelots," *Vanity Fair,* October 2009. www.vanityfair .com/politics/features/2009/10/death-of-a-president200910.
22. Joseph A. Pechman, "Individual Income Tax Provisions of the Revenue Act of 1964," *Journal of Finance,* Vol. 20, No. 2 (May 1965), 247–272.
23. Goldwater, *With No Apologies,* 156.
24. Douglas Dillon Oral History, November 10, 1964, 130; September 22, 1964, 141, 143.
25. Savage, *JFK, LBJ, and the Democratic Party,* 133–134.
26. "Notes on Meeting with Lyndon Johnson," Heller Papers, Box 7, November 23, 1963, JFKL, cited in Brauer, "Kennedy, Johnson, and the War on Poverty."
27. www.criticalpast.com/video/65675069651_Robert-Francis-Kennedy_Jagiellonian -University_Jagiellonian-globe_Tadeusz-Kosciuszko.
28. Milton Gwirtzman Oral History, December 23, 1971, JFKL.
29. Goodwin, *Remembering America,* 296.
30. Milton Gwirtzman Oral History, December 23, 1971.
31. O'Donnell and Powers, *"Johnny, We Hardly Knew Ye,"* 13, 383.
32. Robert S. McNamara, *In Retrospect: The Tragedy and Lessons of Vietnam* (New York: Times Books, 1995), 71, 97.
33. Edward M. Kennedy, *True Compass: A Memoir* (New York: Twelve, 2009), 212.
34. State Department Human Rights Report, Vietnam, 2010. www.state.gov/j/drl/rls/ hrrpt/2010/eap/154408.htm.
35. A transcript is at reagan2020.us/speeches/reagan_kennedy_debate.asp.
36. Remarks of Robert F. Kennedy at the University of Kansas, March 18, 1968. www .jfklibrary.org/Research/Ready-Reference/RFK-Speeches/Remarks-of-Robert-F -Kennedy-at-the-University-of-Kansas-March-18-1968.aspx.
37. Talbot, *Brothers,* 358.
38. Daniel Patrick Moynihan, *A Portrait in Letters of an American Visionary* (New York: PublicAffairs, 2010), 150–153.
39. Beran, *The Last Patrician,* 106.

10. PASSING THE TORCH: 1968 TO THE FUTURE

1. Quoted by Tom Putnam in his remarks at the Fiftieth Anniversary Conference and Reunion, February 21, 2011, JFKL.
2. On Nixon's liberalism, see Jodie T. Allen, "Last of the Big Spenders: Richard Nixon and the Greater Society," *Washington Post,* February 24, 1983, A15, and David Greenberg, "Richard the Bleeding Hearted," *Reviews in American History*

30 (2002), 156–167. See also Dylan R. Matthews, "The Cards and How You Play Them," *Harvard Crimson,* March 7, 2012. www.thecrimson.com/column/broom -of-the-system/article/2012/3/7/matthews-nixon-obama.

3. Tom Wicker, *One of Us: Richard Nixon and the American Dream* (New York: Random House, 1991), 481.

4. Nixon, *RN,* 560–561.

5. Gal Beckerman, *When They Come for Us, We'll Be Gone: The Epic Struggle to Save Soviet Jewry* (New York: Houghton Mifflin Harcourt, 2010), 293–294.

6. "U.S.-Russian Relations: The Legacy of Jackson-Vanik," *Centerpoint,* March 2010. www.wilsoncenter.org/islamists/article/us-russian-relations-the-legacy-jackson -vanik.

7. Richard Nixon interview with Frank Gannon, February 9, 1983, Walter J. Brown Media Archives, University of Georgia Libraries. www.libs.uga.edu/media/collec tions/nixon/nixonday1.html.

8. Special Message to the Congress Proposing a Comprehensive Health Insurance Plan, February 6, 1974. www.presidency.ucsb.edu/ws/index.php?pid=4337.

9. Ronald Reagan, *Reagan: A Life in Letters* (New York: Free Press, 2003), 348.

10. Wicker, *One of Us,* 562.

11. Jimmy Carter, Carter/Kennedy Unity Celebration Remarks at the Democratic Party Dinner, October 19, 1980.

12. www.taxpolicycenter.org/taxtopics/encyclopedia/Capital-Gains-Taxation.cfm. See also Robert L. Bartley and Amity Shlaes, "The Supply-Side Revolution," in Brian Anderson, ed., *Turning Intellect into Influence* (New York: Reed Press, 2004).

13. Presidential press conference, June 26, 1978.

14. Nick Gillespie and Matt Welch, *The Declaration of Independents: How Libertarian Politics Can Fix What's Wrong with America* (New York: PublicAffairs, 2011), 98–101.

15. Remarks at State Democratic Party Rally, Miami Beach, Florida, October 26, 1978.

16. George Will, "My Role in the Reagan-Carter Debate," *Gainesville Sun,* July 12, 1983, www.pinkpillbox.com/wexford.htm; Harry Rosenthal, "Reagan Moves to Virginia," Associated Press, August 1980.

17. Televised Address by Governor Ronald Reagan, "A Strategy for Peace in the '80s," October 19, 1980.

18. Remarks at the Illinois Forum Reception in Chicago, September 2, 1981.

19. Remarks at Ohio State Republican Fundraising Reception in Cincinnati, November 30, 1981.

20. Remarks at a Rally Supporting a Proposed Constitutional Amendment for a Balanced Federal Budget, July 19, 1982.

21. Remarks to the Students and Faculty at St. John's University in New York, March 28, 1985.

22. Address to the Nation on the Federal Budget and Deficit Reduction, April 24, 1985.

23. Remarks to the United States Chamber of Commerce on the Economy and Deficit Reduction, November 19, 1987.

24. Address to the Nation on Strategic Arms Reduction and Nuclear Deterrence, November 22, 1982.

25. Remarks at the National Leadership Forum of the Center for International and Strategic Studies of Georgetown University, April 6, 1984.

26. Remarks to the Students and Faculty at St. John's University in New York, March 28, 1985.

27. Address to the Nation on United States Policy in Latin America, May 9, 1984.

28. Remarks at a Fundraising Reception for the John F. Kennedy Library Foundation, June 24, 1985.

29. Robert L. Bartley, *The Seven Fat Years and How to Do It Again* (New York: Free Press, 1992), 18, 74.

30. www.polyconomics.com/index.php?option=com_content&view=article&id =1854:jfk-and-taxes&catid=54:2005&Itemid=31.

31. Richard J. Walton, "Dangerous President," *Newsweek,* November 28, 1983, 76.

32. www.c-spanvideo.org/program/37821-1.

33. Remarks at the American University Centennial Celebration, February 26, 1993.

34. Remarks on Signing the National and Community Service Trust Act, September 21, 1993.

35. Remarks at the Dedication of the John F. Kennedy Presidential Library Museum, October 29, 1993.

36. Remarks on Arrival in Caracas, Venezuela, October 12, 1997.

37. Remarks at the John F. Kennedy Presidential Library Foundation Dinner, March 8, 1998.

38. See, for example, Susan Estrich, "A True Baptism by Fire: The Waco Legacy," *Los Angeles Times,* April 25, 1993. articles.latimes.com/1993-04-25/opinion/op -27045_1_janet-reno.

39. Joe Klein, *The Natural: The Misunderstood Presidency of Bill Clinton* (New York: Broadway, 2003), 79.

40. Remarks on Transmitting the Tax Relief Plan to the Congress, February 8, 2001.

41. Remarks at a Dinner for Senator Jeff Sessions in Birmingham, June 21, 2001.

42. Franklin Foer, "John Kerry, Teen Outcast." www.cbsnews.com/2100-215_162 -610517.html.

43. Remarks by Secretary Geithner Before the Economic Club of New York, March 15, 2012. www.treasury.gov/press-center/press-releases/Pages/tg1452.aspx.

44. www.futureofcapitalism.com/2010/09/lieberman-on-taxes.

45. See Jon C. Hopwood, "Mitt Romney: In the Shadow of JFK," November 23, 2011. news.yahoo.com/mitt-romney-shadow-jfk-223800016.html.

46. Leuchtenburg, *In the Shadow of FDR,* ix.

47. O'Brien, *John F. Kennedy,* 721.

48. Filmed remarks in support of New York gubernatorial candidate Robert Morgenthau, October 11, 1962. www.jfklibrary.org/Asset-Viewer/Archives/JFKWHA-136 -003.aspx.

Bibliography

ARCHIVES AND MANUSCRIPT COLLECTIONS

JFK Library, Boston, Massachusetts (JFKL). David Powers Papers. Pre-Presidential Papers. Presidential Papers. Theodore C. Sorensen Papers. **Oral Histories:** Joseph W. Alsop, David E. Bell, Hyman Bookbinder, Chester Bowles, Council of Economic Advisers, Cuban Prisoners Exchange Panel (John B. Jones, Louis B. Oberdorfer, and Mitchell Rogovin), Richard Cardinal Cushing, Mary Davis, Douglas Dillon, Ralph Dungan, Albert Gore, Milton Gwirtzman, Walter Heller and Kermit Gordon, Andrew J. Houvouras, Robert F. Kennedy, Robert Lovett, James A. Reed, Theodore Sorensen, Lewis H. Weinstein, White House Staff Reflections on the New Frontier.

Columbia University, Oral History Research Office. John F. Kennedy Project: John Hersey. David Powers. Theodore C. Sorensen.

Cornell University, Kheel Center for Labor-Management Documentation and Archives, Martin Catherwood Library. International Ladies' Garment Workers' Union. David Dubinsky. President's Records, 1932–1966.

College of the Holy Cross, Archives and Special Collections. James Michael Curley Papers.

University of North Carolina, Chapel Hill, Louis Round Wilson Special Collections Library, Southern Historical Collection. Vermont Connecticut Royster Papers.

Wisconsin Historical Society, Madison, Wisconsin. Harold R. Christoffel Papers.

BOOKS

Ball, George. *The Past Has Another Pattern.* New York: W. W. Norton, 1982.

Bartley, Robert L. *The Seven Fat Years and How to Do It Again.* New York: Free Press, 1992.

Bass, Warren. *Support Any Friend: Kennedy's Middle East and the Making of the U.S.-Israel Alliance.* New York: Oxford University Press, 2003.

Beckerman, Gal. *When They Come for Us, We'll Be Gone: The Epic Struggle to Save Soviet Jewry.* Boston: Houghton Mifflin Harcourt, 2010.

Beran, Michael Knox. *The Last Patrician: Bobby Kennedy and the End of American Aristocracy.* New York: St. Martin's Press, 1998.

Bernstein, Irving. *Promises Kept: John F. Kennedy's New Frontier.* New York: Oxford University Press, 1991.

Black, Conrad. *Richard M. Nixon: A Life in Full.* New York: PublicAffairs, 2007.

Bowles, Chester. *Promises to Keep: My Years in Public Life, 1941–1969.* New York: Harper & Row, 1971.

Bradlee, Benjamin C. *Conversations with Kennedy.* New York: Pocket Books, 1976.

Branch, Taylor. *Parting the Waters: America in the King Years, 1954–63.* New York: Simon & Schuster, 1988.

Brinkley, Alan. *John F. Kennedy.* New York: Times Books, 2012.

Bryant, Nick. *The Bystander: John F. Kennedy and the Struggle for Black Equality.* New York: Basic Books, 2006.

Caro, Robert A. *The Years of Lyndon Johnson: The Passage of Power.* New York: Knopf, 2012.

Clarke, Thurston. *Ask Not: The Inauguration of John F. Kennedy and the Speech That Changed America.* New York: Henry Holt, 2004.

Cochran, Bert. *Labor and Communism: The Conflict That Shaped American Unions.* Princeton, N.J.: Princeton University Press, 1977.

Collins, Robert M. *More: The Politics of Economic Growth in Postwar America.* New York: Oxford University Press, 2002.

Dallek, Robert. *An Unfinished Life: John F. Kennedy, 1917–1963.* Boston: Little, Brown, 2003.

Dershowitz, Alan. *Rights from Wrongs: A Secular Theory of the Origins of Rights.* New York: Basic Books, 2005.

Donovan, Robert J. *PT 109: John F. Kennedy in World War II.* New York: McGraw-Hill, 1961.

Evers, Myrlie. *For Us, the Living.* Jackson: University Press of Mississippi, 1996.

Evers-Williams, Myrlie, and Manning Marable, eds. *The Autobiography of Medgar Evers.* New York: Basic Civitas Books, 2005.

Fanta, J. Julius. *Sailing with President Kennedy.* New York: Sea Lore Publishing, 1968.

Fay, Paul B., Jr. *The Pleasure of His Company.* New York: Harper & Row, 1966.

Fea, John. *Was America Founded as a Christian Nation?: A Historical Introduction.* Louisville: Westminster John Knox Press, 2011.

Galbraith, John Kenneth. *Letters to Kennedy.* Cambridge, Mass.: Harvard University Press, 1998.

Ghaemi, Nassir. *A First-Rate Madness: Uncovering the Links Between Leadership and Mental Illness.* New York: Penguin, 2011.

Gillespie, Nick, and Matt Welch. *The Declaration of Independents: How Libertarian Politics Can Fix What's Wrong with America.* New York: PublicAffairs, 2011.

Gitell, Seth. *Broken Promise: The Story of U.S. Army Special Forces and the Dega People in the Central Highlands of South Vietnam, 1961–1965. Houston: Radix Press, 1996.

Goldwater, Barry. *Conscience of a Conservative*. Blacksburg, Va.: Wilder Publications, 2009.

———. *With No Apologies*. New York: William Morrow, 1979.

Goodwin, Doris Kearns. *The Fitzgeralds and the Kennedys*. New York: Simon & Schuster, 1987.

Goodwin, Richard. *Remembering America: A Voice from the Sixties*. New York: Harper & Row, 1988.

Gore, Albert. *Let the Glory Out: My South and Its Politics*. New York: Viking, 1972.

Greeley, Andrew M. *The Irish Americans: The Rise to Money and Power*. New York: Harper & Row, 1981.

Griffith, Winthrop. *Humphrey: A Candid Biography*. New York: William Morrow, 1965.

Hacker, Barton C., and James M. Grimwood. *On the Shoulders of Titans: A History of Project Gemini*. Washington: NASA, 1977.

Halberstam, David. *The Best and the Brightest*. New York: Penguin, 1972.

Hayek, F. A. *The Road to Serfdom*. Chicago: University of Chicago Press, 2007.

Hershberg, James G. *James B. Conant: Harvard to Hiroshima and the Making of the Nuclear Age*. New York: Knopf, 1993.

Higham, John. *Strangers in the Land: Patterns of American Nativism, 1860–1925*, second edition. New Brunswick, N.J.: Rutgers University Press, 1988.

Hill, Clint, with Lisa McCubbin. *Mrs. Kennedy and Me*. New York: Gallery Books, 2012.

Jackson, Kenneth T. *The Ku Klux Klan in the City, 1915–1930*. New York: Oxford University Press, 1967.

Johnson, Robert David. *Congress and the Cold War*. New York: Cambridge University Press, 2005.

Judt, Tony. *Reappraisals: Reflections on the Forgotten Twentieth Century*. New York: Penguin, 2008.

Kempe, Frederick. *Berlin 1961: Kennedy, Khrushchev, and the Most Dangerous Place on Earth*. New York: G. P. Putnam's Sons, 2011.

Kennedy, Edward M. *True Compass: A Memoir*. New York: Twelve, 2009.

Kennedy, Jacqueline. *Historic Conversations on Life with John F. Kennedy*. New York: Hyperion, 2011.

Kennedy, John F. *A Nation of Immigrants*. New York: Harper Perennial, 2008.

———. *Profiles in Courage*. New York: HarperCollins, 2003.

———. *The Strategy of Peace*. New York: Popular Library, 1961.

———. *Why England Slept*. New York: Wilfred Funk, 1940.

Kennedy, Robert. *The Enemy Within*. New York: Harper & Brothers, 1960.

———. *Thirteen Days: A Memoir of the Cuban Missile Crisis*. New York: W. W. Norton, 1969.

Kennedy, Rose Fitzgerald. *Times to Remember*. Garden City, N.Y.: Doubleday, 1974.

Klein, Joe. *The Natural: The Misunderstood Presidency of Bill Clinton*. New York: Broadway, 2003.

Leamer, Lawrence. *The Kennedy Men*. New York: William Morrow, 2001.

Leuchtenburg, William E. *In the Shadow of FDR: From Harry Truman to Bill Clinton*. Ithaca, N.Y.: Cornell University Press, 1983 (second edition, 1994).

Lichtenstein, Nelson. *Labor's War at Home: The CIO in World War II*. New York: Cambridge University Press, 1982.

Lincoln, Evelyn. *My Twelve Years with John F. Kennedy*. New York: David McKay, 1965.

Lomazow, Steven, and Eric Fettman. *FDR's Deadly Secret*. New York: PublicAffairs, 2010.

Longley, Kyle. *Senator Albert Gore, Sr.: Tennessee Maverick*. Baton Rouge: Louisiana State University Press, 2004.

Lukas, J. Anthony. *Common Ground*. New York: Vintage Books, 1986.

Mackenzie, G. Calvin, and Robert Weisbrot. *The Liberal Hour: Washington and the Politics of Change in the 1960s*. New York: Penguin, 2008.

Manchester, William. *The Death of a President*. New York: Harper & Row, 1967.

Marlin, George. *The American Catholic Voter: 200 Years of Political Impact*. South Bend, Ind.: St. Augustine's Press, 2006.

Matthews, Chris. *Jack Kennedy: Elusive Hero*. New York: Simon & Schuster, 2011.

——. *Kennedy and Nixon: The Rivalry That Shaped Postwar America*. New York: Simon & Schuster, 1996.

McNamara, Robert S. *In Retrospect: The Tragedy and Lessons of Vietnam*. New York: Times Books, 1995.

Moyar, Mark. *Triumph Forsaken: The Vietnam War, 1954–1965*. New York: Cambridge University Press, 2006.

Moynihan, Daniel Patrick. *A Portrait in Letters of an American Visionary*. New York: PublicAffairs, 2010.

Naftali, Timothy, Ernest May, and Philip Zelikow, eds. *The Presidential Recordings: John F. Kennedy*. New York: W. W. Norton, 2001.

Navasky, Victor. *Kennedy Justice*. New York: Atheneum, 1971.

Nixon, Richard. *In the Arena*. New York: Simon & Schuster, 1990.

——. *RN: The Memoirs of Richard Nixon*. New York: Grosset & Dunlap, 1978.

Nossiter, Adam. *Of Long Memory: Mississippi and the Murder of Medgar Evers*. Reading, Mass.: Addison-Wesley, 1994.

O'Brien, Lawrence F. *No Final Victories: A Life in Politics from John F. Kennedy to Watergate*. Garden City, N.Y.: Doubleday, 1974.

O'Brien, Michael. *John F. Kennedy: A Biography*. New York: Thomas Dunne Books, 2005.

O'Donnell, Kenneth P., and David Powers, with Joe McCarthy. *"Johnny, We Hardly Knew Ye": Memories of John Fitzgerald Kennedy*. Boston: Little, Brown, 1970.

Okrent, Daniel. *Last Call: The Rise and Fall of Prohibition*. New York: Scribner, 2010.

Oshinsky, David M. *A Conspiracy So Immense: The World of Joe McCarthy*. New York: Free Press, 1983.

Pakula, Hannah. *The Last Empress: Madame Chiang Kai-shek and the Birth of Modern China*. New York: Simon & Schuster, 2009.

Parmet, Robert D. *The Master of Seventh Avenue: David Dubinsky and the American Labor Movement*. New York: NYU Press, 2005.

Piereson, James. *Camelot and the Cultural Revolution*. New York: Encounter Books, 2007.

Reagan, Ronald. *Reagan: A Life in Letters*. New York: Free Press, 2003.

Reeves, Richard. *President Kennedy: Profile of Power*. New York: Simon & Schuster, 1993.

Salinger, Pierre. *With Kennedy*. Garden City, N.Y.: Doubleday, 1966.

Savage, Sean J. *JFK, LBJ, and the Democratic Party*. Albany: State University of New York Press, 2004.

Schlesinger, Arthur M., Jr. *A Thousand Days: John F. Kennedy in the White House*. Boston: Houghton Mifflin, 1965.

Semple, Robert B., Jr., ed. *Four Days in November: The Original Coverage of the John F. Kennedy Assassination by the Staff of the* New York Times. New York: St. Martin's Press, 2003.

Sinatra, Barbara. *Lady Blue Eyes: My Life with Frank*. New York: Crown Archetype, 2011.

Solberg, Carl. *Hubert Humphrey: A Biography*. New York: W. W. Norton, 1984.

Sorensen, Theodore. *Counselor: A Life at the Edge of History*. New York: Harper, 2008.

———. *Kennedy*. New York: Harper & Row, 1965.

Stebenne, David L. *Arthur J. Goldberg: New Deal Liberal*. New York: Oxford University Press, 1996.

Stein, Herbert. *The Fiscal Revolution in America*. Chicago: University of Chicago Press, 1969.

Stoll, Ira. *Samuel Adams: A Life*. New York: Free Press, 2008.

Talbot, David. *Brothers: The Hidden History of the Kennedy Years*. New York: Free Press, 2007.

Tifft, Susan E., and Alex S. Jones. *The Trust: The Private and Powerful Family Behind the* New York Times. Boston: Little, Brown, 1999.

Tofel, Richard J. *Sounding the Trumpet: The Making of John F. Kennedy's Inaugural Address*. Chicago: Ivan R. Dee, 2005.

Weiner, Timothy. *Legacy of Ashes*. New York: Doubleday, 2007.

Whalen, Richard J. *The Founding Father: The Story of Joseph P. Kennedy*. New York: New American Library, 1964.

Whalen, Thomas J. *Kennedy Versus Lodge: The 1952 Massachusetts Senate Race*. Boston: Northeastern University Press, 2000.

White, Theodore. *In Search of History*. New York: Harper & Row, 1978.

———. *The Making of the President 1960*. Cutchogue, N.Y.: Buccaneer Books, 1961.

Wicker, Tom. *One of Us: Richard Nixon and the American Dream*. New York: Random House, 1991.

Wills, Garry. *The Kennedy Imprisonment*. Boston: Atlantic–Little, Brown, 1981.

Wofford, Harris. *Of Kennedys and Kings: Making Sense of the Sixties*. Pittsburgh: University of Pittsburgh Press, 1980 (reprint 1992).

Zieger, Robert H. *John L. Lewis: Labor Leader*. Boston: Twayne, 1988.

ARTICLES

Listed below are major articles that may be of interest to those pursuing further research on Kennedy. Most articles from magazines and newspapers cited in the endnotes are omitted here.

Brauer, Carl M. "Kennedy, Johnson, and the War on Poverty." *Journal of American History*, Vol. 69, No. 1 (June 1982), 98–119.

Land, Guy Paul. "John F. Kennedy's Southern Strategy, 1956–1960." *North Carolina Historical Review*, Vol. 56, No. 1 (January 1979), 41–63.

Parmet, Herbert S. "The Kennedy Myth and American Politics." *History Teacher*, Vol. 24, No. 1 (November 1990), 31–39.

Pechman, Joseph A. "Individual Income Tax Provisions of the Revenue Act of 1964." *Journal of Finance*, Vol. 20, No. 2 (May 1965), 247–272.

Weinstein, Lewis H. "John F. Kennedy: A Personal Memoir, 1946–1963." *American Jewish History*, Vol. 75, No. 1 (September 1985), 5–30.

INTERNET RESOURCES

The **John F. Kennedy Presidential Library and Museum,** www.jfklibrary.org, has placed online many of Kennedy's presidential records and speeches and some, but not all, of the oral history interviews conducted by the library after Kennedy's death.

The **Miller Center at the University of Virginia** makes available on its website, millercenter.org/scripps/archive/presidentialrecordings/kennedy, the recordings and transcripts of about 260 hours of President Kennedy's Oval Office meetings and telephone conversations.

The **State Department Office of the Historian** has posted, at history.state.gov/ historicaldocuments/kennedy, many of the thirty volumes covering the Kennedy administration in its series *Foreign Relations of the United States,* which gathers diplomatic cables, meeting records, and other valuable foreign policy sources.

The **University of California, Santa Barbara, American Presidency Project,** run by a UCSB political science professor, John T. Woolley, and Gerhard Peters, has placed online in searchable text form the public papers of all the presidents, including Kennedy. The Kennedy material is at www.presidency.ucsb.edu/ john_f_kennedy.php. The site also includes Kennedy's 1960 presidential campaign speeches as they were compiled and published by the U.S. Government Printing Office after the campaign.

Index